THE KLEINMAN EDITION

A Torah theme for every day of every week,
blending profound perspectives
from all areas of Torah literature –
Scripture, Mishnah, Jewish Law, Mussar/Ethics,
Tefillah/Prayer, and Hashkafah/Jewish Thought –
collected for daily study.

ArtScroll Series®

THE KLEINMAN EDITION

A TORAH THEME FOR EVERY DAY OF EVERY WEEK FROM ALL AREAS OF TORAH LITERATURE — COLLECTED FOR DAILY STUDY.

Rabbi Yosaif Asher Weiss
General Editor

OF TORAH

VOLUME 5

DAILY STUDY FOR THE WEEKS OF

יתרו-תצוה

YISRO–TETZAVEH

Published by

ARTSCROLL • Mesorah Publications, ltd

FIRST EDITION
First Impression … January 2007

Published and Distributed by
MESORAH PUBLICATIONS, LTD.
4401 Second Avenue / Brooklyn, N.Y 11232

Distributed in Europe by
LEHMANNS
Unit E, Viking Business Park
Rolling Mill Road
Jarow, Tyne & Wear, NE32 3DP
England

Distributed in Australia and New Zealand by
GOLDS WORLDS OF JUDAICA
3-13 William Street
Balaclava, Melbourne 3183
Victoria, Australia

Distributed in Israel by
SIFRIATI / A. GITLER — BOOKS
6 Hayarkon Street
Bnei Brak 51127

Distributed in South Africa by
KOLLEL BOOKSHOP
Ivy Common
105 William Road
Norwood 2192, Johannesburg, South Africa

ARTSCROLL SERIES®
THE KLEINMAN EDITION — LIMUD YOMI / A DAILY DOSE OF TORAH
VOL. 5: YISRO–TETZAVEH

ISBN:
ISBN 10: 1-4226-0144-7 (hard cover)
ISBN 13: 978-1-4226-0144-0 (hard cover)

Typography by CompuScribe at ArtScroll Studios, Ltd.

Printed in the United States of America by Noble Book Press Corp.
Bound by Sefercraft, Quality Bookbinders, Ltd., Brooklyn N.Y. 11232

DEDICATION OF THIS VOLUME

This volume is dedicated
in honor of our children

Alison, Martin and Bonnie,

in honor of our parents

Eddie and Irma Muller,
and Ruth Leventhal,

and in beloved memory of

Bernard E. Leventhal ז״ל
ברוך בן משה ז״ל
כ׳ אב תשנ״א

We are grateful to *Hakadosh Baruch Hu*
for blessing us with the ability to
participate in Artscroll's revolutionary work.
We pray that this *sefer* and the whole
Limud Yomi Series will be an inspiration to all
for daily learning and spiritual growth,
and that our parents and children,
to whom this volume is dedicated,
will be blessed with the merit of the
countless hours and days of Torah study
that will flow from this series.

Edward J. and Rose F. Leventhal

The Kleinman Edition

To our fathers and grandfathers, daily Torah study was the first priority. It is fitting, therefore, that we dedicate this Limud Yomi Series in their memory

Avrohom Kleinman ז״ל

ר׳ אברהם אייזיק ב״ר אלכסנדר ז״ל

נפ׳ י״ב שבט תשנ״ט

After years of slave labor and concentration camps — years when he risked his life to put on *tefillin* every day! — he courageously rebuilt. Wherever he was — in DP camps, Poughkeepsie, Borough Park, or Forest Hills — he was a one-man *kiruv* movement, before "*kiruv rechokim*" was a familiar phrase. Everyone was drawn to his enthusiasm for Yiddishkeit.

His home was open to anyone in need, even when there was barely enough for family.

All his life he felt close to his Rebbe, the Nitra Rav, and to the father-in-law he never knew; their *sefarim*, *Naos Desheh* and *Lechem Abirim*, were part of our Shabbos table. He was a caring and gentle man whose life was defined by his love of learning Torah, *gemillas chasadim*, *kiruv* work, *hachnasas orchim*, *askanus*, and love for his family. He left a noble legacy that we are honored to perpetuate.

Mendel Indig ז״ל

ר׳ מנחם דוד ב״ר מרדכי שמואל ז״ל

נפ׳ ט׳ אדר ב׳ תשס״ג

"It was as if a *maloch* protected us," he used to say about the dark years of Churban Europa. He lost almost everything — even the *tefillin* that he put on every day until the very end — but he kept his spirit, his *emunah*, his dedication to Torah, and his resolve to rebuild.

He became a living legend of Torah, *chesed*, and service to his Bensonhurst community. His home was open to anyone in need, and there was always enough room for guests. His *succah* was the largest in the neighborhood, and he always found a way to bring endangered relatives to America and help them become established.

After he retired, he devoted himself to learning and bringing others close to Yiddishkeit, especially immigrants from the former Soviet Union, teaching them to put on *tefillin* and reuniting them with the Judaism of their ancestors. It is our privilege to carry on his glorious legacy.

We pay tribute to our mothers

Ethel Kleinman תחי׳

Rose Indig תחי׳

To us and our children and grandchildren — and to all who know them — they are role models of *emunah*, *chesed*, love and wisdom.

Our mothers שיחיו and our fathers ז״ל planted seeds of Torah in America and produced magnificent *doros* of children, grandchildren, and great-grandchildren following their example. May Hashem continue to bless our mothers with good health and many nachas-filled years.

Elly and Brochie Kleinman and their children

Deenie and Yitzy Schuss   Yossie Kleinman   Aliza and Lavey Freedman

and families

PATRONS OF LIMUD YOMI / A DAILY DOSE OF TORAH

With dedication to the principle that Torah study should always be available,
the following generous and visionary patrons
have dedicated volumes of this series:

VOL. 1: BEREISHIS-VAYEIRA / בראשית-וירא

Elly and Brochie Kleinman and family

In memory of their fathers

ר׳ אברהם אייזיק ב״ר אלכסנדר ז״ל – Avrohom Kleinman ז״ל

ר׳ מנחם דוד ב״ר מרדכי שמואל ז״ל – Mendel Indig ז״ל

and יבלח״ט in tribute to their mothers שתחי׳ לאוי״ט

Ethel Kleinman

Rose Indig

VOL. 2: CHAYEI SARAH-VAYISHLACH / חיי שרה-וישלח

Motty and Malka Klein

for the merit of their children שיחי׳

Esther and Chaim Baruch Fogel   Dovid and Chavie   Binyomin Zvi

Elana Leah and Natan Goldstein   Moshe Yosef   Yaakov Eliyahu

In honor of his mother שתחי׳

Mrs. Suri Klein לאוי״ט

In memory of his father

ר׳ יהודה ב״ר דוד הלוי ז״ל נפ׳ כ״ז אדר ב׳ תשס״ג – Yidel Klein

In memory of her parents

ר׳ אשר אנשיל ב״ר משה יוסף ז״ל נפ׳ ג׳ שבט תשנ״ט – Anchel Gross

שרה בת ר׳ חיים אליהו ע״ה נפ׳ כ״ד סיון תשס״א – Suri Gross

And in memory of their grandparents who perished על קידוש השם in the Holocaust

ר׳ דוד ב״ר יעקב הלוי ע״ה ופערל בת ר׳ צבי ע״ה הי״ד – Klein

ר׳ מרדכי ב״ר דוד הלוי ע״ה ולאה בת ר׳ יעקב הלוי ע״ה הי״ד – Klein

ר׳ משה יוסף ב״ר בנימין צבי ע״ה ומלכה בת ר׳ יחיאל מיכל ע״ה הי״ד – Gross

ר׳ חיים אליהו ב״ר מרדכי ע״ה ויוטא בת ר׳ שלמה אליעזר ע״ה הי״ד – Gartenberg

VOL. 3: VAYEISHEV-VAYECHI / וישב-ויחי

Leon and Agi Goldenberg

Mendy and Estie Blau – Efraim, Rivka, and Chava

Shiffie Grossman – Chanie, and Rikki

Abi and Shoshana Goldenberg – Yehudis

Tzvi and Leilie Fertig

and Yitzy Goldenberg

In memory of their fathers and uncle

ר׳ אברהם אבא ב״ר צבי ז״ל – Abba Goldenberg ז״ל

ר׳ יוסף אליעזר ב״ר יעקב יצחק ז״ל – Joseph Brieger ז״ל

ר׳ יעקב שלמה ב״ר משה הלוי ז״ל – Yaakov Shlomeh Lebovits ז״ל

and יבלח״ט in tribute to their mothers שתחי׳ לאוי״ט

Chaya (Sicherman) Goldenberg   Malka (Karfunkel) Brieger

and their aunt – Faiga (Sicherman) Lebovits

VOL. 4: SHEMOS-BESHALACH / שמות־בשלח
Yossi and Bella Essas (Los Angeles)
Noam Zvi Hillel Avraham Adina Batya Ashira Miriam
In honor of his parents
Rabbi Eliyahu and Anya Essas שליט״א

VOL. 5: YISRO-TETZAVEH / יתרו־תצוה
Edward J. and Rose F. Leventhal
in honor of their children,
Alison, Martin and Bonnie,
and in honor of their parents
Eddie and Irma Muller,
and Ruth Leventhal,
and in beloved memory of his father,
ברוך בן משה ז״ל – Bernard E. Leventhal ז״ל

VOL. 14: THE FESTIVALS / מועדי השנה
The Teichman Family (Los Angeles)
In memory of their parents and grandparents
שמואל ב״ר יששכר דוב ז״ל – Sam Teichman ז״ל
ליבה בריינדל בת ר׳ יהושע הלוי ע״ה – Lujza Teichman ע״ה
רחל בת ר׳ אלכסנר סנדר ע״ה – Rose Teichman ע״ה
יצחק אייזיק ב״ר אברהם חיים ז״ל – Isaac Nae ז״ל

☙ Publisher's Preface

King David said: גַּל עֵינַי וְאַבִּיטָה נִפְלָאוֹת מִתּוֹרָתֶךָ, *Unveil my eyes that I may perceive wonders from your Torah* (*Psalms* 119:18).

Shammai said: עֲשֵׂה תּוֹרָתְךָ קֶבַע, *Make your Torah study a fixed practice* (*Avos* 1:15).

Rav Saadiah Gaon said: The Jewish people is a nation only by virtue of the Torah.

The Torah is the essence of the Jewish people, and not a day should go by without Torah study. How much learning should there be? Just as the Torah itself is infinite, there is no limit to the effort to master its contents. The task does not end when one bids farewell to the academy and enters the world of work and business. All over the world, study halls are filled before dawn and after dark with men plumbing the depths of the Talmud and other works. Before and after their workdays, they overcome fatigue with a relentless desire to absorb more and more of God's word.

To such people, **The Kleinman Edition: Limud Yomi / A Daily Dose of Torah** will be a welcome supplement, an enrichment that offers glimpses of additional topics and a means of filling the day's spare minutes with nourishment for the mind and spirit.

To those who as yet have not been able to savor the beauty of immersion in the sea of study, this new series will be a vehicle to enrich their every day with an assortment of stimulating Torah content.

We are gratified that Volumes 1 through 4 of this new series have been phenomenally well received. Many people have told us how they are filling once-empty gaps in their day with these "daily doses," and how this work has stimulated them to do further research in these subjects. As King Solomon said, תֵּן לְחָכָם וְיֶחְכַּם־עוֹד הוֹדַע לְצַדִּיק וְיוֹסֶף לֶקַח, *Give the wise man and he will become wiser; make known to the righteous and he will add [to his] learning* (*Proverbs* 9:9).

Each "Daily Dose of Torah" includes selections from a broad spectrum of Torah sources (see below); in combination they provide a multi-dimensional study program. Each selection can stand on its own, or, ideally, serve as a vehicle for further research and enrichment. These components are as follows:

- ❑ ***A Torah Thought for the Day***, focusing on a verse in the weekly *parashah.* The discussion may revolve around various classic interpretations, or it may offer a selection of insights and lessons that are derived from the verse. This section will draw from a wide gamut of early and later commentators, and will enhance the reader's appreciation for the wealth of Torah interpretation and its lessons for life.
- ❑ ***The Mishnah of the Day,*** presenting a Mishnah selection every day, with text, translation, and concise commentary, adapted from the classic ArtScroll Mishnah Series and the Schottenstein Edition of the Talmud. This daily dose will begin with Tractate Shabbos, and continue through Seder Moed.
- ❑ ***Gems from the Gemara,*** presenting some of the Talmud's discussion of the daily Mishnah. Thus the reader will "join the academy" of the Talmud's question-and-answer clarification of the laws and underlying principles of the Mishnah.
- ❑ ***A Mussar Thought for the Day,*** building upon the theme of the *Torah Thought for the Day*, by presenting an ethical or moral lesson drawn from the masters of Mussar, Hashkafah, and Chassidus. This selection will stimulate thought and growth — and be a welcome source of uplifting ideas for times when the reader is called upon to speak at a *simchah.*
- ❑ ***The Halachah of the Day,*** presenting a practical, relevant halachic discussion, beginning with the thirty-nine forbidden categories of Shabbos labor. The selections are adapted from Rabbi Simcha Bunim Cohen's popular and authoritative works, which are part of the ArtScroll Series. [These brief discussions are not intended to be definitive. Questions should be directed to a qualified rav.]
- ❑ ***A Closer Look at the Siddur,*** broadening the reader's understanding of the rich tapestry of *tefillah*/prayer. The Shabbos Daily Dose will focus on the Shabbos prayers. And once a week, this section will discuss such universal themes as the Thirteen Principles of Faith or the Six Constant Commandments.

❑ ***A Taste of Lomdus,*** a special weekly feature that will present a brief but in-depth discussion of a Talmudic subject, in the tradition of the Torah giants whose reasoning and novellae are the basis of research and study in advanced yeshivas. Every day, there will be a challenging "Question of the Day," related to the theme of the day. The answers for the questions will come at the end of each week.

Each volume of the Daily Dose of Torah Series will present a capsule study program for twenty-eight days. The annual cycle will be comprised of thirteen four-week volumes, covering all fifty-two weeks of the year, and a fourteenth volume devoted to Rosh Hashanah, Yom Kippur, and the festivals. We are confident that the complete series will bring the excitement of Torah study to countless people, and that many of them will use it as a springboard to further learning, both independently and by joining *shiurim.*

The Kleinman Edition: Limud Yomi / A Daily Dose of Torah is dedicated by **ELLY AND BROCHIE KLEINMAN,** in memory of their fathers ז"ל and in honor of their mothers שיחיו. The Kleinmans have long distinguished themselves as generous and imaginative supporters of Torah and *chesed* causes. With warmth and kindness, they have opened their home countless times to help institutions and individuals. They have richly earned the respect and affection of all who know them, and we are honored to count them not only as major supporters of our work, but as personal friends. They and their family bring honor to the legacy of their parents.

We are proud to welcome **ED AND ROSE LEVENTHAL** to the ArtScroll family. They prefer to do good things without receiving recognition, but as our Sages teach, when people flee from honor, it pursues them. The Leventhals are leaders of their community, and are involved in a host of activities to spread Torah study and observance. As they say in their dedication of this work, they consider themselves blessed to help bring daily learning and spiritual growth to others.They do so in many ways, and now, by adding the Daily Dose to their list, they are enriching the days and lives of many thousands of Jews.

The editor of this new series is **RABBI YOSAIF ASHER WEISS,** Rosh Yeshivas Ohr Hadaas, Staten Island, who is also a distinguished editor of the Schottenstein Editions of the Talmud Bavli and Yerushalmi. Rabbi Weiss' reputation as a noted scholar and educator will be justly embellished by the Daily Dose Series.

We are grateful to **RABBI RAPHAEL BUTLER,** the dynamic and innovative founder and president of the Afikim Foundation, who conceived of this concept and had a significant role in its development. We are proud to enjoy his friendship.

We are grateful to the outstanding *talmidei chachamim* who are contributing to this series: **RABBI YOSEF GAVRIEL BECHHOFER, RABBI REUVEN BUTLER, RABBI ELIYAHU COHEN, RABBI ASHER DICKER, RABBI MAYER GOLDSTEIN, RABBI MOSHE YEHUDA GLUCK, RABBI BERYL SCHIFF, RABBI MORDECHAI SONNENSCHEIN, RABBI MOSHE UNGAR, AND RABBI YISROEL DOV WEISS.** The quality of their scholarship shines through every page. We thank **RABBI SIMCHA SHAFRAN** for allowing us to use his *sefer Maadanei Simchah* as a source for some of the Questions of the Day.

The beauty and clarity of the book's design is yet another tribute to the graphics genius of our friend and colleague **REB SHEAH BRANDER**. As someone once said in a different context, "I can't put it into words, but I know it when I see it." It is hard to define good taste and graphics beauty in words, but when one sees Reb Sheah's work, one knows it.

ELI KROEN, a master of graphics in his own right, designed the cover with his typical creativity and good taste. **MOSHE DEUTSCH** had an important hand in the typesetting and general design. **MRS. CHUMIE LIPSCHITZ**, a key member of our staff, paginated the book. **TOBY GOLDZWEIG, SURY REINHOLD, AND SARA RIFKA SPIRA** typed and corrected the manuscript. **MRS. ESTHER FEIERSTEIN** proofread the final copy.

MRS. MINDY STERN proofread and made many important suggestions. **AVROHOM BIDERMAN** was involved in virtually every aspect of the work from its inception, and **MENDY HERZBERG** assisted in shepherding the project to completion.

As this new series continues to take shape, we express our great appreciation to our long-time friend and colleague **SHMUEL BLITZ**, head of ArtScroll Jerusalem. His dedication and judgment have been indispensable components of virtually every ArtScroll/Mesorah project.

We are grateful to them all. The contributions of ArtScroll/Mesorah to the cause of Jewish life and Torah study are possible because of the skill and dedication of the above staff members and their colleagues.

It is an enormous privilege to have been instrumental in bringing Torah knowledge to the people of Torah. There are no words to express our gratitude to Hashem Yisbarach for permitting us to disseminate His Word to His children.

Rabbi Meir Zlotowitz / Rabbi Nosson Scherman

Kislev 5767 / December 2006

פרשת יתרו

Parashas Yisro

פרשת
יתרו

SUNDAY

PARASHAS
YISRO

A TORAH THOUGHT FOR THE DAY

וַיִּשְׁמַע יִתְרוֹ כֹהֵן מִדְיָן חֹתֵן מֹשֶׁה אֵת כָּל־אֲשֶׁר עָשָׂה אֱלֹהִים לְמֹשֶׁה וּלְיִשְׂרָאֵל עַמּוֹ כִּי־הוֹצִיא ה׳ אֶת־יִשְׂרָאֵל מִמִּצְרָיִם

Yisro, the minister of Midian, the father-in-law of Moshe, heard about everything that HASHEM had done for Moshe and for Israel, His people — that HASHEM had taken Israel out of Egypt (*Shemos* 18:1).

Rashi cites the *Mechilta* that asks: What report did he hear that made him come? He heard about the Splitting of the *Yam Suf* and the war with Amalek.

Now, the verse itself states that Yisro *heard about everything that HASHEM had done for Moshe and for Israel, His people — that HASHEM had taken Israel out of Egypt.* Thus, the verse itself points to the Exodus from Egypt as that which Yisro heard. Nevertheless, *Rashi* apparently understands that the verse refers to two separate occurrences. First, Yisro heard about what "Hashem had done for Moshe and for all of Israel." This refers to some happening, not identified in the verse, that was the reason behind Yisro's coming, and that motivated him to join the ranks of Bnei Yisrael. Second, Yisro also heard "that Hashem had taken Israel out of Egypt." This latter part of the verse does not mention Moshe, as he was in Midian for a great part of the exile, and was not himself enslaved. It is regarding the *first* part of the verse that *Mechilta* identifies the events that Yisro heard about as being the Splitting of the Sea and the war with Amalek — these were events in which Moshe *did* play an active role (*Maharsha* to *Zevachim* 116a).

An obvious question still remains, however. Hadn't the whole world heard about the Splitting of the Sea? In last week's *parashah* we read (15:14-15): שָׁמְעוּ עַמִּים יִרְגָּזוּן חִיל אָחַז יֹשְׁבֵי פְּלָשֶׁת. אָז נִבְהֲלוּ אַלּוּפֵי אֱדוֹם . . . נָמֹגוּ כֹּל יֹשְׁבֵי כְנָעַן, *Peoples heard — they trembled; terror gripped the inhabitants of Philistia. Then the chieftains of Edom were confounded . . . all the dwellers of Canaan melted.* Moreover, the Midrash relates that at the time the *Yam Suf* split, all the waters in the world split as well. Thus, one could scarcely have avoided knowing about this great miracle. What was so unusual about Yisro's hearing that caused it to be singled out by the Torah?

The answer lies in the one additional word found in *Rashi*: "What report did he hear that made him *come*?"

Sometimes, says *Rav Sholom Schwadron,* two people can hear about the same incident, but they will react in totally different ways. He

illustrates this with a story that is told of Rav Baruch Ber Lebovitz. It was well known that Rav Baruch Ber had great reverence for Torah scholars. Once, he heard that there was an old man who still remembered the great *gaon,* Rav Akiva Eiger; Rav Baruch Ber decided to go through the great hardship of finding and visiting this man, thinking that he might hear a new Torah thought from him.

He asked his famous student, Rav Shlomo Heiman, to join him on this venture, and after much difficulty they succeeded in locating the man. Rav Baruch Ber could hardly contain his excitement, and with great feeling asked the man whether he had indeed known Rav Akiva Eiger.

The old man, very coldly and unenthusiastically, answered: "You mean the Posner Rav. Yes, I knew him."

Immediately, Rav Baruch Ber stood up and turned to his student, stating, "We have nothing to gain here. This man did not *know* Rav Akiva Eiger! True, he might have seen him and even conversed with him, but the Rav Akiva Eiger I wish to hear about, he obviously never knew. If he had, he would be able to speak of him only with awe and admiration. It is as if we are talking about two different people."

Everyone heard about the great miracles of the Splitting of the Sea and the war with Amalek, but only Yisro understood the message and made a decision to change his life. As *Rashi* says: What did he hear that made such a great impact on him and caused him to come? It was something that everyone heard, but only Yisro got the message.

MISHNAH OF THE DAY: SHABBOS 18:3

The following Mishnah discusses the extent to which a person may assist a woman or an animal in giving birth on the Sabbath or Yom Tov:

אֵין מְיַלְּדִין אֶת הַבְּהֵמָה — ***We may not assist an animal in delivering its young***[1] **בְּיוֹם טוֹב** — ***on Yom Tov,***[2] **אֲבָל מְסַעֲדִין** — ***but we may support*** it.[3] **וּמְיַלְּדִין אֶת הָאִשָּׁה בַּשַּׁבָּת** — ***We may assist a woman in***

NOTES

1. I.e., we may not draw the fetus from the uterus, since this is considered excessive toil (*Rav*).

2. I.e., not even on a festival may we assist an animal in delivering its young, and it goes without saying that we may not do so on the Sabbath (*Meiri*).

3. I.e., we may catch the newborn animal so that it does not fall to the ground (*Rav*).

childbirth on the Sabbath;[4] **וְקוֹרִין לָהּ חֲכָמָה מִמָּקוֹם לְמָקוֹם** — ***and we may call a midwife*** [lit., *a wise woman*] ***from place to place for her;***[5] **וּמְחַלְּלִין עָלֶיהָ אֶת הַשַּׁבָּת** — ***and we may desecrate the Sabbath on her behalf;***[6] **וְקוֹשְׁרִין אֶת הַטַּבּוּר** — ***and we may tie the umbilical cord.***[7] **רַבִּי יוֹסֵי אוֹמֵר אַף חוֹתְכִין** — ***R' Yose says: We may even cut*** it.[8] **וְכָל צָרְכֵי מִילָה עוֹשִׂין בַּשַּׁבָּת** — ***And all requirements of circumcision may be performed on the Sabbath.***[9]

NOTES

4. I.e., even on the Sabbath we may draw the fetus from the uterus of the woman, and it goes without saying that we may do so on a festival. Moreover, it goes without saying that we may support the infant.

5. Even if there is a midwife here, but there is a more expert one elsewhere, the distant one may be summoned (*Tiferes Yisrael*). In fact, we may even summon a midwife from beyond the 12 *mil* (24,000 *amos*) maximum travel area, although this travel is proscribed by a Biblical prohibition (*Tos. Yom Tov; Tiferes Yisrael*).

6. The Gemara (129a) inquires why this statement is necessary, since the Mishnah previously stated: *We may assist a woman in childbirth on the Sabbath.* The Gemara explains that this statement teaches us that candles may be lit even for a blind woman in childbirth. Although she does not benefit directly from the light, she nevertheless feels more at ease with the knowledge that there is adequate light for the midwives.

7. Tying the umbilical cord is permitted in order to prevent the infant's intestines from protruding through the open navel when he is picked up (*Rav; Rashi*). This Tanna, however, permits only tying the cord, not cutting it off (*Rav*).

8. R' Yose permits cutting off the umbilical cord, cleansing the navel, and applying the necessary medications, such as myrtle powder (*Rav; Rambam Commentary*).

9. All these requirements are expounded in the following chapter (*Rav; Rambam Commentary*).

GEMS FROM THE GEMARA

The Gemara (128b-129a) explains that there are three distinct rules that apply to a woman who has given birth, regarding the criteria that must be satisfied in order for the Sabbath to be desecrated for her. The first rule: At the time that a woman is actually giving birth, she is automatically *presumed* to be in a life-threatening situation. Therefore, no *specific* indications of danger are necessary to allow us to do whatever is deemed essential in providing care for a woman giving birth, even if these things involve desecration of the Sabbath. A woman remains in this presumed status from the time she goes into labor or begins to bleed, and it remains in effect until three days after the delivery. During this time, if *we* believe it to be necessary, we may desecrate the Sabbath for her whether or not *she* feels that it is necessary. [However, whatever can be done in an unusual manner (thereby avoiding a Biblical violation) should be done in that manner (*Shulchan Aruch* 330:1). Although this is not usually required in life-threatening situations, the threat to life involved in childbirth is not considered as great — under ordinary circumstances — and therefore we avoid a Biblical violation whenever possible (*Mishnah Berurah* 330:5).]

From the third until the seventh day after birth, a second rule applies: We may desecrate the Sabbath to provide care for the new mother only when she states that it is absolutely necessary for her health that it be provided. From the eighth day after the birth until the thirtieth day, the third rule applies: During this period, even if the mother claims that it is necessary to her health to desecrate the Sabbath, we may not do so ourselves. However, we may call a non-Jew to give her the necessary care. Her situation is then analogous to that of a sick person whose life is not in danger. For such a patient, too, a non-Jew may be summoned to perform any necessary treatment. [This rule applies only to a woman who has no other medical condition besides having delivered a baby. Where life-threatening complications arise from the delivery of a baby because of other medical issues that are present, a woman may obviously be treated even by Jews in any way necessary, since such a woman is certainly no different than any other person whose life is in danger on the Sabbath.]

A MUSSAR THOUGHT FOR THE DAY

We discussed in *A Torah Thought for the Day* how although everyone heard about and even saw the miracle of the Splitting of the Sea, only Yisro took a lesson from it and was motivated to join the Bnei Yisrael.

This concept is discussed by *Rabbeinu Yonah* in *Shaarei Teshuvah* (2:26), where he notes that often, when people hear a very moving lecture or are shaken up by terrible news, they are prompted to change their ways. However, the impact does not last long, for the *yetzer hara* tries hard to make the person forget the lesson. In just a few days, he will be back to normal.

The only way to insure a lasting message from an inspiring incident

or the like is for a person to consciously "wake himself up" and discern what lessons can be learned from that incident, and how those lessons can impact upon and change his life.

He quotes the words of Hillel (*Avos* 1:14): אִם אֵין אֲנִי לִי מִי לִי, *If I am not for myself, who will be for me*? This means that although a person can hear speeches and lectures given by others, nothing will become a part of him unless he is actively involved in internalizing the message, utilizing his own understanding and intellect.

This is what Yisro did. He did not simply *hear* the facts of the great miracles as everyone else did; he took it a step further. He asked himself: "What does my knowledge of those miracles obligate me to do? What lessons do they teach me? Who is really in charge of everything in this world? And what can I do to become close to the true God?"

In the *Yiddish* language there are two very similar words, whose meanings are worlds apart. One is הערען, *heren,* which means *hearing,* and the other is דערהערען, *derheren,* which means *comprehending.* Someone can talk in a foreign language and he will be heard by everyone in the room, but not everyone will understand and comprehend what is being said.

This is why so many times, even after being exposed to clear indications of the hand of Hashem (such as the hurricanes and tsunamis of recent years), it does not take long for us to shake off our inspiration and go back to our regular routine. If we only *hear* current events, but fail to *understand* their messages and internalize their lessons, then the *yetzer hara* will do a fine job of helping us to forget the initial impact.

Rav Chaim Shmulevitz put it so perfectly. The Midrash (*Yalkut* §244) tells us that a maidservant saw at the Sea what even the great Yechezkel the prophet did not see (this refers to visions of Hashem's Throne). He asks: Why, then, did the maidservant not become a prophet like Yechezkel? And he answers: Because even after she saw the great vision, she remained a maidservant; she did nothing more than see. Thus, while she may have indeed seen great things, this did not motivate her to grow spiritually and change her ways.

QUESTION OF THE DAY:

When did Yisro come to visit Moshe?

For the answer, see page 58.

HALACHAH OF THE DAY

Yesterday, we discussed two sets of circumstances where one is permitted to untie Rabbinically prohibited knots — cases of physical distress, and cases where the knot in question precludes the proper observance of a mitzvah. In other cases of necessity, where the knot is the cause of significant inconvenience but not physical distress, the following two types of Rabbinically prohibited knots may be untied: a double knot that was intended to remain in place for less than twenty-four hours, and a knot/bow combination that was intended to remain in place for less than seven days. As we explained above in our discussion of tying, these two knots are a matter of dispute among the *poskim,* and according to some opinions, are not even forbidden by Rabbinic decree. We may therefore rely on these opinions in cases of necessity.

For example, if a woman needs to wear a particular dress on Shabbos but its belt has been tied with a double knot that had been intended to remain intact for less than twenty-four hours, she may undo the belt and wear the dress. The same ruling would apply if the belt were tied in a knot/bow combination that had been tied with intent that it remain in place for less than seven days. If, however, the belt was tied in a double knot with intent that it remain for more than twenty-four hours, or a knot and bow was tied with intent that it remain for more than seven days, it may not be untied on Shabbos.

In cases of great necessity, one may ask a non-Jew to open any Rabbinically prohibited knot.

Now that we have discussed the intricacies of the laws governing tying and untying knots on Shabbos, we can discuss some practical applications of these laws. While we will approach these cases from the perspective of tying the knot, one must remember that it is forbidden to untie any knot which may not be tied on Shabbos.

One may not tighten or loosen the knots of *tzitzis* on Shabbos. Additionally, individual *tzitzis* strands often have a knot at the end of the strand, which is tied there to prevent the strand from unraveling. One may not tie or untie such a knot on Shabbos.

It is forbidden to tie even a single knot on a loose thread of a garment in order to prevent the thread from slipping out of the garment. This is true even if one intends to leave the knot in place for less than twenty-four hours.

We will continue with other practical applications of the laws of tying and untying tomorrow.

פרשת יתרו

SUNDAY

PARASHAS YISRO

A CLOSER LOOK AT THE SIDDUR

The first verse of *Krias Shema,* which we say twice daily, states: שְׁמַע יִשְׂרָאֵל ה׳ אֱלֹהֵינוּ ה׳ אֶחָד, *Hear, O Israel: HASHEM is our God, HASHEM is One.*

Rashba (*Responsa* 5:55) explains that the word שְׁמַע, *hear,* has three meanings: (1) the physical act of hearing; (2) understanding and comprehending the message (see *A Torah Thought for the Day* and *A Mussar Thought for the Day*); and (3) the acceptance and belief of the message.

In reciting *Shema* we are accepting the yoke of Hashem, twice every day, obligating us to learn His Torah and obey His mitzvos. *Rashba* explains that the first step in this process is for us to fully understand the fundamental concept that Hashem is One.

From there we must proceed to the knowledge and acceptance that He is the only One, and that He watches our every move. This will enable us to fulfill the commandments stated in the next verse of the *Shema*: to love Hashem, to be ready to sacrifice one's life for the sake of Hashem, and to forgo our desires or forfeit our wealth if they stand in the way of serving only Hashem.

Rashba says that part of this mitzvah is for one to actually visualize and imagine himself giving up all his money and even his life for Hashem. It is not enough to just say the words. Rather, to completely fulfill these mitzvos, one must use his imagination to picture a scene where he is tested and required to sacrifice his life for Hashem. If a person does this, says *Rashba,* Hashem views it as if he had actually been so tested, and it is as if he withstood his trial and gave up his life for the sake of Hashem. This is the highest level of fulfillment that can be accomplished, short of actual sacrifice of one's life.

In this way, the recital of the *Shema* must be different than reading a portion of the Torah, where a person receives a mitzvah simply for reading. To properly fulfill the mitzvos of reciting this passage, one must accept upon himself not to compromise in any way, and to stand ready to make any sacrifice necessary for the sake of sanctifying Hashem's Name.

Rashba underscores the critical nature of this by adding a prayer: "May Hashem help me from belonging to the group about which it is said: *They honored Me only with their lips and mouths, but their hearts were removed from this.*"

Thus, when we say the first word of the *Shema,* we are required to be mindful of all its meanings: We must *hear* these truths, *understand* them, and be willing to fully *accept* them.

A TORAH THOUGHT FOR THE DAY

וְאַתָּה תֶחֱזֶה מִכָּל־הָעָם אַנְשֵׁי־חַיִל יִרְאֵי אֱלֹהִים אַנְשֵׁי אֱמֶת שֹׂנְאֵי בָצַע . . . וְשָׁפְטוּ אֶת־הָעָם בְּכָל־עֵת

And you shall see from among the entire people, men of valor, God-fearing men, men of truth, men who despise money . . . They shall judge the people at all times (*Shemos* 18:21-22).

The events as they are related here by the Torah bear further scrutiny. Yisro, a relative newcomer, offered a suggestion as to how to change the entire judicial system that was in place at the time, and his suggestion received the approval of Moshe and Hashem. He also merited getting a special name in recognition of having added this portion of the Torah. As *Rashi* states in the beginning of this *parashah* (18:1): "He was called Yeser, which means *extra* or *more,* because he caused one more passage of the Torah to be written, namely the passage וְאַתָּה תֶחֱזֶה, *and you shall see,* etc." Obviously, Yisro's advice must have been very astute.

Indeed, the main thrust of his advice was very logical — to appoint many lower judges to deal with the simpler problems, thus leaving Moshe Rabbeinu the time to be available for the difficult issues, which only someone of Moshe's caliber could judge.

Let us delve a bit further, and examine the four qualifications that Yisro enumerates for the lower judges: (1) men of valor; (2) God-fearing men; (3) men of truth; (4) men who despise money. The importance of the last three attributes in a judge are self-understood, as they enable him to carry out the laws of Hashem without any corruption. However, the first one, אַנְשֵׁי־חַיִל, *men of valor,* needs some clarification. What does it mean, and why is it necessary for a judge to be a man of valor?

Rashi explains that *men of valor* means men of means — rich men, who have no need to flatter or show recognition. This definition is difficult to understand, however, for one of the other qualities mentioned was despising money — and, as the Midrash explains, this refers to men who do not attach importance even to their own money. Why, then, was it necessary to add a separate qualification that the judge must be rich? If he has no desire or respect for money, what difference would his financial status make?

In the *Mechilta* that *Rashi* cites, there is also another interpretation of אַנְשֵׁי־חַיִל, stated in the name of R' Elazar HaModa'i. *Men of valor* — these are men who inspire confidence, for they are worthy enough that their words may always be relied upon (this is similar to the interpretation that *Rashi* uses for *men of truth*).

The *Bad Kodesh* explains this quality and shows how it is derived from the word חַיִל. In the famous last chapter of *Mishlei,* we find the statement: אֵשֶׁת־חַיִל מִי יִמְצָא, *A woman of valor, who can find?* (31:10). It would seem from here that it is almost impossible to find such a person. Nevertheless, a few verses later it says: רַבּוֹת בָּנוֹת עָשׂוּ חָיִל, *many women have attained valor* (v. 29), from which it would seem that it is not hard at all to find this quality! The answer to this seeming contradiction is that there is a big difference between "performing acts of valor" and being "a person of valor." Many people can periodically perform worthy acts; but a person whose very essence is one of valor, meaning that his or her life is one continuous act of valor, is extremely difficult to find.

This, says the *Bad Kodesh,* is what the *Mechilta* means by "men of valor." Such men inspire confidence in everything they say or do, because their very essence is valor. Men such as these are qualified to serve in the position of judges.

MISHNAH OF THE DAY: SHABBOS 19:1

The final Mishnah in the preceding chapter concluded with the statement: "And all requirements of circumcision may be performed on the Sabbath" (128b). The following Mishnah elaborates on this statement, discussing whether the preliminaries to circumcision are also permitted, even if they involve labors that are usually forbidden on the Sabbath:

רַבִּי אֱלִיעֶזֶר אוֹמֵר — ***R' Eliezer says:*** **אִם לֹא הֵבִיא כְּלִי מֵעֶרֶב שַׁבָּת** — ***If one did not bring an instrument*** for circumcising ***on the Sabbath eve,***[1] **מְבִיאוֹ בַּשַּׁבָּת** — ***he should bring it on the Sabbath*** itself,[2] **מְגוּלֶּה** — ***exposed;***[3] **וּבְסַכָּנָה מְכַסֵּהוּ עַל פִּי עֵדִים** — ***but in*** times of

NOTES

1. I.e., he did not bring the circumcision knife on Friday to the house where the infant's Sabbath circumcision is scheduled to take place (*Rashi*).

2. R' Eliezer rules that in order to perform the circumcision on the Sabbath, it is permissible to engage even in activities that are only preliminaries to the circumcision, even when such preliminaries could have been prepared prior to the Sabbath (Gemara 131a).

3. He should carry it in full view, in order to demonstrate the preciousness of this mitzvah, by showing that one is even permitted to violate the Sabbath in order to fulfill it (*Rav, Tiferes Yisrael* from Gemara 130a).

danger,[4] ***he should cover it in the presence of witnesses.***[5]

וְעוֹד אָמַר רַבִּי אֱלִיעֶזֶר — ***And R' Eliezer said further:*** **כּוֹרְתִים עֵצִים לַעֲשׂוֹת פֶּחָמִין**— ***We may fell trees to make charcoal***[6] **וְלַעֲשׂוֹת כְּלִי בַרְזֶל** — ***and to make iron instruments.***[7]

כְּלָל אָמַר רַבִּי עֲקִיבָא — But ***R' Akiva stated a general rule:*** **כָּל מְלָאכָה שֶׁאֶפְשָׁר לַעֲשׂוֹתָהּ מֵעֶרֶב שַׁבָּת** — ***Any labor that can be performed on the Sabbath eve*** before the onset of the Sabbath, **אֵינָהּ דּוֹחָה אֶת הַשַּׁבָּת** — ***does not override*** [lit., *push aside*] ***the Sabbath,***[8] **וְשֶׁאִי אֶפְשָׁר לַעֲשׂוֹתָהּ מֵעֶרֶב שַׁבָּת** — and any labor ***that cannot be performed on the Sabbath eve,***[9] **דּוֹחָה אֶת הַשַּׁבָּת** — ***does override the Sabbath.***

NOTES

4. At times when idolaters prohibited the performance of circumcision upon pain of death. This occurred specifically during the Roman occupation of Israel (*Rav; Rashi;* see *Me'ilah* 17a, *Mechilta* 20:6), during the reign of Hadrian. It was one of the prime causes of the Bar Kochba uprising (*Doros HaRishonim* vol. 4 [of the reprinted edition, published in Jerusalem 1967], Ch. 27).

5. [Literally, *upon the word of witnesses.*] The purpose of having witnesses is so that if necessary they can later attest that he carried the knife for purposes of performing a mitzvah, thereby deflecting from him any suspicion of wrongdoing (*Rashi;* see *Tiferes Yisrael; Shoshanim LeDavid*).

6. If there is no knife available, they may even fell trees to make the charcoal necessary to forge iron in order to make a knife. R' Eliezer teaches us here that even these remote preliminaries to the circumcision, which could easily have been arranged before the Sabbath, also override the Sabbath (*Tiferes Yisrael*).

7. I.e., a circumcision knife (*Rav*).

8. R' Akiva argues with R' Eliezer, who permits the performance of preliminaries to a mitzvah (even if they involve forbidden labor) on the Sabbath. R' Akiva maintains, on the other hand, that when a preliminary could have been performed before the Sabbath, one may not perform it on the Sabbath (*Rav; Rashi*).

9. Such as the circumcision itself, which may not be performed before the eighth day (*Rav; Rashi*).

QUESTION OF THE DAY:

Why did Yisro stress that the newly appointed judges would judge the nation "at all times"?

For the answer, see page 58.

פרשת יתרו

MONDAY

PARASHAS YISRO

GEMS FROM THE GEMARA

The Gemara (130a) presents several Aggadic teachings that touch upon the subject of the mitzvah of circumcision. Among them is the statement of R' Shimon ben Elazar, that any commandment for which the Jewish people gave themselves over to death at the time of a government edict directed against that commandment — such as their edicts forcing Jews to perform idolatry, and their edicts to prevent Jews from performing circumcision — is still strongly held (i.e., widely observed) by the Jewish people. But any commandment for which the Jewish people did not give themselves over to death at the time of a government edict directed against the commandment — such as the decree banning the wearing of *tefillin* — is only weakly held by the Jews.

The Gemara, citing R' Yannai, then establishes that the Jewish people as a whole were not totally dedicated to the mitzvah of *tefillin.* The Gemara states: "*Tefillin* require their wearer to maintain a clean body, as Elisha the Winged One maintained." While it was true that Elisha was scrupulous in maintaining the cleanliness of body required for wearing *tefillin* constantly (see Gemara there for details), most people were not, and thus they were not totally dedicated to the mitzvah of *tefillin.*

The Gemara then explains how "Elisha the Winged One" earned his title. Once, the Roman government issued a decree that anyone found with *tefillin* on his head would have his skull pierced and his brain gouged out. Yet Elisha would don *tefillin* and go out into the marketplace, in defiance of the decree. One day, a certain official spied Elisha while he was wearing his *tefillin,* and pursued him. As the official caught up to him, Elisha took the *tefillin* from his head and grasped them in his hand. The official said to him: What is in your hand? Elisha answered him: Dove's wings. Whereupon Elisha opened his hand, and miraculously, in it were a pair of dove's wings. On account of this miracle, they would call him "Elisha the Winged One."

The Gemara inquires: What is unique about dove's wings that caused Elisha to answer the official as he did? The Gemara explains that Elisha specifically mentioned dove's wings because the Congregation of Israel is compared to a dove, for it is written of Israel (*Tehillim* 68:14): כַּנְפֵי יוֹנָה נֶחְפָּה בַכֶּסֶף, *[You will be like] the wings of a dove covered with silver.* This analogy teaches that just as in the case of the dove, its wings protect it (a dove shields itself with its wings as it fights), so in the case of Israel — the commandments that they observe protect them. Since the commandments — one of which is the donning of *tefillin* — are compared to the wings of a dove, and since Elisha was in need of the commandments' protection, it is fitting that he referred to his *tefillin* specifically as *dove's* wings.

A MUSSAR THOUGHT FOR THE DAY

In *A Torah Thought for the Day,* we discussed some of the qualifications required in order for a person to be appointed as a judge. We explained the importance of אַנְשֵׁי־חַיִל, *men of valor*, which, according to the *Mechilta,* means men who inspire confidence. In truth, Moshe could not find people who possessed all of the attributes suggested by Yisro. He was, however, able to find men of valor (see verse 25).

We can learn from this passage about the great responsibility that rests upon the shoulders of judges. If they cannot inspire full confidence in the fact that they will carry out their duties to the fullest, they are not fit to be the ones who carry out the laws of Hashem. The same is true regarding a Rav of a city or community, who shoulders enormous responsibility with every decision he makes.

There is an amazing story told of the Chofetz Chaim that drives home this message very clearly. The Chofetz Chaim had a son-in-law, Rav Aharon HaKohen, who was a Torah genius. There was once an opportunity for him, at a young age, to become a rabbi in a prominent city, and the position was very appealing to him. When his efforts to secure the appointment ended in failure, he related his disappointment to his illustrious father-in-law. The Chofetz Chaim first tried calming him by saying that the responsibilities of a Rav are extremely taxing, and therefore he should not be upset that he had not been chosen. When some time had elapsed and the Chofetz Chaim saw that his son-in-law was still crestfallen, he related the following story to him:

[The Chofetz Chaim himself had actually served as Rav of Radin for a very short time, until the following incident occurred, which caused him to give up his post. He told his son-in-law the story on the condition that he would not reveal it to anyone as long as the Chofetz Chaim lived.]

"One of the local butchers in town was once caught selling nonkosher meat. Naturally, he was banned from selling any meat in the city. After some time had passed, however, he came before me with a very heavy heart and full of regret, promising never to do such a thing again. When

I realized that he was sincere about his repentance, and I knew the fate his children were facing without any food to eat at home, I agreed to restore his livelihood to him, on the condition that he would pay a large penalty to the town's *beis midrash.* A short time later, the butcher passed on, and the story was forgotten.

"One day as I was learning in the *beis midrash* I dozed off. In my dream, I saw three prestigious-looking people. They asked me what I had had in mind at the time I had penalized the butcher. Was my intention to ensure that a repeat transgression would not occur? Or did I wish to fine him as an atonement for his sin? At first, I did not recall which purpose I had had in mind, but upon reflection, I replied that my main intention had been to prevent a recurrence of the misdeed. The men thanked me and left.

"When I awoke," continued the Chofetz Chaim, "I felt very sick about this whole thing, and couldn't calm myself. I fell back asleep and this time the butcher, totally broken and sobbing uncontrollably, appeared in my dream. 'Rebbi, do you know what you did to me when you answered the Heavenly Court? When my sin was being judged and they wanted to punish me and sent me to Gehinnom, I claimed that I had received my atonement for this sin while living, as I was forced to pay that large sum of money. So they decided to ask you what you had in mind when you issued that penalty. But now I have no hope. What will become of me?'

"After this dream, I realized the awesome responsibility of a Rav, and it was just too much for me to bear. So do not be upset, my dear son-in-law, if Hashem has decided that the time is not yet ripe for you to take a Rabbinic post!"

HALACHAH OF THE DAY

We continue our discussion of practical applications of the laws of *tying* and *untying* on Shabbos.

According to most *poskim,* it is forbidden to tie shoes with a double knot on Shabbos. Furthermore, one may not tie his shoes with a single knot and bow combination if he intends to leave the knot in place for more than twenty-four hours. [For example, if the person tends to slip his shoes off at night without undoing the knot, such a knot may have been tied with intent to leave it in place for several days.] If, however, the knot will be undone within twenty-four hours, one may use a knot/bow combination. In such cases, some *poskim* permit even the use of a double knot; this opinion may be relied upon in cases of necessity (such as where the shoelaces constantly come loose unless such a knot is tied).

It is forbidden to untie laces that were tied in a double knot or in a bow/knot combination for more than twenty-four hours. (An exception to this rule is cases of necessity or where the laces are causing physical distress, as explained above.) However, if the person did not intend for the bow/knot combination to remain in place for longer than twenty-four hours, he may untie it — even if it was in fact in place for more than twenty-four hours. Thus, if a person slipped his shoes off on Friday night without untying the bow/knot, and he wants to untie the shoes Shabbos morning in order to put them on, he may do so. The reason for this is that we assume that his original intention was not to leave the knot in place for so long a period, since people generally untie their shoes at night.

We explained previously that a knot that is customarily left in place for more than twenty-four hours is considered a permanent knot, and that one is therefore Biblically forbidden to tie or untie such a knot on Shabbos. Nowadays, when one receives a tied-up parcel, it would seem that most people leave the knots in the string intact, and open the parcel by cutting the string. If this is the case, it would seem to be a Biblical violation of the *melachah* of *untying* to untie such a knot on Shabbos. A common application of this rule would be a bakery box that is tied with a string. In order to open the box, one should not untie the string; rather, he should cut the string in a destructive manner.

There are two different prevalent methods of tying a necktie — one is permissible, the other is questionable. If the knot is tied in such a way that when pulling the narrow end out of the knot the entire knot becomes undone, it is considered a bow, and may be tied on Shabbos even if one desires to leave the knot in place indefinitely. If, however, a knot is still left in place after pulling the narrow end through, the tie should be untied within twenty-four hours. Some *poskim* rule more leniently, stating that a necktie may be tied in any manner.

A CLOSER LOOK AT THE SIDDUR

The eleventh blessing of the weekday *Shemoneh Esrei* begins: הָשִׁיבָה שׁוֹפְטֵינוּ כְּבָרִאשׁוֹנָה וְיוֹעֲצֵינוּ כְּבַתְּחִלָּה וְהָסֵר מִמֶּנּוּ יָגוֹן וַאֲנָחָה, *Restore our judges as in earliest times, and our counselors as at first; remove from us sorrow and groans.*

This blessing, called the "blessing of *din*" by the Gemara, asks for restoration of justice. It follows the blessing that calls for the ingathering

of the exiles. The reestablishment of the proper judicial system is viewed as part of the process of redemption. As *Rambam* says (*Commentary to the Mishnah, Sanhedrin* 1:3), Mashiach will come only after the *Sanhedrin* is returned to its proper judging place.

We add to this a prayer to remove from us sorrow and groans. At first glance, this request does not seem to be at all connected to the request for a rebuilt judicial system. *R' Yonasan Eibeshitz* explains that one should include in this *tefillah* the prayer that Jewish judges should be proper and righteous (as we discussed in *A Torah Thought for the Day),* and that they should not be easily persuaded or bought off by bribery. For if, God forbid, this is the case, Hashem punishes both them and the society that allowed them to be appointed. The Talmud states in *Shabbos* (33a): Because of corruption of law and order, hunger, looting, and death by the sword come to the world. The opposite is true when righteous judges are appointed — they bring blessing to the world. (As we know, reward is always apportioned in greater measure than punishment.)

This is what we intend when we ask Hashem for the restoration of our judges as in earlier times. If justice will rule and prevail in the world, then sorrow and pain will be removed from our midst.

It is interesting to note that the *Baruch She'amar* cites an old version of the blessing that had the following text: וְהָסֵר מִמֶּנּוּ מַלְכוּת יָוָן וְרוֹמִי, *remove from us the Greek and Roman kingdoms.* It seems that these two names were removed by (or because of) censorship, and in their stead the two words יָגוֹן וַאֲנָחָה were inserted, referring more obliquely to the pain and sorrow that these nations caused when they ruled over the Jews. During ancient times, righteous judges and equitable Jewish laws were replaced by corrupt judges and cruel and unfair laws and decrees.

He then goes on to explain our version of the text in a manner similar to that expressed above. He cites another Gemara in *Shabbos* (139a): "If you see a generation that encounters much tragedy and suffering, check into the Jewish judges." Corrupt judges and judgments can be responsible for much pain and suffering. Thus, restoration of proper judges can indeed serve to remove from us much sorrow and groaning, and the link between the two parts of the blessing can then be clearly understood.

A TORAH THOUGHT FOR THE DAY

וַיֹּאמֶר ה׳ אֶל־מֹשֶׁה הִנֵּה אָנֹכִי בָּא אֵלֶיךָ בְּעַב הֶעָנָן בַּעֲבוּר יִשְׁמַע הָעָם בְּדַבְּרִי עִמָּךְ וְגַם־בְּךָ יַאֲמִינוּ לְעוֹלָם

HASHEM said to Moshe, "Behold! I will come to you in a thick cloud, so that the people will hear when I speak to you, and they will also believe in you forever" (*Shemos* 19:9).

There is a basic question that one may ask. The Torah writes clearly that after the drowning of the Egyptians in the *Yam Suf,* the people feared Hashem, and they had faith in Hashem and in Moshe His servant (*Shemos* 14:31). We see that they already had faith in Moshe. What, then, was the point of doing anything at this time to ensure that they would believe in Moshe?

As we know, the belief that Moshe's prophecy was of a higher level than that of all other prophets is the seventh of the Thirteen Principles of Judaism (י״ג עקרים), and here at *Mattan Torah* is where this was established (see *A Closer Look at the Siddur* to Sunday of *Parashas Vayeishev,* where we discussed this). It behooves us to pay close attention to the words of the *Rambam* to understand how he derives this from our verse.

Rambam dedicates an entire chapter in *Hilchos Yesodei HaTorah* (Ch. 5) to this fundamental principle. He says: "The Jews do not believe in Moshe Rabbeinu because of the wonders he performed, for if that would be the case, there would always be a doubt in some people's heart that perhaps they were performed with sorcerous practices. All wonders were carried out only for the necessity of the situation, i.e., the Egyptians had to be drowned so the sea was split, and so on. If so, what was the factor that convinced the people to believe wholeheartedly in Moshe?

"This belief came to us through the awesome sight of the Giving of the Torah, where our own eyes witnessed the 'fire' and 'thunderous noises'; we did not hear of them from a stranger whom we did not know. Every member of the Jewish nation saw how Moshe entered the cloud and then Hashem's voice rang out, 'Moshe, Moshe.' As the Gemara states in *Shabbos* (146), all the souls of the Jewish nation until the end of time were present at Har Sinai when the Torah was given (including those of converts)."

Rambam explains that the belief in Moshe is learned from the above verse, *I will come to you in a thick cloud etc. and they will also believe in you forever.* It would seem that until this point in time, the Jews did not have a total trust and belief in Moshe. There was still room for speculation as to whether their understanding of Moshe's stature was 100 percent correct.

The unshakable belief in Moshe that came with *Mattan Torah,* he explains, itself serves to preserve the truth of the Torah. Even if another prophet comes at a later time to change a certain mitzvah and he performs a wonder to prove his point, we are convinced that he is a false prophet, and we must not listen to him. Since he comes to contradict the words we received from Moshe, we can assume that he is not a true prophet, and that his wonders are performed through sorcery. Had our belief in the prophecy of Moshe been dependent on the wonders that he performed, we would be in a dilemma, trying to decide which wonders were more convincing.

The *Brisker Rav* takes this a step further. The awesome sight of *Mattan Torah,* he states, was not intended to convince us only of the authenticity of Moshe's prophecy. It served also to demonstrate the differences between other prophets and Moshe, which the *Rambam* enumerated in Chapter 7 of *Yesodei HaTorah.* One of the special privileges given to Moshe alone was that he was able to speak to Hashem whenever he wanted, while all other prophets had no way to initiate contact. They were forced to wait until a Divine spirit rested upon them. This distinction was also established at this time, as the verse (19:19) states: מֹשֶׁה יְדַבֵּר וְהָאֱלֹהִים יַעֲנֶנּוּ בְקוֹל, *Moshe would speak and HASHEM would respond to him in a voice,* which means that when Moshe spoke, Hashem answered him (see *Ibn Ezra*). Thus, this unique aspect of Moshe's prophecy was also established here.

MISHNAH OF THE DAY: SHABBOS 19:2

The following Mishnah discusses the circumcision procedure itself, explaining which of its various elements may be performed on the Sabbath, and how:[1]

NOTES

1. In order to understand this Mishnah properly, one must be familiar with the various steps of the circumcision procedure. Prior to circumcision, the corona has two coverings: The outer covering is a thick layer of skin called the foreskin; beneath it lies a thin membrane. The *mohel* first cuts off the foreskin. This act is called מִילָה, *circumcision.* He then tears the membrane and pulls it back, thereby exposing the corona. This is called פְּרִיעָה, *uncovering.* He next performs מְצִיצָה, *drawing* the *blood,* and then dresses the wound.

עוֹשִׂין כָּל צָרְכֵי מִילָה [בְּשַׁבָּת] — ***We may perform all the necessities of circumcision on the Sabbath:***[2] מוֹהֲלִין וּפוֹרְעִין וּמוֹצְצִין — ***We may circumcise,***[3] ***uncover*** the corona,[4] ***draw*** the blood,[5] וְנוֹתְנִין עָלֶיהָ אִיסְפְּלָנִית וְכַמּוֹן — ***and place a bandage and cumin upon it.***[6] אִם לֹא שָׁחַק מֵעֶרֶב שַׁבָּת — ***If one did not crush*** the cumin ***on the Sabbath eve*** before the onset of the Sabbath, לוֹעֵס בְּשִׁינָּיו וְנוֹתֵן — ***he may chew*** it ***with his teeth and apply*** it.[7] אִם לֹא טָרַף יַיִן וָשֶׁמֶן מֵעֶרֶב שַׁבָּת — ***If one did not vigorously mix wine and oil on the Sabbath eve,***[8] יִנָּתֵן זֶה בְּעַצְמוֹ וְזֶה בְּעַצְמוֹ — ***each of these***

NOTES

2. This statement is not intended to be merely an introduction to the Mishnah. Rather, it is meant to teach us that if the person who was performing the circumcision on the Sabbath failed to remove some shreds of flesh whose presence do not invalidate the circumcision (as will be explained below, Mishnah 6), he may nevertheless resume the circumcision and remove them, as long as he is still occupied with the circumcision (*Tos. Yom Tov* from Gemara 133b).

3. I.e., cut off the foreskin (*Rav; Rashi).*

4. By tearing and pulling back the thin membrane under the foreskin, one uncovers the corona (*Rav; Rashi*). This is an essential part of circumcision. If the person performing the circumcision fails to expose the corona, the infant is considered uncircumcised (*Ritva;* see below, Mishnah 6).

5. The blood is drawn out of the wound to prevent it from coagulating under the skin and causing the member to swell (*Tiferes Yisrael*). Normally, one who causes blood to flow on the Sabbath (where it can be considered a constructive act) thereby performs a derivative of the forbidden *melachah* of *slaughtering.* However, in this instance, drawing blood is permissible, since it is done to prevent a potentially fatal condition from developing (*Rav; Rashi*). [Many authorities hold that aside from any medical considerations, drawing out the blood is an inherent part of the mitzvah of circumcision (for further discussion, see *Sefer HaBris,* pp. 185, 216-226).]

6. These are applied for therapeutic purposes (*Ritva*). The cumin must be crushed to be effective, as is evident below.

7. Crushing cumin on the Sabbath in the normal manner is a derivative of the forbidden *melachah* of grinding and is ordinarily prohibited. Hence, although a circumcised person is considered critically ill (חוֹלֶה שֶׁיֵּשׁ בּוֹ סַכָּנָה), and it is therefore permitted to crush the cumin for him, nevertheless we perform this normally forbidden labor in the most unusual manner possible (*Rav; Rashi*).

8. In Mishnaic times it was customary to mix wine and oil by beating them in a bowl (as we do with eggs), and then applying the mixture to the incision as a medication (*Rav; Rashi*). Beating wine with oil on the Sabbath is prohibited by Rabbinic decree, as is beating eggs, for the reason that it appears as though one is preparing food for cooking. Although this is only a Rabbinic prohibition, it nonetheless is in effect even when the mixture is needed for post-circumcision medication (*Tiferes Yisrael*), for it can be prepared in the manner presently described in the Mishnah.

ingredients ***should be placed*** in the bowl ***by itself.***[9] וְאֵין עוֹשִׂין לָהּ חָלוּק לְכַתְּחִילָּה — ***And we may not in the first place fashion a shirt-like bandage for*** the circumcised member,[10] אֲבָל כּוֹרֵךְ עָלֶיהָ סְמַרְטוּט — ***but one may wrap a piece of cloth around it.***[11] אִם לֹא הִתְקִין מֵעֶרֶב שַׁבָּת — ***If he did not prepare*** even an ordinary cloth[12] ***on the Sabbath eve,*** כּוֹרֵךְ עַל אֶצְבָּעוֹ וּמֵבִיא — ***he may wrap*** one ***around his finger***[13] ***and bring*** it; וַאֲפִילּוּ מֵחָצֵר אַחֶרֶת — ***and*** he may bring it ***even from another courtyard.***[14]

NOTES

9. Although one may not vigorously mix them, he may pour first the wine and then the oil (or vice versa) into the same bowl, and then apply the contents of the bowl to the wound (*Meiri*).

10. After medications are applied to the circumcision wound, the wound is bandaged. During the Mishnaic era, it was common to employ for this purpose a cloth shaped like a finger, with openings at either end. This bandage was not essential for the actual treatment of the wound. Rather, it would be drawn over the corona [as if it were a "shirt" for the member], thereby preventing the skin from growing back over it (*Rav, Rashi*). Fashioning such a bandage on the Sabbath is prohibited because it is tantamount to making a utensil (and its purpose here does not address a life-threatening situation). Hence, such a bandage may be used for circumcision only if it has been prepared before the Sabbath (*Meiri*).

11. If one did not prepare a shirt-like bandage before the Sabbath, he may wrap an ordinary piece of cloth around the corona.

12. I.e., if before the Sabbath he did not even bring a piece of cloth to the site where the circumcision was to be performed (*Rav; Rashi; Meiri*).

13. He should wrap it around his finger [like a glove] and transport it in this irregular manner (*Rav; Rashi; Tiferes Yisrael*). Although there is a Rabbinic decree prohibiting the "wearing" of an article that is not considered apparel in a public domain, here it was permitted for the purpose of bandaging the circumcision wound (*Tiferes Yisrael*).

14. By Rabbinic decree it is prohibited to carry articles from one private property to another unless the owners have merged their properties by means of *eruvei chatzeiros* (see above, Mishnah 2:7). The circumcision bandage, however, may be brought from another person's property [i.e., even from one courtyard to another] in the manner prescribed above, even if no *eruv* was made (*Rav*).

GEMS FROM THE GEMARA

As our Mishnah deals with medical issues, the Gemara here expands on this topic. Abaye, in particular, cites many pieces of medical advice that he received from his "mother." In truth, this does not refer to his natural mother, for the Gemara tells us that Abaye was an orphan, whose mother died in childbirth. The various pieces of advice that he cites from his "mother" are actually those of his nurse, who raised him.

The final pieces of advice that the Gemara cites from Abaye's nurse (134a) concern an infant whose body has a reddish hue, and one whose body has a yellowish hue. In the former case, the nurse told Abaye, the problem is that the infant's blood is still not absorbed into his flesh. Therefore, his circumcision should be delayed until his blood is absorbed into his flesh. In the case of the infant who is yellow, the problem is that he is deficient in blood. Therefore, his circumcision should be delayed until his blood supply is sufficient.

The Gemara adduces a Baraisa as support for these last pieces of advice:

R' Nassan said: Once I went to the towns near the sea, and a woman came before me who had circumcised her first son and he died, and then she circumcised her second son, who also died. She now brought her third son before me. I saw that the skin of the infant was red. I told the woman, "Wait for him, and do not circumcise him until his blood is absorbed into his flesh." She waited for him until his blood was absorbed into his flesh, and then she circumcised him, and he lived. And they called the child Nassan the Babylonian after me.

R' Nassan continues his discourse:

On another occasion I traveled to the province of Cappadocia, and one woman came before me who had circumcised her first son and he died, her second son and he died, and now she brought her third son before me. I saw that the skin of the infant was yellow. I looked closely at him, and I did not see in him any covenantal blood. I said to the mother, "Wait for him, and do not circumcise him until he is full-blooded." She waited for him until he became full-blooded, and then she circumcised him, and he lived. And they called his name Nassan the Babylonian after my name.

QUESTION OF THE DAY:

Why does the verse state that Hashem told Moshe that the Jews would "also" believe in him forever?

For the answer, see page 58.

פרשת
יתרו

TUESDAY

PARASHAS
YISRO

A MUSSAR THOUGHT FOR THE DAY

We discussed in *A Torah Thought for the Day* the important principle of נְבוּאַת מֹשֶׁה, Moshe's supreme prophecy. There is a very important thought that is clarified by the *Meshech Chochmah* in his preface to *Shemos.* He asks: How can it be that at *Mattan Torah* it was established that Moshe would forever be the "father of all prophets," both to those who preceded him and those who would follow him? Is there not a fundamental concept that every person has *free choice* (as we have discussed several times in earlier studies)? How, then, can it be said absolutely that Moshe would always maintain his superiority? *Meshech Chochmah* strengthens his question by noting that there were true prophets who became established as prophets through signs and miracles that they performed, and at the end they became false prophets, such as Chananya ben Azur. Why was Moshe not vulnerable to falling from his eminent stature? Was he not also a human being?

Faced by the enormity of this question, *Meshech Chochmah* states that he is compelled to offer a startling interpretation. He suggests that from the time of *Mattan Torah* onward, Hashem liberated Moshe from the challenge of free choice, and he became bound to follow the will of Hashem, just as angels are. This is what the Torah means when it says that Hashem spoke through Moshe's mouth; there were no barriers causing him to misconstrue the message of Hashem, as he was a pure vehicle to deliver the words of Hashem.

Shiras David states that the *Meshech Chochmah* is careful to say that Moshe was elevated to the level of angels, because although angels do not have an evil inclination (*yetzer hara*), they still have the ability to sin (after a fashion), as we see with regard to the angels who came to overturn Sodom (see *Bereishis* 19:22 with *Rashi*). This, explains *Shiras David,* is why, although Moshe no longer had free choice, there was still a possibility for him to err, as occurred at *Mei Merivah,* with the result that he was not allowed to enter Eretz Yisrael.

We must realize that Moshe reached this exalted level only after he succeeded in utilizing all of his abilities to serve Hashem to the fullest extent possible. At that point, he was given this great gift, and it was therefore clear that he would always remain the father of all prophets.

Rambam states in *Hilchos Teshuvah* (5:2), where he elaborates on the concept of free will, that everyone can be a righteous man like Moshe Rabbeinu or a wicked man like Yeravam. Now, obviously, he is not talking about Moshe's level of prophecy, for the Torah testifies that no one else will be able to attain this level of prophecy. Rather, he is referring to what Moshe achieved on his own — success in utilizing his entire being to serve Hashem. Each person can, on his own level, use his abilities to the maximum in the service of Hashem, just as Moshe did.

HALACHAH OF THE DAY

We will conclude our discussion of the *melachos* of *tying* and *untying* with several more common applications of these laws.

When closing a plastic bag on Shabbos, one must take great care that the manner of closing the bag is not in violation of the laws of Shabbos. Many common methods of tying bags are forbidden — some of them Biblically.

One may not gather the two ends of the top of a bag and secure them together with a double knot. Furthermore, one may not gather the top of the bag into one piece and then tie it onto itself in a single knot.

Since garbage bags are usually left tied permanently, one may not tie a trash bag closed with a single knot/bow combination. This is true even if he intends to untie the bag within twenty-four hours.

One may not tie a food storage bag closed with a single knot and bow unless he specifically intends to undo the knot within twenty-four hours. Specific intent is necessary in this case because these bags are often left tied for more than twenty-four hours.

The only permissible method of tying closed a trash bag or a food storage bag that will be closed for more than twenty-four hours is by gathering the two ends of the top and tying them together in a single knot (alternatively, one may use a twist tie to close the bag — see below).

Since one may not untie a knot that it is forbidden to tie on Shabbos, it follows that one may not untie a food storage bag whose top was tied in one of the above listed forbidden manners. Therefore, if one encounters a bag tied in such a way and desires to open it, he should tear the bag open in a destructive fashion. If the bag is imprinted with pictures or letters, one must take care not to tear them.

The use of twist ties on Shabbos is a matter of dispute among the *poskim*. While some *poskim* permit their use, others forbid them to be used on Shabbos. The reasoning for this opinion is as follows: We mentioned earlier that twisting strands together in a fashion that will cause them to remain firmly wound together as one is a form of tying. The nature of twist ties is that once they are wound together they remain wound until they are manually separated. This would seem to be a form of tying on Shabbos. A simple way to avoid this problem is by employing a different method of using the twist tie on Shabbos. Instead of twisting the ends of the tie together, one may simply wind the twist tie around the neck of the bag several times so that it holds the bag closed.

A CLOSER LOOK AT THE SIDDUR

During the introduction to *Az Yashir* (the Song of the Sea) that we recite during *Pesukei D'Zimrah* every morning during *Shacharis,* we cite the verse (*Shemos* 14:31): וַיַּרְא יִשְׂרָאֵל אֶת־הַיָּד הַגְּדֹלָה אֲשֶׁר עָשָׂה ה׳ בְּמִצְרַיִם וַיִּירְאוּ הָעָם אֶת־ה׳ וַיַּאֲמִינוּ בַּה׳ וּבְמֹשֶׁה עַבְדּוֹ, *Israel saw the great hand that HASHEM inflicted upon Egypt, and the people feared HASHEM and they had faith in HASHEM and in Moshe, His servant.*

Although we learned (see *A Torah Thought for the Day* and *A Mussar Thought for the Day*) that the full belief in Moshe's prophecy became firm and established only at the time of receiving the Torah, nevertheless, after the Splitting of the Sea the Jews reached a certain level of belief in Moshe. This belief, as explained by *Rabbeinu Efraim,* was of the form that is described in the verse itself: *they had faith in HASHEM and in Moshe, His servant.* That is, they believed that Moshe was a true servant of Hashem, which means that he carried out his mission faithfully. The mission for which he was chosen while still in Midian, to take the Jews out of Egypt (*Shemos* 3:10), was finally accomplished after the drowning of the Egyptians. As the Midrash states, they were not called גְּאוּלִים, *redeemed ones,* until after their oppressors were punished. It is for this reason that we say in the blessing right before *Shemoneh Esrei,* שִׁירָה חֲדָשָׁה שִׁבְּחוּ גְאוּלִים לְשִׁמְךָ עַל שְׂפַת הַיָּם, *With a new song the redeemed ones praised You on the banks of the Sea.*

Thus, when Moshe successfully completed this assignment, he was recognized by all as a true servant of Hashem. This was the sum total of the faith they had in him — that he was a dedicated servant of Hashem. However, the faith in his unique level of prophecy was established only at *Mattan Torah.*

The *Gra* points out that in the entire *Haggadah Shel Pesach,* wherein we expound all the miracles of the Exodus in great detail, there is no mention of Moshe's name, with the exception of this verse mentioned here. He explains that this is intentional, so no attention would be diverted from Hashem, Who was the true Redeemer of the Jews. This verse, on the other hand, is mentioned in the Haggadah, for it reinforces that message by saying that the Bnei Yisrael saw and acknowledged that Moshe was only a servant of Hashem. He was not looking for any credit or to introduce any ideas of his own. Moshe was interested in only one thing — carrying out the will of Hashem, by fulfilling his tasks as completely and correctly as possible. Such a mention of Moshe is appropriate in the Haggadah, as it underscores the lesson that the Haggadah wishes to teach.

A TORAH THOUGHT FOR THE DAY

זָכוֹר אֶת־יוֹם הַשַּׁבָּת לְקַדְּשׁוֹ
Remember the day of the Sabbath, to sanctify it (*Shemos* 20:8).

This verse, which begins the fourth of the *Aseres HaDibros* (*Ten Commandments*), is the source of the commandment (which, according to most authorities, is Biblical in nature) to make *Kiddush* on the Sabbath. The word *remember* as used in this verse is interpreted not as a directive to hold the Sabbath in one's mind, but to actively speak of it, thus sanctifying it. This "speech" is the recital of *Kiddush.*

In the *Devarim* text of the *Aseres HaDibros* (5:12), the fourth commandment begins with the words: שָׁמוֹר אֶת־יוֹם הַשַּׁבָּת לְקַדְּשׁוֹ, *Guard the Sabbath to sanctify it. Rashi* (to our verse) tells us that when giving the Torah, Hashem said both *"Remember"* and *"Guard"* simultaneously — a miracle that could be performed only by Hashem Himself. The commandment to *guard* the Sabbath is expressed in *refraining* from acts that would desecrate the Sabbath, such as the performance of forbidden labor. The commandment to *remember,* on the other hand, refers to a positive action that establishes the sanctity of the Sabbath. [*Rashi* goes even further, explaining that the commandment to remember the Sabbath is actually in effect all week. He cites this as the source for the statement of the Gemara in *Beitzah* (16a) that if one comes upon an attractive item (such as a prime animal), he should put it away for the Sabbath. Thus, one must keep the Sabbath in the forefront of his mind all week.]

We may ask: If the commands to *remember* and to *guard* the Sabbath are fundamentally different, why did Hashem express them simultaneously? *Gur Aryeh* (to *Devarim* 5:12) answers that in fact the two are connected, for reciting *Kiddush* clarifies the *reason* that we refrain from labor on the Sabbath. Without any formal declaration, it would be easy for one to view the Sabbath as simply a day off from the exertions of the workweek, without any greater purpose. The recital of *Kiddush* makes it clear, however, that we are ceasing our labors in order to commemorate the fact that Hashem rested on the Sabbath after creating the world; therefore, the fulfillment of the commandment to *remember* the Sabbath assists in the proper fulfillment of the command to *guard* the Sabbath.

MISHNAH OF THE DAY: SHABBOS 19:3

פרשת יתרו

WEDNESDAY

PARASHAS YISRO

The following Mishnah discusses the preoperative and postoperative care of the infant who is undergoing circumcision on the Sabbath:

מַרְחִיצִין אֶת הַקָּטָן — ***We may bathe the infant,***[1] בֵּין לִפְנֵי הַמִּילָה וּבֵין לְאַחַר הַמִּילָה — ***both prior to the circumcision, and following the circumcision;***[2] וּמְזַלְּפִין עָלָיו בַּיָּד — ***and we may sprinkle*** water ***upon him by hand,***[3] אֲבָל לֹא בִכְלִי — ***but not with a utensil.***[4] רַבִּי אֶלְעָזָר בֶּן עֲזַרְיָה אוֹמֵר מַרְחִיצִין אֶת הַקָּטָן בַּיּוֹם הַשְּׁלִישִׁי שֶׁחָל לִהְיוֹת בַּשַּׁבָּת — ***R' Elazar ben Azariah says: We may bathe the infant on the third day*** following the circumcision ***when it occurs on the Sabbath.***[5] שֶׁנֶּאֱמַר — ***As it is said:***[6] ,,וַיְהִי בַיּוֹם הַשְּׁלִישִׁי בִּהְיוֹתָם כֹּאֲבִים" — ***"And it came to pass on the third day, when they were in pain"*** (*Genesis* 34:25).[7]

The Mishnah next considers whether the Sabbath can be overridden in cases of doubt:

NOTES

1. I.e., the infant may be bathed with hot water on the day of his circumcision, even when it is on the Sabbath (*Tiferes Yisrael*).

2. In Mishnaic times it was customary to bathe the infant with hot water twice, once prior to the circumcision to strengthen him to endure the circumcision, and again following the circumcision. Failure to perform either of these washings was considered endangering the infant's life. The Rabbis, therefore, permitted bathing the infant on the Sabbath if he is to be circumcised then. [However, the bathing should be done in an unusual manner; see below.]

3. As we saw in the case of the cumin in the previous Mishnah, whatever can be done in an unusual manner should be done in such a manner. Hence, the child should not actually be immersed. Rather, the water should be sprinkled on him (*Rav, Rambam Commentary* from Gemara 134b).

4. Moreover, although sprinkling warm water by hand upon the infant is permitted, sprinkling it from a utensil remains prohibited (*Rav*).

5. R' Elazar ben Azariah differs with the Tanna Kamma on two counts: (a) He permits bathing the infant in the usual manner both before and after the circumcision, whereas the Tanna Kamma permits only sprinkling; (b) he also permits bathing the infant with hot water on the third day following the circumcision (*Rav*).

6. This verse is stated in connection with the people of Shechem, who circumcised themselves and were attacked on the third day after their circumcision by Shimon and Levi.

7. We learn from this verse that the danger to a circumcised person increases on the third day after his circumcision. Accordingly, R' Elazar ben Azariah's lenient ruling applies only to the third day, not to the second (*Rav;* see *Tos. Yom Tov* 9:3).

פרשת יתרו

WEDNESDAY

PARASHAS YISRO

סָפֵק — *A questionable one,* [8] **וְאַנְדְּרוֹגִינוֹס — *or an androgyne,*** [9] **אֵין מְחַלְּלִין עָלָיו אֶת הַשַּׁבָּת — *we may not violate the Sabbath on his behalf.*** [10] **וְרַבִּי יְהוּדָה מַתִּיר בְּאַנְדְּרוֹגִינוֹס — *R' Yehudah, however, permits*** the circumcision to take place on the Sabbath ***in*** the case of ***an androgyne.*** [11]

NOTES

8. I.e., a baby possibly born during the eighth month of pregnancy (*Rav; Rashi*). In Mishnaic times a child born during the eighth month was not considered viable, and it was anticipated that he would soon die. Accordingly, there is no obligation to circumcise him, and his circumcision certainly does not override the Sabbath. Consequently, if there is uncertainty as to whether or not a child was born during the eighth month of his incubation period, his circumcision also does not take place on the Sabbath. A "seven-month child," however, is considered viable, and his circumcision does override the Sabbath (Gemara 135a).

9. An individual possessing both male and female organs (*Tiferes Yisrael*). Since his gender is doubtful (*Rashi* to 135a), the obligation to circumcise him therefore applies only out of doubt as well.

10. I.e., to perform circumcision. Since, in both cases, the obligation of circumcision is questionable, it may not be performed on the Sabbath. Although one is obligated to circumcise even a child whose requirement for circumcision is questionable, this can be done after the Sabbath, when it does not involve any possibly unwarranted desecration of the Sabbath.

11. R' Yehudah bases his view on the passage (*Bereishis* 17:10): הִמּוֹל לָכֶם כָּל־זָכָר, *Every male among you shall be circumcised.* The word, כָּל, *every,* is taken to allude to the androgyne [*every male* being interpreted as *every type of male*], teaching us that his obligation to be circumcised is definite. The Tanna Kamma, however, bases his ruling on the verse (*Vayikra* 12:3): וּבַיּוֹם הַשְּׁמִינִי יִמּוֹל בְּשַׂר עָרְלָתוֹ, *And on the eighth day, the flesh of his foreskin shall be circumcised.* The words וּבַיּוֹם הַשְּׁמִינִי, *and on the eighth day,* imply that we shall perform the circumcision on the eighth day even if it should occur on the Sabbath. The term עָרְלָתוֹ, *his foreskin,* implies a foreskin that must definitely be circumcised, not one whose obligation is doubtful. Accordingly, we deduce that only a definitely obligatory circumcision overrides the Sabbath, and not a doubtful one such as that of an androgyne (Gemara 135a, as understood by *Rashi*).

GEMS FROM THE GEMARA

The Gemara (134b-135a) cites a Baraisa that expands upon our Mishnah. We saw in the Mishnah that the term עָרְלָתוֹ, *his foreskin,* implies a foreskin that must definitely be circumcised, not the foreskin of one whose obligation of circumcision is doubtful. The Baraisa states that the term *his foreskin* teaches further that circumcising the foreskin of one who was certainly born on the previous Sabbath overrides the

Sabbath, but circumcising one who was born during twilight on Friday evening does not override the Sabbath. [Since there is a question whether twilight is part of the outgoing or the incoming day, one born during twilight on Friday may not be circumcised on the following Sabbath day, for perhaps he was born on Friday and the following Sabbath is, in fact, the *ninth* day after his birth, not the eighth. Similarly, one born during twilight on the Sabbath may not be circumcised on the following Sabbath day, for perhaps he was born at night and the following Sabbath is only the *seventh* day.]

Moreover, states the Baraisa, the term *his foreskin* teaches that circumcising the foreskin of one who is certainly uncircumcised overrides the Sabbath, but "circumcising" one who was born circumcised does not override the Sabbath.

What circumcision can be performed upon an infant that was born circumcised (i.e., without a foreskin)? The Baraisa relates that Beis Shammai say that one must cause "covenantal blood" to flow from a naturally circumcised infant, while Beis Hillel say that it is not necessary.

The Baraisa then presents a conflicting Tannaic interpretation of the dispute between Beis Shammai and Beis Hillel: R' Shimon ben Elazar maintained that Beis Shammai and Beis Hillel did not disagree regarding the case of one who was born circumcised, for all agree in that case that one must cause covenantal blood to flow from the infant. In what case, then, did they disagree? In the case of a convert who converts to Judaism when he is already circumcised. Beis Shammai say that such a convert must undergo a "circumcision" — that is, one must cause covenantal blood to flow from such a convert, while Beis Hillel say that one need not cause covenantal blood to flow from him.

A MUSSAR THOUGHT FOR THE DAY

In the fourth of the *Aseres HaDibros,* we are commanded to remember the Sabbath, and also to refrain from forbidden *melachah.* The scope of the prohibition is wide-ranging, forbidding a wide variety of actions (as we have seen in our studies of the *Halachah of the Day*). Indeed, we are enjoined from even *thinking* on the Sabbath about how to proceed with our weekday work.

The *Dubno Maggid* once asked: The prophet Michah tells us that Hashem challenges the Jews, saying: "Have I ever oppressed you with My mitzvos?" The commentators explain this to mean, "Are any of My

mitzvos oppressive and difficult to keep?" Now, seemingly, one could view the Sabbath restrictions as a very great burden, for they completely forbid a Jew from performing or even thinking about his labors. Is this not a severe restriction?

The Maggid answered that Sabbath is restrictive only for those who have no faith in Hashem. For those who do have faith, however, the opposite is true. Sabbath is not restrictive, it is liberating! He illustrates his meaning with a famous parable:

Once, a poor man was walking down the road, bent almost double under his heavy pack. A wealthy merchant passed by in his fine carriage and graciously offered the fellow a ride. The poor man gratefully accepted, and clambered up into the back of the wagon, pack and all.

A bit later, the merchant looked into the rear of the wagon to see how his passenger was faring. To his great surprise, he saw that the poor man was sitting in the wagon with his pack on his shoulders! He asked in amazement, "Why are you still carrying your pack?! Put it down on the seat beside you, and relax!" The poor man looked at him and replied, "My master! You are doing me a great service by offering me a ride; I would not presume to make you carry my pack as well!" The merchant laughed, and said, "Dear man! You are being foolish. It matters not whether your pack is on your shoulders or on the seat; both are being carried by the wagon in any case!"

So too, says the Maggid, is it with us. Hashem "carries" us all and provides for all of our needs. During the week, it is our responsibility to work to provide for ourselves, but on the Sabbath He takes us onto His wagon, as it were, and tells us that we need not worry. If we take our mundane worries with us into the Sabbath, we are no different than that poor man, who failed to realize the true source of his aid.

HALACHAH OF THE DAY

The next of the thirty-nine forbidden *melachos* of Shabbos is the melachah of תּוֹפֵר, *sewing.* Sewing was necessary as part of the construction of the Mishkan, since it was sometimes necessary to repair curtains or other woven articles that had become torn.

The *melachah* of *sewing* may be defined as the uniting of two items (or two parts of one item) into one. This definition is not limited to the specific common case of using thread to sew together two strips of cloth; rather, it also includes all forms of mending such as gluing and taping. Additionally, it applies to materials of all textures, such as paper, soft plastic, leather, and wood. We will focus first upon the act of sewing itself, and then move on to other forms of mending.

The minimal act of sewing that is forbidden under Biblical law is the drawing of a thread back and forth through two pieces of fabric, such that both ends of the thread emerge on the same side, *and then tying the ends.* This may be done either by tying the ends together, or by tying a knot in each end so that the thread cannot slide back out through the fabric. The stitch is now fastened securely, and the pieces of fabric are considered to be bonded together as one. Even if the ends are knotted with non-professional and non-permanent knots (which would themselves not be prohibited under the *melachah* of *tying*), one still violates the *melachah* of *sewing,* since the prohibition of sewing is independent of the prohibition of tying. If one draws a thread back and forth through two pieces of fabric and ties the ends in a permanent or professional knot, he violates both the prohibition against *tying* and the prohibition against *sewing.*

Another act that is considered sewing under the Biblical guidelines of this prohibition is drawing a thread through two fabrics three or more times, even without tying the ends. This also securely fastens two pieces of fabric, since a triple stitch does not normally come free by itself.

It is forbidden by Rabbinic decree to draw a thread back and forth through two pieces of fabric even without tying the ends of the thread. One is permitted, however, to draw a thread through fabric once even if he then ties the ends of the thread (with a permissible type of knot), because drawing a thread through only once is not considered *sewing* at all.

A CLOSER LOOK AT THE SIDDUR

In connection with the fourth of the *Aseres HaDibros,* let us take a closer look at the text of the Friday night *Kiddush.*

We begin *Kiddush* on Friday night with the recitation of the *Vayechulu* prayer, which, as we have discussed earlier in our studies, attests to our belief that Hashem created the world in six days and rested on the seventh. Indeed, we say this prayer during *Maariv* of Friday night as well, and some authorities explain that we include it in *Kiddush* to fulfill the obligation that rests upon those household members who did not *daven Maariv* (see *Tosafos* to *Pesachim* 106a).

Following this passage, we recite a blessing over wine (בּוֹרֵא פְּרִי הַגָּפֶן,

borei pri hagafen). *Kiddush* is recited over wine because we are commanded to *remember* the Sabbath with *Kiddush;* the term *remember* is often used in association with wine (see, for example, *Shir HaShirim* 1:4), and therefore we recite *Kiddush* over wine (see *Tosafos* ibid.). After the blessing over the wine, we recite the main *Kiddush* blessing. This blessing notes that we, the Jewish nation, were given the special gift of the Sabbath as our heritage, as a mark of Hashem's love and favor. It continues by identifying the Sabbath as זִכָּרוֹן לְמַעֲשֵׂה בְרֵאשִׁית, *a remembrance of the Creation* — that is, a testimony to Hashem's creation of the world.

We also speak of the Sabbath as תְּחִלָּה לְמִקְרָאֵי קֹדֶשׁ, *the prologue to the [days] that are designated as holy.* These "days" are the festivals, which would receive their holy status each year as a result of the Jewish court's declaration of the new month (before the advent of the fixed calendar). The Sabbath is called the *prologue* to the festivals because in *Vayikra* Ch. 23, where the festivals are listed, the passage begins with mention of the Sabbath. Alternatively, it is because its holiness stems from the beginning of Creation, while the festivals came into existence only later.

We also mention the Exodus from Egypt in *Kiddush,* stating that it is a זֵכֶר לִיצִיאַת מִצְרָיִם, *a remembrance of the Exodus from Egypt. Ramban* explains that while the Sabbath attests to our belief in Hashem's creation of the world, the Exodus from Egypt proved to the world that Hashem continues to control and supervise the world as He sees fit. Thus, the Sabbath and the Exodus are interconnected, in that both attest to Hashem's mastery of the world. It is thus fitting to speak of the Exodus during *Kiddush.*

QUESTION OF THE DAY:

What other obligation, aside from Kiddush, is derived from this verse (Shemos 20:8): "Remember the day of the Sabbath, to sanctify it"?

For the answer, see page 58.

A TORAH THOUGHT FOR THE DAY

לֹא תִגְנֹב
You shall not steal (*Shemos* 20:13).

The Gemara in *Sanhedrin* (86a) observes that the prohibition against theft included in the *Aseres HaDibros* is speaking not about ordinary theft, but rather about the capital crime of kidnaping. This is known, explains the Gemara, by looking at the context into which this commandment was placed. Since the two commandments that immediately precede the prohibition of לֹא תִגְנֹב, *You shall not steal* — namely, לֹא תִרְצָח, *You shall not kill,* and לֹא תִנְאָף, *You shall not commit adultery* — are both capital offenses, by utilizing the Scriptural exegesis of דָּבָר הַלָּמֵד מֵעִנְיָנוֹ, *something that is derived from context,* we may learn that the commandment of *You shall not steal* is also a crime that warrants the death penalty. Since it is clear from other passages in the Torah [such as the verse שַׁלֵּם יְשַׁלֵּם, *he must repay* (*Shemos* 22:2; see *Rashi* there)] that an ordinary thief is not killed, but is required to return the object that he stole or its value, and the only capital crime involving stealing is kidnaping [as the Torah tells us elsewhere (ibid. 21:16): וְגֹנֵב אִישׁ וּמְכָרוֹ וְנִמְצָא בְיָדוֹ מוֹת יוּמָת, *One who kidnaps a man and sells him, and he was found to have been in his hand, shall be put to death*], it is understood that this commandment is also referring to kidnaping.

Even so, many Midrashim and commentaries explain that all types of theft are included in this prohibition. *Targum Onkelos* translates לֹא תִגְנֹב literally as *do not steal,* and does not specify *do not steal another person.* This understanding, however, does not contradict the Gemara's exegesis, for it is possible that the Gemara is telling us only that it is evident from the placement of this commandment that kidnaping is *included* in the prohibition of *You shall not steal.* It does not mean that *all* theft dealt with in this commandment is subject to the death penalty (see *Ibn Ezra* and *Sforno*). Thus, according to these commentators, the commandment includes a prohibition against all types of theft, including kidnaping, theft of property, robbery, fraud or damage.

Many commentaries ask a basic question about the inclusion of לֹא תִגְנֹב, *You shall not steal* — as well as the accompanying commandments of לֹא תִרְצָח, *You shall not kill,* and לֹא תִנְאָף, *You shall not commit adultery* — in the *Aseres HaDibros.* Unlike the other commandments — such as לֹא תַחְמֹד, *You shall not covet,* and זָכוֹר אֶת־יוֹם הַשַּׁבָּת לְקַדְּשׁוֹ, *Remember the Sabbath day to keep it holy* — which instructed the Jewish people to observe new commandments, the prohibitions against theft, murder and adultery

פרשת יתרו

THURSDAY

PARASHAS YISRO

were already incumbent on all of mankind by their inclusion in the *Sheva Mitzvos Bnei Noach,* the seven Noahide commandments. Accordingly, the Jewish people had been required to observe these laws even before receiving the Torah. This being the case, what was the purpose of including these already familiar laws in Hashem's Divine Revelation at Sinai? What new instructions were the Bnei Yisrael given regarding these mitzvos when they received the Torah?

R' Yaakov Weinberg explained that the difference between the seven Noahide mitzvos (which were incumbent upon all the nations of the world, including the Jewish people even before they accepted the Torah) and the 613 mitzvos in the Torah is that these two sets of mitzvos were intended to achieve two totally separate purposes. The seven commandments that were given to all of mankind are preconditions that are needed for people to simply exist and live as human beings; in order for people to enjoy the world that Hashem created, the Creator determined that these rules must be followed. Accordingly, humanity was not given a choice as to whether or not they wanted to accept these obligations. Moreover, since the only purpose of these commandments is to allow a person to live in this world, a person who successfully fulfills them does not impact anything beyond his own existence.

The Torah that was given to the Bnei Yisrael at Sinai was different. Observing the mitzvos of the Torah is not, as are the seven Noahide mitzvos, necessary for basic human survival. Rather, the Torah was — and is — a covenant offered by Hashem to the Jewish people that allows us an opportunity to live a life of elevated spiritual benefit beyond simple, mundane existence. Through the Torah, we enjoy the opportunity to become close — and bring the entire world closer — to Him. [It was for this reason that the Jews had to *choose* to accept the Torah, for a covenant is obviously meaningless when forced upon one of the parties.]

Understanding that the Torah is a relationship with Hashem designed to bring humanity closer to Him also allows us to understand that its mitzvos are far more than a long list of do's and don't's. In giving us the mitzvos, Hashem is telling us that this is the way we must live in order to continuously refine and develop our bond with Him. Successfully fulfilling the mitzvos of the Torah creates a closer connection between Hashem and the world, and disobeying them distances us from Him.

With this in mind, we now understand that although some of the Noahide laws were "repeated" in the *Aseres HaDibros,* this inclusion gave these mitzvos a new world of meaning. Although theft was forbidden before *Mattan Torah,* a person who did not steal carried out the basic responsibilities that allowed him to live a physical life; nothing beyond this was achieved. However, after the Torah was given and "*you shall not steal*" was included in the covenant of mitzvos, the very same action took on added spiritual importance. Hashem told us that living an honest life is one of the criteria for becoming close to Him. After *Mattan Torah,* a person who does not steal (or kill or commit adultery) impacts not only himself, but spiritually improves the entire world.

MISHNAH OF THE DAY: SHABBOS 19:4

Only a circumcision performed on the eighth day overrides the Sabbath prohibition against inflicting a wound. The following Mishnah discusses the liability of a person who inadvertently performed circumcision on the Sabbath upon a baby that was either less or more than eight days old:

מִי שֶׁהָיוּ לוֹ שְׁנֵי תִינוֹקוֹת — ***One who had two infants*** to circumcise, אֶחָד לָמוּל אַחַר הַשַּׁבָּת — ***one to circumcise after the Sabbath,*** וְאֶחָד לָמוּל בְּשַׁבָּת — ***and one to circumcise on the Sabbath,***[1] וְשָׁכַח וּמָל אֶת שֶׁל אַחַר הַשַּׁבָּת בְּשַׁבָּת — ***and he forgot*** which one was which ***and circumcised the one due after the Sabbath on the Sabbath,***[2] חַיָּיב — ***he is liable*** to a *chatas* for having inadvertently desecrated the Sabbath.[3] אֶחָד לָמוּל בְּעֶרֶב שַׁבָּת — If he had two infants, ***one to circumcise on Friday,***[4] וְאֶחָד לָמוּל בְּשַׁבָּת — ***and one to circumcise on the Sabbath,*** וְשָׁכַח וּמָל אֶת שֶׁל עֶרֶב שַׁבָּת בְּשַׁבָּת — ***and he forgot and circumcised the***

NOTES

1. For example, one was born the previous Sabbath, and the other on the previous Sunday.

2. I.e., he mixed up the infants, and circumcised the infant that was supposed to be circumcised on Sunday a day early, on the Sabbath.

3. Since the circumcision, having been performed prior to the eighth day, is invalid, he is liable to a *chatas* for making a wound — a derivative of the forbidden *melachah* of *slaughtering* (*Rav* from Gemara 137a). [Although this act of wounding is completely destructive (since it is not a valid circumcision), and generally there is no liability for forbidden labors that are destructive, our Mishnah nonetheless considers him liable, for the Tanna of our Mishnah is R' Shimon, who rules (see Gemara 106a) that wounding and burning are exceptions to the general rule that exempts destructive acts (see *Kereisos* 19b).]

4. I.e., the infant was born on Friday and should therefore have been circumcised before the Sabbath. For some reason, however, he was not circumcised on that day. Since the Sabbath is not his eighth day of life, he may not be circumcised then, but must wait until Sunday.

Friday one on the Sabbath: רַבִּי אֱלִיעֶזֶר מְחַיֵּיב חַטָּאת — ***R' Eliezer holds*** him ***liable*** to ***a chatas,***[5] וְרַבִּי יְהוֹשֻׁעַ פּוֹטֵר — ***but R' Yehoshua exempts*** him.[6]

NOTES

5. Although he performed a mitzvah of circumcision (since the infant is more than eight days old), R' Eliezer holds that he is nevertheless liable to a *chatas,* because the mitzvah of circumcising an infant that is more than eight days old does not override the Sabbath (*Rav; Rashi*).

6. R' Yehoshua holds that since he erred while attempting to perform a mitzvah (the circumcision of the child born on the preceding Sabbath), and the end result was that he did, in fact, fulfill a mitzvah (circumcising the child born Friday of the previous week, who is more than eight days old), albeit the wrong one, he is not liable to a *chatas.* This is because R' Yehoshua considers one liable for inadvertently performing a forbidden labor only if he is engaged in an optional activity at the time. However, if he is engaged at the time in a mitzvah — such as circumcision — he is exempt. However, in the first case of this Mishnah (regarding a baby not yet eight days old), R' Yehoshua agrees that he is liable. This is because a child less than eight days old is not yet eligible for circumcision. Hence, the person who circumcises him cannot be considered to be engaged in a mitzvah (*Rav* from Gemara ibid.).

GEMS FROM THE GEMARA

According to our reading of the Mishnah, the opening case is not subject to a dispute: Everyone agrees that the circumciser is liable to a *chatas* for mistakenly circumcising a seven-day-old baby on the Sabbath. However, the Gemara (137a) records that there is an Amoraic dispute as to how the Mishnah's opening case should read.

Rav Huna's version of the Mishnah is exactly as we have it: The Mishnah begins by saying that where one mistakenly circumcised an after-Sabbath infant on the Sabbath, all agree that he *is* liable to a *chatas* [since he did not actually perform a mitzvah, as the circumcision of a seven-day-old baby is meaningless]. The case of the dispute between R' Eliezer and R' Yehoshua is where he circumcised a Friday child (i.e., a nine-day-old baby) on the Sabbath — where his error *did* result in the performance of a mitzvah.

Rav Yehudah, however, had a different version of the Mishnah. In his version, the first case of the Mishnah involves a case where one accidentally circumcised a *nine*-day-old baby on the Sabbath (the case that is second in our reading of the Mishnah), and according to his reading, both R' Eliezer and R' Yehoshua agree in this case that the circumciser is *exempt* from a *chatas* [since he did in fact perform a mitzvah]. The Mishnah then goes on to state in its second case that R' Eliezer and

R' Yehoshua disagree in a case where he mistakenly circumcised a *seven*-day-old infant on the Sabbath instead of the eight-day-old one (in Rav Huna's reading, this is the first case of the Mishnah, and all agree that he *is* liable to a *chatas*). Although in this case he did not in the end perform a mitzvah, R' Yehoshua nevertheless exempts him (according to Rav Yehudah's reading) because he erred while *attempting* to perform a mitzvah.

Both Rav Huna and Rav Yehudah derive R' Yehoshua's position (according to their respective versions) from a comparison between our Mishnah and the laws of the *chatas* that is brought for idolatry. [The rules for all questions of liability to a *chatas* are derived from the *chatas* brought for the sin of idolatry (see *Rashi* from Gemara 68b-69a).]

According to both Rav Huna and Rav Yehudah, R' Eliezer holds that this case is comparable to the case of idolatry: Just as in the case of idolatry the Torah says: "You shall not do it," and when one does do it inadvertently he is liable to a *chatas,* here too, in the case of a mistaken circumcision on the Sabbath, one who circumcises in error is liable.

On the other hand, R' Yehoshua distinguishes between the cases, and therefore exempts the circumciser. According to Rav Huna, the distinction is that in the case of idolatry he is liable because no mitzvah is actually performed, whereas in the case of a mistaken circumcision on the Sabbath, a mitzvah is actually performed. Hence, only in a case in which a proper circumcision is performed (such as where the nine-day-old baby is in fact circumcised on the Sabbath), which does not match the *chatas* model of idolatry, is the circumciser exempt from a *chatas.*

However, according to Rav Yehudah, R' Yehoshua's distinction is that in the case of idolatry, the sinner is *not* occupied with attempting to perform a mitzvah, whereas the circumciser in our case *is* occupied with attempting to perform a mitzvah. Accordingly, even in a case in which a proper circumcision is *not* performed (because the baby circumcised was only seven days old), which does not match the *chatas* model of idolatry, the circumciser is exempt from a *chatas.*

QUESTION OF THE DAY:

Is a person liable to execution for kidnaping his own child?

For the answer, see page 58.

A MUSSAR THOUGHT FOR THE DAY

In *A Torah Thought for the Day,* we noted that the commentaries ask why mitzvos such as the prohibitions against murder, theft and adultery, already included in the seven Noahide mitzvos, were repeated as part of the *Aseres HaDibros.* The *Alter of Slabodka* also raises another point. The Jewish people standing at Har Sinai were the loftiest spiritual generation that had ever existed in the history of mankind. Why did Hashem have to tell them such things as *You shall not steal*? Clearly, the base action of illegally taking another person's property would have been beneath them?

In answer to this question, the Alter states that a great difference exists between the Noahide prohibition against stealing, and the commandment of *You shall not steal* that was said at Sinai. The motive behind the Noahide prohibition against theft was (like all of the seven mitzvos that the entire world must obey) a necessary safeguard needed to maintain society. Since it is clear that society is unable to exist when open robbery is condoned, a person is not permitted to take an object that belongs to somebody else. The prohibition of *You shall not steal* in the *Aseres HaDibros,* however, includes an entirely different, and far more encompassing, message than the need to refrain from simple theft.

One aspect of this wider perspective of theft is seen in *Targum Yonason ben Uziel's* explanation of לֹא תִגְנֹב. He explains that in this commandment, Hashem told *My nation, the Bnei Yisrael: You may not steal, you may not associate or be a partner with a thief, you may not have any thieves in your midst, so you can train your children that they are not to steal. Me'am Loez* adds other actions included in the prohibition of לֹא תִגְנֹב, such as the restriction against buying stolen goods, for if a thief knows that he has no outlet for his stolen items, he will no longer steal. While the basic Noahide prohibition against theft does not allow a person to actually pocket his friend's article, לֹא תִגְנֹב requires a much higher level of responsibility in regard to theft. A Jew must measure every one of his actions and ensure that they are totally honest, so that theft will never even indirectly occur because of something that he does.

The Alter goes even further. He explains that לֹא תִגְנֹב also instructs more: beyond the Noahide prohibition, and even the additional facets of responsibility mentioned by *Targum Yonason ben Uziel,* לֹא תִגְנֹב does not allow a person to "steal" even if the stolen item is intangible, such as taking someone else's opportunity to perform a mitzvah (*Chullin* 133a) or being *goneiv daas* (literally, *stealing a mind*), by tricking a person or misleading him to believe something that is not true. It is similarly forbidden to take something for a few moments as a "joke" to annoy a person, even if the intent is not to keep the object. In short, any action that in any way *resembles* taking something illicitly was also included in the commandment of לֹא תִּגְנֹב said at Sinai.

Continuing, the Alter explains why this is so. In including all of these actions in the *Aseres HaDibros,* the Torah is telling us that the hurt a person feels when he realizes that his "mind has been stolen" — i.e., that he has been taken advantage of — is a feeling of vulnerability that, in a small but real way, is similar to how a person feels when he returns home to find that his house has been burglarized. Similarly, the loss that a person about to excitedly perform a mitzvah feels when the opportunity to do so is snatched from him is also one of being robbed. Even though a person may not react with the same feeling of outrage, and it is easy to rationalize that these sins are not as severe, the Torah tells us the truth — the person who caused this hurt is no less guilty than a thief.

The same concept, says the Alter, must be applied to the inclusion of לֹא תִּרְצָח, *You shall not kill,* and לֹא תִּנְאָף, *You shall not commit adultery,* in the *Aseres HaDibros.* The Gemara gives examples of many actions that are considered as severe as murder (such as shaming a person in public) and many inappropriate modes of behavior that are compared to adultery. The Torah, in including these previously forbidden actions in the *Aseres HaDibros,* was teaching the Jewish people a lesson that applies to everyone, even to the lofty generation that stood at Sinai — the *middos* (character traits) that give rise to performing these prohibitions may not be present in our lives in any form.

HALACHAH OF THE DAY

As mentioned above, the *melachah* of *sewing* is distinct from that of tying a knot. Nonetheless, since they are both means of fastening, some *poskim* permit non-permanent sewing, just as they permit non-permanent tying. According to these *poskim,* it is permitted to sew two items together if the intent is to separate them within twenty-four hours, [and, in cases of necessity, within seven days]. Since other *poskim* dispute this ruling, stating that non-permanent sewing is prohibited, the halachah follows the stringent view. However, in the presence of mitigating factors, one may rely upon the more lenient view, as we will explain below. Some *poskim* rule that taping for a short term is permitted. This is because taping things together with the intent to separate them shortly is more similar to buttoning than to sewing. This leniency does not apply to gluing.

Fastening two items by tightening a thread that had connected them loosely is considered a transgression of the *av melachah* of *sewing.* Thus, if a hem or a seam became loose and the ends spread apart slightly, it is forbidden to pull the thread in order to bring the loose edges together tightly. Similarly, it is forbidden to secure a loose button by pulling a loose thread and thereby re-tightening the button.

The *Shulchan Aruch* cites an interesting application of this rule. It was common in earlier times for people to tighten their sleeves by pulling on a strap that was threaded through it. The *Shulchan Aruch* rules that tightening one's sleeve in this manner is forbidden, unless the holes through which the strap is threaded are loose and are stitched around the edges (like buttonholes). If the holes are tight and unstitched, tightening the strap is tantamount to sewing the ends of the sleeve together. By contrast, when the holes are spacious and stitched, tightening the strap is more like buttoning one's sleeve, rather than like sewing. Nevertheless, even when the holes are spacious and stitched, the *poskim* permit tightening the sleeve in this manner only if one's intent is to loosen it later when one removes the garment. It is forbidden to tighten the strap partially on Shabbos if one's intent is to leave it in that position permanently, and to always slide one's hand into and out of the partially tightened sleeve.

This principle applies also to tying shoelaces. Shoelaces are threaded through holes on opposite sides of a shoe. Pulling the shoelace tight and tying it is akin to pulling on the strap to tighten the sleeve in the previous example. However, since the holes in the shoes have eyelets that are designed to allow the laces to be drawn through them smoothly, facilitating tightening and loosening the laces, this is similar to the permissible case of the *Shulchan Aruch,* as long as it is not done in a permanent manner. Thus, it is prohibited for one to tighten his laces partially and to tie them in a manner that allows him to always slip his feet in and out of his shoes. (The tying and untying of shoelaces was discussed in greater detail in our discussion of the labor of *untying.*)

A CLOSER LOOK AT THE SIDDUR

The *Yerushalmi* (*Berachos* 1:5) teaches that one of the reasons that *Krias Shema* is recited twice daily is because references to the *Aseres HaDibros* are included in its passages. The *Yerushalmi* explains: The opening words of the *Shema,* שְׁמַע יִשְׂרָאֵל ה׳ אֱלֹהֵינוּ, *Hear O Israel, HASHEM is our God,* exemplify the first commandment: אָנֹכִי ה׳ אֱלֹהֶיךָ, *I am HASHEM, your God.* And the next words of that verse, ה׳ אֶחָד, *HASHEM is the One and Only,* represent a warning against idolatry, the subject of the second commandment: לֹא־יִהְיֶה לְךָ אֱלֹהִים אֲחֵרִים עַל־פָּנָי, *You shall not recognize the gods of others in My presence.* The *Shema* includes the command to love Hashem, and one who loves Hashem will not swear falsely in His Name (the third commandment). In the third chapter of the *Shema* we say: לְמַעַן תִּזְכְּרוּ וַעֲשִׂיתֶם אֶת־כָּל־מִצְוֹתָי, *so that you will remember, and observe all of My commandments. Yerushalmi* explains this as an allusion to the fourth commandment to *remember the Sabbath,* which is deemed equivalent to all the mitzvos of the Torah. The *Shema* tells us to keep the mitzvos *so that your days will be lengthened* (לְמַעַן יִרְבּוּ יְמֵיכֶם); this alludes to the fifth commandment to honor one's parents, for which the Torah writes the reward: לְמַעַן יַאֲרִכוּן יָמֶיךָ, *so that your days will be lengthened.*

Yerushalmi finds an allusion to the sixth commandment (that prohibits murder) in the words וַאֲבַדְתֶּם מְהֵרָה, *and you will be swiftly annihilated,* for he who murders eventually suffers a similar fate (see *Avos* 2:7). The seventh commandment, that prohibits adultery, is alluded to in the verse: וְלֹא תָתוּרוּ אַחֲרֵי לְבַבְכֶם וְאַחֲרֵי עֵינֵיכֶם, *and you shall not stray after your hearts and after your eyes.* The eighth commandment, לֹא תִגְנֹב, *You shall not steal,* is hinted at in the verse: וְנָתַתִּי מְטַר־אַרְצְכֶם בְּעִתּוֹ יוֹרֶה וּמַלְקוֹשׁ וְאָסַפְתָּ דְגָנֶךָ וְתִירֹשְׁךָ וְיִצְהָרֶךָ, *then I will provide rain for your Land in its proper time, the early and the late rains, that you may gather in your grain, your wine, and your oil* (*Devarim* 11:14). The Torah's specification *that you may gather in* ***your*** *grain,* explains the *Yerushalmi,* implies that you are not allowed to gather in the grain of others; i.e., by stealing it.

The ninth commandment, the prohibition against bearing false witness, is alluded to in the closing words of the *Shema*: ה׳ אֱלֹהֵיכֶם אֱמֶת, *Hashem, your God, is True.* Since Hashem is True, we must emulate Him by speaking only the truth. Finally, the tenth commandment, which forbids us to covet the possessions of others, is alluded to in the directive found in *Shema* to place *mezuzos* on the doors of *your houses*

(בֵּיתֶךָ). The Torah bids us to be concerned with our own houses, and not those of our neighbors.

Mishnah Berurah (61:2, citing *Elyah Rabbah*) writes that it is proper, while reciting the *Shema,* to concentrate on the Ten Commandments, as this helps ensure that one will not come to transgress any of them.

A TASTE OF LOMDUS

Although the specific commandment of לֹא תִגְנֹב (*Shemos* 20:13) is understood by the Gemara (*Sanhedrin* 86a) to be referring to the prohibition of kidnaping, we explained in *A Torah Thought for the Day* that many Midrashim see a greater message in this commandment, the need to avoid any kind of theft in all areas of life.

The Gemara in *Bava Kamma* (60b) inquires as to whether a person in life-threatening danger is permitted to use someone else's property to rescue himself. Most commentaries (see *Tosafos* there ד"ה מהו להציל) understand that the Gemara is not asking whether one may resort to theft to save his life. It is obvious that the preservation of a human life overrides every prohibition in the Torah (besides the three cardinal sins of idolatry, adultery, and murder), and a person is thus clearly allowed to use another's property in order to save his own life. Rather, the Gemara inquires as to whether the person must repay the owner for his loss in such a case. Do we say that such compensation is required, or does the fact that one's life was in danger allow him to use the object without need for remuneration?

Rashi explains differently, maintaining that the Gemara's question is exactly what it appears to be at first glance. In his view, the Gemara is asking whether theft with intent to repay is permitted in order to save a life, or, is the person obligated to lose his life and never take someone else's object or property without the owner's explicit permission. [*Raavad* (*Bava Kamma* 117b) notes that the Gemara is asking this question on a *Biblical* level, for practically, one of Yehoshua's ten ordinances (see ibid. 81a) permits people to use another person's property to save their life if they will repay the owner for the loss. However, he appears to agree with *Rashi* that, this Rabbinic edict notwithstanding, a person in mortal danger would not be allowed to use another person's property to save himself.]

How can this be understood? What does *Rashi* see in the prohibition of theft that makes it as stringent as the three cardinal sins, to the extent

that the Gemara in fact rules that it is forbidden to save one's life with another's money or property?

R' Shimon Shkop (*Nedarim* §1) asks a similar question. One of the principles employed to determine the course of action when two mitzvos come into conflict with each other and are impossible to reconcile is *asei docheh lo saaseh,* a positive commandment overrides a negative commandment. If this is the case, asks R' Shimon, why can't a person in need of *tefillin* use someone else's *tefillin* without permission, reasoning that the positive commandment of *tefillin* should override the negative commandment of theft?

R' Shimon answers that the reason why a person cannot make an *asei docheh lo saaseh* determination and steal the *tefillin* is because, simply put, the *tefillin* are not his; they belong to someone else. The only reason that a positive commandment defers a negative one is because when they are in conflict the person is unable to perform both of them, and the Torah determines that it is more important, as it were, for a person to perform a *mitzvas asei* than it is to refrain from a prohibition. However, this assessment may be made only when a person is faced with two conflicting mitzvos, such as the need to wear *tzitzis* and the requirement to refrain from wearing forbidden *kilayim* mixtures; since either way he will perform one of Hashem's mitzvos, the Torah instructs him to do the positive commandment.

Theft, however, is different in the sense that it impacts upon two people; the prohibition of *lo signov* does not allow a thief to steal, and at the same time protects the property owner from having his possessions stolen. Thus, although it may be argued that the positive commandment of *tefillin* overrides the need to refrain from theft from the thief's perspective, the person who stands to lose his *tefillin* will not gain anything from the other person's performance of this mitzvah. All that applies to him is that he will lose his *tefillin;* accordingly, the prohibition of *lo signov* that protects his property is not deferred. In short, the fact that the *tefillin* belong to someone else precludes their inclusion in any determination that someone who is not their owner may make, in a way that has nothing to do with *asei docheh lo saaseh* or the systems by which certain mitzvos override others; the object is not his, and there is never any justification to deprive the rightful owner of his property.

R' Shimon Shkop's disciple, *R' Shmuel Rozovsky* (*Zichron Shmuel* §83), applies this idea to explain why *Rashi* maintains that a person is not allowed to steal in order to save his life. Although almost every Torah prohibition is overridden in a case of life-threatening danger, and a person may perform any otherwise forbidden action to save his life, the

license allowed is confined to actions that he performs that do not infringe on others. The reason for this limit is not so much the *prohibition* of theft, which would be permitted like everything else, but is because theft, by its very nature, deprives the rightful owner of his property in a situation where he is possibly unwilling to allow this. Since the owner cannot be compelled to give up his property, there is no way that another person — even when faced with a life-threatening danger — is permitted to take it.

R' Shmuel observes that although most other commentaries explain the Gemara's question differently (as noted above), they do not dispute *Rashi's* premise that someone else's possessions are totally precluded from my use to the extent that no determination — such as *asei docheh lo saaseh* — may ever permit me to take them. However, these opinions maintain that with regard to a life-threatening situation there is a difference. If the owner of the object was standing there at the time, he would be obligated by the dictate of לֹא תַעֲמֹד עַל־דַּם רֵעֶךָ, *you shall not stand aside while your brother's blood is being shed* (*Vayikra* 19:16), to do all he can, including spending money, to save the other person's life. Thus, they maintain, the necessary resources may be taken, even when the owner is not present and cannot be asked for his permission. However, when there is no clear mitzvah directed at the property owner compelling him to give up his possessions, theft may never be committed under any circumstances.

A TORAH THOUGHT FOR THE DAY

לֹא תַחְמֹד בֵּית רֵעֶךָ לֹא־תַחְמֹד אֵשֶׁת רֵעֶךָ
וְעַבְדּוֹ וַאֲמָתוֹ וְשׁוֹרוֹ וַחֲמֹרוֹ וְכֹל אֲשֶׁר לְרֵעֶךָ
You shall not covet your fellow's house;
you shall not covet your fellow's wife,
his manservant, his maidservant, his ox, his donkey,
or anything that belongs to your fellow (*Shemos* 20:14).

The *Rishonim* dispute the scope of the prohibition of לֹא תַחְמֹד, *Lo Sachmod,* which prohibits coveting another's possessions. *Rambam* (in *Hilchos Gezeilah* 1:9) maintains that simply desiring another's possessions does not violate לֹא תַחְמֹד; it is violated only when one sets into motion a scheme to obtain the coveted item. Moreover, according to *Rambam,* one does not violate the prohibition unless his scheme is successful, and he actually succeeds in obtaining the coveted item. If he is unsuccessful, he has not violated לֹא תַחְמֹד; according to *Rambam* in *Sefer HaMitzvos* (*Lo Saaseh* §266), though, he *has* violated the prohibition of לֹא תִתְאַוֶּה, *Lo Sis'aveh* (*You shall not desire*), which appears in the *Devarim* version of the *Aseres HaDibros.* [As was mentioned in Tuesday's *Torah Thought for the Day,* there are several differences between the *Shemos* and *Devarim* versions.]

Smag (*Lo Saaseh* §158) disagrees with *Sefer HaMitzvos* and maintains that both *Lo Sis'aveh* and *Lo Sachmod* do forbid simply scheming to obtain another's property, even if the plans are not actually carried out and the property is never obtained. He supports this with the observation that in the *Shemos* version of the *Aseres HaDibros,* the prohibition against coveting another's wife is mentioned, while with respect to *Lo Sis'aveh,* in the *Devarim* version, the wife of another is not mentioned; *Lo Sis'aveh* is written with respect to the *house* of another. It defies logic, says *Smag,* to say that the Torah forbade even scheming to obtain another's house, while it was more lenient with regard to coveting another's wife. Rather, concludes *Smag,* it must be that there is only one prohibition — and it forbids scheming to obtain either the wife *or* the property of another, even if the schemes are not set into motion.

Both of the aforementioned views are in agreement that simply *desiring* the wife or property of another person, while certainly not a desirable trait, does not violate the prohibition of לֹא תַחְמֹד. However, this is not universally accepted either. From *Rabbeinu Bachya* and *Ibn Ezra* to *Shemos* 20:14 it is clear that they are of the opinion that even wishing in one's heart that he could obtain that which is not his violates the prohibition of *Lo Sachmod.* We will discuss this opinion further in *A Mussar Thought for the Day.*

פרשת יתרו

FRIDAY

PARASHAS YISRO

MISHNAH OF THE DAY: SHABBOS 19:5

The following Mishnah identifies circumstances under which circumcision must be postponed until the ninth, tenth, eleventh, or twelfth day, because of a doubt as to whether the Sabbath was the child's eighth day of life:

קָטָן נִימּוֹל לִשְׁמוֹנָה לְתִשְׁעָה וְלַעֲשָׂרָה וּלְאַחַד עָשָׂר וְלִשְׁנֵים עָשָׂר — ***A child is*** sometimes ***circumcised on the eighth, ninth, tenth, eleventh, or twelfth*** day after his birth, לֹא פָּחוֹת וְלֹא יוֹתֵר — ***not earlier nor later.***[1] הָא כֵּיצַד — ***How is this?*** כְּדַרְכּוֹ לִשְׁמוֹנָה — ***In the normal manner,*** a child is circumcised ***on the eighth*** day. נוֹלַד לְבֵין הַשְּׁמָשׁוֹת נִימּוֹל לְתִשְׁעָה — ***If he was born during twilight, he is circumcised on the ninth*** day.[2] בֵּין הַשְּׁמָשׁוֹת שֶׁל עֶרֶב שַׁבָּת נִימּוֹל לַעֲשָׂרָה — If he was born during ***twilight on the eve of the Sabbath, he is circumcised on the tenth*** day.[3] יוֹם טוֹב לְאַחַר הַשַּׁבָּת נִימּוֹל לְאַחַד עָשָׂר — ***If,*** in the previous case, ***Yom Tov falls*** on the day ***after the Sabbath, he is circumcised on the eleventh*** day.[4] שְׁנֵי יָמִים שֶׁל רֹאשׁ הַשָּׁנָה נִימּוֹל לִשְׁנֵים עָשָׂר — ***If the two days of Rosh***

NOTES

1. I.e., there are circumstances in which even a perfectly healthy child is prevented by law from having its circumcision performed on the eighth day, but rather has it postponed to a later day. However, a circumcision is never advanced to before the eighth day, nor is it ever postponed beyond the twelfth day for reasons of uncertainty. [In cases of illness, it can be postponed further, as the Mishnah will state below.]

2. Twilight is the period of time between sunset and nightfall (see above, Mishnah 2:7). There is a halachic question as to whether it is to be judged the end of the preceding day or the onset of the following night. Since the twilight period may actually be part of the incoming night, the child may not be circumcised until the eighth day from that night. Counting from the day preceding the twilight (of which the twilight may actually be a part), that "eighth" day is actually the ninth day (*Rav; Rashi*).

3. If he was born at twilight of Friday evening, there is doubt whether the day of his birth is Friday or Saturday. Hence, we are uncertain whether his circumcision should be performed on Friday or on the Sabbath. The Mishnah rules that he is circumcised on the tenth day — e.g., Sunday. He cannot be circumcised on Friday, since perhaps the time of his birth was actually Saturday and Friday's circumcision would be premature. Similarly, he cannot be circumcised on the Sabbath, since perhaps the time of his birth was actually Friday, and the Sabbath would be the ninth day, when a postponed circumcision may not take place. The circumcision must therefore be postponed until Sunday, which is the tenth day (*Rav*).

4. If Yom Tov falls on the Sunday upon which the child mentioned in the previous case is scheduled to be circumcised, he is circumcised on the eleventh day. Since his circumcision is a postponed one, it does not override Yom Tov either. It is therefore postponed until Monday (the day following Yom Tov), which is the eleventh day after his birth (*Rav; Rashi*).

Hashanah fall immediately after the Sabbath, ***he is circumcised on the twelfth*** day.[5] **קָטָן הַחוֹלֶה אֵין מוֹהֲלִין אוֹתוֹ עַד שֶׁיַּבְרִיא** — In the case of ***a sick child, we do not circumcise him until he becomes healthy.***[6]

NOTES

5. If the two days of Rosh Hashanah fall on Sunday and Monday in the aforementioned case (of a boy born during twilight of Friday evening), the circumcision may not be performed on Monday either, for a postponed circumcision does not override the prohibition of the second day of Rosh Hashanah either. Thus, the circumcision must be delayed until Tuesday — the twelfth day.

6. I.e., we must wait seven full days (i.e., 168 hours) after his recovery before circumcising him (*Rav, Tiferes Yisrael* from Gemara).

[The regulation of waiting seven full days applies only to children who suffer illnesses that affect their whole body. However, an ailment which is limited to but one of his limbs does not require this waiting period, and the child should be circumcised as soon as he has recuperated from his illness (*Shulchan Aruch, Yoreh Deah* 262:2).]

GEMS FROM THE GEMARA

The Gemara (137a) considers the Mishnah's last statement that we do not circumcise a sick child until he becomes healthy. The Gemara cites a ruling in the name of Shmuel that once the fever has left the infant, we must wait seven days from the time of his recovery before circumcising him. [From *Rosh* and *Ran* here, it would seem that this is based on the medical concern that the infant may possibly still be too weak to survive the circumcision (see *Teshuvos Binyan Tziyon* §87).]

The Gemara inquires: Does Shmuel require seven days, or an interval of seven full twenty-four-hour periods? [Under normal circumstances, a child is circumcised on the eighth day of his life although seven full twenty-four-hour periods have not passed since his birth. This is because we apply the legal principle of מִקְצָת הַיּוֹם כְּכֻלּוֹ, *part of a day is equivalent to a whole day,* and we consider the period from the time of his birth to the end of that day as a complete twenty-four-hour period (see *Teshuvos Mahari Weil* §158). But perhaps in the case of an infant who was ill, seven full twenty-four-hour periods must pass, to insure that the infant is fully recovered and able to survive the circumcision.

The Gemara attempts to resolve this inquiry from a Baraisa, in which Luda taught that: "The day of his recovery is the same as the day of his birth." This comparison would seem to mean that just as in the case of the day of his birth, we do not require an interval of seven full twenty-four-hour periods to pass before circumcising him, so too, in the case of

the day of his recovery (i.e., an infant recovering from illness), we do not require an interval of seven full twenty-four-hour periods to pass before circumcising him.

However, the Gemara rejects this inference, countering that even Luda might agree that the day of his recovery is treated more stringently than the day of his birth. He may have only meant to compare the day of birth with the day of recovery in terms of the number of days that must elapse before the circumcision is performed.

[Since the question is not resolved by the Gemara, we would rule stringently and require a full seven twenty-four-hour periods to elapse before circumcising the child, for it is a question of possible danger to the child to do it earlier (*Rosh*). However, although the Gemara does not resolve the question here, the Gemara in *Yevamos* 71b does reach the conclusion that a recovered infant needs a waiting period of seven full days before undergoing circumcision (*Ran; Shulchan Aruch, Yoreh Deah* 262:2; cf. *Korban Nesanel*).]

A MUSSAR THOUGHT FOR THE DAY

In *A Torah Thought for the Day,* we noted the opinion of *Ibn Ezra* and *Rabbeinu Bachya,* that even harboring a desire in one's heart to obtain the property of another constitutes a violation of the prohibition of לֹא תַחְמֹד. With respect to this, *Ibn Ezra* asks a powerful question. It is understandable that the Torah can expect a person not to commit forbidden acts, and can forbid a person to take steps to obtain that which is not his. But how can a person be expected to exercise such control over his very thoughts? Is it not human nature for a person to see something precious or beautiful and desire to have it for himself? Yet, the Torah here seems to be saying that this control is required of every Jew, and lacking it will result in the transgression of a prohibition!

Ibn Ezra answers that indeed, we are expected to reach this level of control. As to how one may achieve this, he offers a parable. A simple peasant, says *Ibn Ezra,* is capable of seeing the queen as she passes through his village, and admiring her great beauty. However, it will not even *occur* to him to desire her as his wife. Why is this so? Because she is so far above his station that to dream of her as a mate is simply not sane; it would be comparable, he says, to wishing for wings so that one could fly.

The parallel, says *Ibn Ezra,* is that Hashem grants every person the material possessions that he is supposed to have. Items that belong to another have been granted to that person. If Hashem wants a certain beautiful item to arrive in a person's possession, He will put into action the necessary steps to insure that it happens. But desiring to take property from another is denying the fact that Hashem apportions all material things. Moreover, if Hashem does *not* wish for a certain person to obtain something, all the scheming in the world is doomed to fail.

It is the responsibility of every Jew, says *Ibn Ezra,* to regard everything that Hashem has granted another as being completely out of his purview, in the same way that the peasant regards the queen. In this way, he will succeed in banishing all covetous thoughts from his mind.

[It is noteworthy that even according to *Ibn Ezra,* seeing the beautiful possessions of another and desiring that Hashem will grant him *similar* possessions does not violate לֹא תַחְמֹד. It is only desiring that which has been granted to another by Hashem that is forbidden.]

HALACHAH OF THE DAY

There is a question whether fastening with a safety pin (by threading it back and forth through two pieces of cloth and then closing the end) is considered a form of *sewing.* Many *poskim* rule that this is no different than sewing with a thread, while others contend that it is not considered sewing. There is yet a third opinion which differentiates between a pin that is attached temporarily and one that is attached permanently. Since a Biblical prohibition may be involved, we must follow the stringent view in this matter. However, there are circumstances in which the use of a pin can be permitted.

One may insert a safety pin through fabric in a manner where the pin pierces each piece of fabric only once and emerges from the other side. As we learned earlier, passing a thread through fabric only once is not considered sewing at all, even if the ends of the thread are tied. Thus, after piercing the fabric with a safety pin, one may close the pin. [Practically speaking, one must pierce the fabric near the ends of the item being fastened in order to be able to close the pin without piercing the fabric a second time.]

One is also permitted to use a safety pin to fasten an item temporarily. We mentioned earlier that there is a view that permits sewing when the

stitches will be left in place for less than twenty-four hours (and in case of necessity less than seven days). We ordinarily do not rely on this view, but in the case of safety pins, which some *poskim* permit altogether, we may do so. Therefore, one may fasten items temporarily — i.e., for less than twenty-four hours — even by passing the pin through the fabric twice. However, it must be clear that the attachment is of a temporary nature. Thus, the pin must be inserted in a manner that ensures that it will be removed after Shabbos. For example, if a hem became loose, one may fasten it with large safety pins that will be bothersome if left in place permanently. If one uses small pins, he should thread them through the fabric so that they are somewhat visible from the outside, as that will surely cause him to remove the pins as soon as possible.

A CLOSER LOOK AT THE SIDDUR

After the conclusion of the Friday night *Shemoneh Esrei,* we recite the *Vayechulu* prayer once more. Although it is recited within the *Shemoneh Esrei* prayer, as we have previously discussed, it is nevertheless repeated (according to most customs; it is omitted by some Yemenite congregations). What is the reason for this additional repetition?

Tosafos to *Pesachim* (106a ד״ה זוכרהו; see also *Tur* §268) offers a possible explanation. He notes that when a festival falls on a Friday evening, the regular Friday night *Shemoneh Esrei* is replaced with the special *Shemoneh Esrei* that is reserved for festivals. Although special insertions are included in the festival *Shemoneh Esrei* to be added when a festival falls on the Sabbath, the *Vayechulu* prayer is *not* recited in the *Shemoneh Esrei.* Thus, if *Vayechulu* were recited only as part of the *Shemoneh Esrei,* it would emerge that on a Friday night that was a festival, the *Vayechulu* prayer would not be recited during prayer at all. To forestall this possibility, the Sages instituted that when a festival falls on the Sabbath, *Vayechulu* should be recited *after* the *Shemoneh Esrei.* And once this custom was in effect, they instituted also that it be said every Friday night, so that there should not be a difference from one Friday night to the next with respect to the *Vayechulu* prayer. [That is, so that one should not get the mistaken impression that the *Vayechulu* prayer recited after *Shemoneh Esrei* on festival Friday nights was only a function of the *festival.*]

In total, then, the *Vayechulu* prayer is recited three times on Friday night — once during the *Maariv Shemoneh Esrei,* once after *Shemoneh Esrei,* and once during the Friday night *Kiddush. Nesiv Binah* cites *Abudraham,* who finds an allusion to this practice in the Midrash. The Midrash states that in the passage of *Vayechulu* we find the word אֲשֶׁר three times, and we also find the word אֲשֶׁר three times in the verses that introduce the subject of the *parah adumah* — the Red Cow whose ashes are used for purification from corpse contamination (*Bamidbar* 19:1-2). The Midrash thus establishes a connection between the two passages, and concludes: "If one recites the *Vayechulu* prayer, with its three mentions of אֲשֶׁר, three times, it will provide him with purification, just as the *parah adumah* does."

QUESTION OF THE DAY:

Does a person violate the prohibition to covet if, in the end, the seller gives in and sells him the item willingly?

For the answer, see page 58.

פרשת יתרו

SHABBOS

PARASHAS YISRO

A TORAH THOUGHT FOR THE DAY

וְלֹא־תַעֲלֶה בְמַעֲלֹת עַל־מִזְבְּחִי אֲשֶׁר לֹא־תִגָּלֶה עֶרְוָתְךָ עָלָיו

And you shall not ascend with steps upon My Altar, so that your nakedness will not be uncovered upon it (*Shemos* 20:23).

This verse commands that the ascent to the Altar be built as a ramp, rather than stairs. A ramp allows one to ascend with smaller steps, which is a more modest method of walking, rather than with larger steps that stairs would require.

Rashi, citing *Mechilta,* notes that even if the Kohanim would ascend upon stairs, there would be no actual revealing of nakedness opposite the stairs, for the Kohanim wore linen pants under their robes, and their bodies would thus be concealed. Nevertheless, explains *Rashi,* walking in such a manner would be degrading to the steps of the Altar. And from the fact that the Torah commands us not to treat the stones of the Altar in a degrading manner, *Mechilta* makes the following *kal vachomer* argument: If, regarding these stones, that cannot perceive their humiliation, the Torah requires that we act in a manner that they not be humiliated — simply because we have need of them — how much more so must we be mindful never to humiliate our fellow man, who is created in the image of the Creator, and who *does* perceive it when he is humiliated! Thus, this command actually carries within itself two separate directives — instructions as to how the Altar must be built, and advice concerning the way that we must treat our fellow man.

It is noteworthy that the Torah includes a message concerning the proper treatment of one's fellow man in the context of the Altar, which is the repository of atonement. We are bidden to always emulate the ways of Hashem. Just as Hashem does not refuse to be pacified, but provides us with the Altar upon which to offer sacrifices and attain forgiveness, it behooves us to do the same for our fellow man. This practice will in itself ensure that the prospect of treating our fellows with a lack of respect will become more distant. Moreover, the *Mechilta* makes a point of saying that the stones are worthy of respect because they are *useful.* If we strive to realize that each of our fellow Jews is a vital component of Bnei Yisrael, then it will be easier for us to treat each Jew with the respect that he deserves.

For another lesson that can be gleaned from this verse, see *A Mussar Thought for the Day.*

MISHNAH OF THE DAY: SHABBOS 19:6

The following Mishnah teaches how much of the foreskin must be removed for the circumcision to be considered valid:

אֵלּוּ הֵן צִיצִין הַמְעַכְּבִין אֶת הַמִּילָה — ***These are the strips*** of flesh ***that impede*** the validity of ***the circumcision*** if they are not removed:[1] **בָּשָׂר הַחוֹפֶה אֶת רוֹב הָעֲטָרָה** — the ***flesh that covers most of the corona.***[2] **וְאֵינוֹ אוֹכֵל בִּתְרוּמָה** — ***And*** a Kohen whose circumcision left him with such strips ***may not eat terumah.***[3] **וְאִם הָיָה בַּעַל בָּשָׂר** — ***If*** a child ***was fleshy*** and thus gave the appearance of being uncircumcised even after his foreskin was removed, **מְתַקְּנוֹ מִפְּנֵי מַרְאִית הָעַיִן** — ***[the circumciser] should rectify this because of the appearance*** of wrongdoing.[4]

The Mishnah now teaches that an additional procedure needs to be performed for the circumcision to be valid:

מָל וְלֹא פָּרַע אֶת הַמִּילָה כְּאִילוּ לֹא מָל — If ***he circumcised but did not uncover the circumcision, it is as if he did not circumcise.***[5]

NOTES

1. When performing the circumcision on a weekday, it is proper to remove all the remaining strips of flesh that adhere to the corona. Many authorities maintain that even if the circumcision procedure has been completed, one should, nevertheless, return to remove even those strips that do not invalidate the circumcision. [This is considered adorning the mitzvah (הִדּוּר מִצְוָה), by making the person appear properly circumcised.] On the Sabbath, however, he may return to remove only those strips of skin whose presence invalidates the circumcision. Those strips that do not invalidate the circumcision may be removed only as long as one is still occupied with the initial circumcision. After he withdraws his hands, he may not return to remove the remaining strips (*Tiferes Yisrael* from Gemara 133b).

2. I.e., the ridge surrounding the membrum, from which it tapers to a point. If this ridge is still covered with flesh, either over the majority of its circumference, or over the majority of its height (even in just one spot), the person is regarded as uncircumcised (*Rav; Rashi; Ran;* cf. *Beis Yosef* to *Tur, Yoreh Deah* §264).

3. A Kohen may not eat *terumah* unless he is circumcised. [Even if he is uncircumcised for a valid reason (e.g., two of his older brothers died from circumcision), he may not eat *terumah.*] Hence, if any strips that invalidate the circumcision remain on a Kohen, he is disqualified from eating *terumah* (*Rav; Rashi*).

4. If, as a result of a child's plumpness, the excess flesh above the foreskin hangs down and appears to cover the corona after the foreskin is removed, the circumciser should trim away the excess flesh so that the child should not appear to be uncircumcised (*Rav; Rashi*).

5. I.e., he removed the foreskin, but did not split the membrane underneath it and pull it back to expose the glans (see above, Mishnah 2 of this chapter). He must return and complete the operation, even if he has already withdrawn from it and is no longer engaged in the circumcision (*Rav*).

GEMS FROM THE GEMARA

The Gemara (137b) cites a Baraisa that lists the blessings recited at various circumcision ceremonies:

At a regular circumcision, the circumciser says: "Blessed are You, Hashem, our God, King of the universe, Who has sanctified us with His commandments and commanded us regarding circumcision." The father of the child says: "Blessed are You, Hashem, our God, King of the universe, Who has sanctified us with His commandments and commanded us to bring him (the infant) into the covenant of Abraham our forefather." The people present at the ceremony then proclaim: "Just as he has entered into the covenant, so may he enter into the study of Torah, the marriage canopy, and the performance of good deeds!" Subsequently, a designated honoree recites the following blessing: "Blessed are You, Hashem, our God, King of the universe, Who has sanctified the beloved one from the womb, placed the mark of the decree in his flesh, and sealed His offspring with the sign of the holy covenant. Therefore, as reward for this, O living God, our Portion [and] our Rock, give the command to rescue the beloved of our flesh from destruction, for the sake of His covenant that He has placed in our flesh. Blessed are You, Hashem, Who establishes the covenant."

At the circumcision of a convert, the circumciser says: "Blessed are You, Hashem, our God, King of the universe, Who has sanctified us with His commandments and commanded us regarding circumcision." And the one designated to recite the blessing says: "Blessed are You, Hashem, our God, King of the universe, Who has sanctified us with his commandments and commanded us to circumcise the converts, and to draw from them blood of the covenant. For without blood of the covenant, heaven and earth would not endure, as it is stated (*Jeremiah* 33:25): *If not for My covenant of day and night, the statutes of heaven and earth I would not have established.* Blessed are You, Hashem, Who establishes the covenant."

At the circumcision of a Canaanite slave, the circumciser says: "Blessed are You, Hashem, our God, King of the universe, Who has sanctified us with His commandments and commanded us regarding circumcision." And the one designated to recite the blessing says: "Blessed are You, Hashem, our God, King of the universe, Who has sanctified us with His commandments and commanded us to circumcise the slaves, and to draw from them blood of the covenant. For without blood of the covenant, heaven and earth would not endure, as it is stated (ibid.): *If not for My covenant of day and night, the statutes of heaven and earth I would not have established.* Blessed are You, Hashem, Who establishes the covenant."

A MUSSAR THOUGHT FOR THE DAY

In *A Torah Thought for the Day,* we discussed how the commandment to avoid stairs when constructing the Altar carries a message to respect every Jew. One may ask, however: Why did the Torah deem it necessary to issue this particular directive right after the Jews received the Torah? What is the significance of its placement here, before the command to build an Altar is even discussed in the Torah at all?

We can perhaps explain this by citing a famous aphorism quoted in the name of *R' Yisrael Salanter.* R' Yisrael would say: "A person running to do a mitzvah can tear down an entire world on his way." Good intentions are wonderful, but they are not a substitute for care and respect. It is true that one must do the right thing, but it also must be done in the right way.

After *Mattan Torah,* the Jews were enthusiastic and full of energy, ready and willing to tackle the new status and responsibilities that had been placed upon them. Sadly, when people are full of zeal, it is all too common for them to pursue their aims with great gusto, while failing to consider how their actions impact upon others. It is also common that in their enthusiasm, they come to regard others who are not as eager as they are in a jaundiced manner, even when this is unwarranted. To forestall these unwelcome side effects, it was necessary for the Torah to issue a warning: In your newfound zeal, do not step upon those whom you should respect.

R' Reuven Feinstein would often say that the idea of avoiding "stairs" is applicable as well to one's attempts to ascend the ladder of spiritual growth. If one tries to climb too quickly, his weaknesses will become exposed. It is better to climb slowly, being sure of one's spiritual footing, than to attempt to jump to a level that one is not ready to attain.

Another level of meaning is found in the interpretation of *Orach LeChaim.* He explains that the verse is advocating humility. The sense of his interpretation is that when one wishes to ascend in his service of Hashem, he should take care not to place himself on any kind of pedestal (this is the meaning of מַעֲלוֹת according to his explanation). If a person approaches the service of Hashem with true humility, he will succeed in ascending to great heights.

QUESTION OF THE DAY:

Where could stairs be found in the Mishkan?

For the answer, see page 58.

HALACHAH OF THE DAY

Yesterday, we discussed some cases where the use of safety pins are permitted on Shabbos. We will now discuss other cases where the use of pins is permitted.

An alternative method of ensuring that one will remove pins from the fabric is to use straight pins instead of safety pins, since one will certainly not leave the straight pins in place permanently (for there is a danger that the pins will prick him). [It is forbidden for one to permanently fasten something with a straight pin, since it is prohibited Rabbinically for one to sew a double stitch (i.e., piercing the fabric twice) even if the ends are not fastened.]

In cases of necessity, where none of the aforementioned methods are feasible, one may rely on the *poskim* who permit the use of safety pins.

Since the *melachah* of *sewing* is defined as uniting two items (or two parts of an item) into one, it applies to pasting with glue or tape as well as sewing with thread. Pasting applies to attaching separate items, such as paper, with glue or tape, as well as attaching an adhesive item, such as a postage stamp or sticker, to another item.

There is a leniency that applies specifically to taping. Whereas sewing is generally forbidden even when it is intended to remain for a short period of time (i.e., less than twenty-four hours), some *poskim* rule that taping for a short term is permitted. This is because taping things together with the intent to separate them shortly is more similar to buttoning than to sewing. This leniency does not apply to gluing.

Based on this leniency, some *poskim* permit securing a disposable diaper with adhesive tape, since the tape will surely be unfastened in a short time, when the diaper is removed. One should note that since taping something permanently is prohibited, one must later unfasten the adhesive tapes when removing the diaper, as opposed to slipping the diaper off the child. Furthermore, when disposing of the diaper, one must be careful not to fasten the adhesive strips to the side of the diaper.

Stapling two items together is a form of *sewing* and is thus forbidden.

According to some *poskim,* the *melachah* of *sewing* pertains even to mending the human body. Thus, it would be forbidden to close a wound with sutures or with a butterfly or steri-strip bandage. In cases of necessity, a competent halachic authority should be consulted. The use of Band-aids will be discussed later in our discussion of this *melachah.*

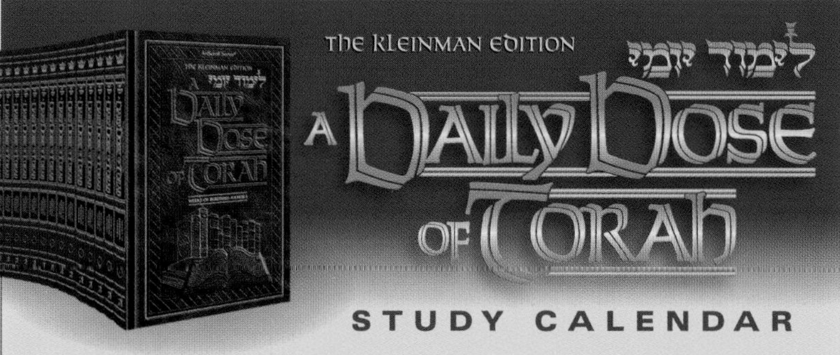

Week preceding *Parashas*	5767 / 2006-2007	5768 / 2007-2008	5769 / 2008-2009
BEREISHIS	Oct. 15-21, 2006	Sep. 30-Oct. 6, 2007	Oct. 19-25, 2008
NOACH	Oct. 22-28, 2006	Oct. 7-13, 2007	Oct. 26-Nov. 1, 2008
LECH LECHA	Oct. 29-Nov. 4, 2006	Oct. 14-20, 2007	Nov. 2-8, 2008
VAYEIRA	Nov. 5-11, 2006	Oct. 21-27, 2007	Nov. 9-15, 2008
CHAYEI SARA	Nov. 12-18, 2006	Oct. 28-Nov. 3, 2007	Nov. 16-22, 2008
TOLDOS	Nov. 19-25, 2006	Nov. 4-10, 2007	Nov. 23-29, 2008
VAYEITZEI	Nov. 26-Dec. 2, 2006	Nov. 11-17, 2007	Nov. 30-Dec. 6, 2008
VAYISHLACH	Dec. 3-9, 2006	Nov. 18-24, 2007	Dec. 7-13, 2008
VAYEISHEV	Dec. 10-16, 2006	Nov. 25-Dec. 1, 2007	Dec. 14-20, 2008
MIKEITZ	Dec. 17-23, 2006	Dec. 2-8, 2007	Dec. 21-27, 2008
VAYIGASH	Dec. 24-30, 2006	Dec. 9-15, 2007	Dec. 28, 2008-Jan. 3, 2009
VAYECHI	Dec. 31, 2006-Jan. 6, 2007	Dec. 16-22, 2007	Jan. 4-10, 2009
SHEMOS	Jan. 7-13, 2007	Dec. 23-29, 2007	Jan. 11-17, 2009
VA'EIRA	Jan. 14-20, 2007	Dec. 30, 2007-Jan. 5, 2008	Jan. 18-24, 2009
BO	Jan. 21-27, 2007	Jan. 6-12, 2008	Jan. 25-31, 2009
BESHALACH	Jan. 28-Feb. 3, 2007	Jan. 13-19, 2008	Feb. 1-7, 2009
YISRO	Feb. 4-10, 2007	Jan. 20-26, 2008	Feb. 8-14, 2009
MISHPATIM	Feb. 11-17, 2007	Jan. 27-Feb. 2, 2008	Feb. 15-21, 2009
TERUMAH	Feb. 18-24, 2007	Feb. 3-9, 2008	Feb. 22-28, 2009
TETZAVEH	Feb. 25-Mar. 3, 2007	Feb. 10-16, 2008	Mar. 1-7, 2009
KI SISA	Mar. 4-10, 2007	Feb. 17-23, 2008	Mar. 8-14, 2009
VAYAKHEL	[Mar. 11-17, 2007]	Feb. 24-Mar. 1, 2008	[Mar. 15-21, 2009]
PEKUDEI		Mar. 2-8, 2008	
VAYIKRA	Mar. 18-24, 2007	Mar. 9-15, 2008	Mar. 22-28, 2009
TZAV	Mar. 25-31, 2007	Mar. 16-22, 2008	Mar. 29-Apr. 4, 2009
SHEMINI	* Apr. 8-14, 2007	Mar. 23-29, 2008	* Apr. 12-18, 2009
TAZRIA	[Apr. 15-21, 2007]	Mar. 30-Apr. 5, 2008	[Apr. 19-25, 2009]
METZORA		Apr. 6-12, 2008	

Week preceding *Parashas*	5767 / 2006-2007	5768 / 2007-2008	5769 / 2008-2009
ACHAREI MOS	[Apr. 22-28, 2007]	Apr. 13-19, 2008	[Apr. 26-May 2, 2009]
KEDOSHIM		Apr. 27-May 3, 2008	
EMOR	Apr. 29-May 5, 2007	May 4-10, 2008	May 3-9, 2009
BEHAR	[May 6-12, 2007]	May 11-17, 2008	[May 10-16, 2009]
BECHUKOSAI		May 18-24, 2008	
BAMIDBAR	May 13-19, 2007	May 25-31, 2008	May 17-23, 2009
NASSO	May 20-26, 2007	Jun. 1-7, 2008	In Israel: May 24-30, 2009 Diaspora: May 31-Jun. 6, 2009
BEHA'ALOSCHA	May 27-Jun. 2, 2007	Jun. 8-14, 2008	In Israel: May 31-Jun. 6, 2009 Diaspora: Jun. 7-13, 2009
SHELACH	Jun. 3-9, 2007	Jun. 15-21, 2008	In Israel: Jun. 7-13, 2009 Diaspora: Jun. 14-20, 2009
KORACH	Jun. 10-16, 2007	Jun. 22-28, 2008	In Israel: Jun. 14-20, 2009 Diaspora: Jun. 21-27, 2009
CHUKAS	Jun. 17-23, 2007	Jun. 29-Jul. 5, 2008	In Israel: Jun. 21-27, 2009 Diaspora: Jun. 28-Jul. 4, 2009
BALAK	Jun. 24-30, 2007	Jul. 6-12, 2008	In Israel: Jun. 28-Jul. 4, 2009 Diaspora: Jun. 28-Jul. 4, 2009
PINCHAS	Jul. 1-7, 2007	Jul. 13-19, 2008	Jul. 5-11, 2009
MATTOS	[Jul. 8-14, 2007]	Jul. 20-26, 2008	[Jul. 12-18, 2009]
MASEI		Jul. 27-Aug. 2, 2008	
DEVARIM	Jul. 15-21, 2007	Aug. 3-9, 2008	Jul. 19-25, 2009
VA'ESCHANAN	Jul. 22-28, 2007	Aug. 10-16, 2008	Jul. 26-Aug. 1, 2009
EIKEV	Jul. 29-Aug. 4, 2007	Aug. 17-23, 2008	Aug. 2-8, 2009
RE'EH	Aug. 5-11, 2007	Aug. 24-30, 2008	Aug. 9-15, 2009
SHOFTIM	Aug. 12-18, 2007	Aug. 31-Sep. 6, 2008	Aug. 16-22, 2009
KI SEITZEI	Aug. 19-25, 2007	Sep. 7-13, 2008	Aug. 23-29, 2009
KI SAVO	Aug. 26-Sep. 1, 2007	Sep. 14-20, 2008	Aug. 30-Sep. 5, 2009
NITZAVIM	[Sep. 2-8, 2007]	Sep. 21-27, 2008	[Sep. 6-12, 2009]
VAYEILECH		Sep. 28-Oct. 4, 2008	
HA'AZINU	Sep. 9-15, 2007	Oct. 5-11, 2008	Sep. 20-26, 2009
VEZOS HABERACHAH IS READ ON SHEMINI ATZERES/SIMCHAS TORAH			

* The Torah reading of the intervening week is superseded by a festival Torah reading. Study for the festivals appears in a festival volume of *A Daily Dose of Torah.*

CALENDAR OF THE FESTIVALS

	5767 / 2006-2007	5768 / 2007-2008	5769 / 2008-2009
Rosh Hashanah		Sep. 13-Sep. 14, 2007	Sep. 30-Oct. 1, 2008
Yom Kippur		Sep. 22, 2007	Oct. 9, 2008
Succos – Shemini Atzeres / Simchas Torah		In Israel: Sep. 27-Oct. 4, 2007 Diaspora: Sep. 27-Oct. 5, 2007	In Israel: Oct. 14-Oct. 21,2008 Diaspora: Oct. 14-Oct. 22, 2008
Pesach	In Israel: Apr. 3-9, 2007 Diaspora: Apr. 3-10, 2007	In Israel: Apr. 20-26, 2008 Diaspora: Apr. 20-27, 2008	In Israel: Apr. 9-15, 2009 Diaspora: Apr. 9-16, 2009
Shavuos	May 23-24, 2007	Jun. 9-10, 2008	May 29-30, 2009

A CLOSER LOOK AT THE SIDDUR

This week, we will continue our discussion of the eleventh of the Thirteen Fundamental Principles (י״ג עיקרים) enumerated by *Rambam,* which states:

אֲנִי מַאֲמִין בֶּאֱמוּנָה שְׁלֵמָה שֶׁהַבּוֹרֵא יִתְבָּרַךְ שְׁמוֹ גּוֹמֵל טוֹב לְשׁוֹמְרֵי מִצְוֹתָיו וּמַעֲנִישׁ לְעוֹבְרֵי מִצְוֹתָיו.

I believe with complete faith that the Creator, Blessed be His Name, rewards with good those who observe His commandments, and punishes those who violate His commandments.

It is important to note that *Rambam* does *not* state that those who observe the commandments will have happy, prosperous lives, and that those who violate them will live lives of privation and want. Indeed, our eyes tell us that often the opposite is true — righteous men live their lives simply, and often in great need, while wicked men live lives filled with material indulgence and splendor. *Rambam* simply states that good awaits those who obey, while punishment will come to those who sin. He does not specify that the reward or punishment will come in this world, because often it does not. Indeed, the Gemara (*Kiddushin* 38b) tells us that שְׂכַר מִצְוָה בְּהַאי עָלְמָא לֵיכָּא, *there is no reward for mitzvos in this world.* While there are mitzvos that are singled out as providing reward in this world (such as the mitzvah to honor one's parents, for which the Torah promises longevity), in the main we are told that the reward will be received in the World to Come.

This is one of the reasons that we often encounter the twin phenomena of צַדִּיק וְרַע לוֹ, *a righteous man and [his material situation] is bad, and* רָשָׁע וְטוֹב לוֹ, *a wicked man and [his material situation] is good.* These situations are not signs that the system of reward and punishment is breaking down. To the contrary! Hashem wishes to reward the *tzaddik* for his good deeds in the World to Come, where reward is eternal. Thus, Hashem "settles his account," as it were, with the *tzaddik* by punishing him while he is still alive for the few sins he may have committed, so that his reward in the next world will be full and unblemished. The wicked man, on the other hand, is destined to eternal punishment in the next world for his many sins (assuming that he does not repent). Nevertheless, even wicked men occasionally perform good deeds. Therefore, Hashem will often grant a wicked person prosperity in this world as compensation for the few good deeds that he has performed, so that he will be utterly undeserving in the next world. Although what we see in our lifetimes does not seem to dovetail with the system of reward and punishment, the truth is that Hashem ultimately balances the scales, and everyone receives what he deserves, be it reward or punishment.

We will continue our discussion of this principle next week.

ANSWERS TO QUESTIONS OF THE DAY

Sunday:

The Gemara in *Zevachim* (116a) records a dispute between the sons of R' Chiya and R' Yehoshua ben Levi. One side maintained that he came before the Torah was given, while the other held that he came afterward.

Monday:

Yisro meant to point out that Moshe was often unavailable to judge because he was speaking to Hashem, while these judges would be available at all times (*Ohr HaChaim*).

Tuesday:

Rashi states that the word "also" means that they would not only believe in Moshe, but also in all the prophets that would follow after him.

Wednesday:

According to many Rishonim, this verse teaches a Biblical requirement to recite *Havdalah* as well (see *Rambam, Sefer HaMitzvos, Asei* §155).

Thursday:

The Gemara in *Sanhedrin* (86a) states that one is liable to execution only for kidnaping someone who was not already in his control *before* the kidnaping. One who kidnaps his own child, therefore, would not be liable.

Friday:

The Rishonim are in dispute: *Rambam* maintains that he still has transgressed, while *Raavad* maintains that he has not. [Of course, as discussed above, some hold that merely *desiring* the item is a transgression.]

Shabbos:

There was a stepladder with three steps in front of the *Menorah.*

פרשת משפטים

Parashas Mishpatim

פרשת משפטים

SUNDAY

PARASHAS MISHPATIM

A TORAH THOUGHT FOR THE DAY

וְאֵלֶּה הַמִּשְׁפָּטִים אֲשֶׁר תָּשִׂים לִפְנֵיהֶם

And these are the statutes that you shall place before them (*Shemos* 21:1).

R*ashi,* in one of his comments on this verse, notes that this passage, which speaks of many monetary laws, immediately follows the closing passage of *Parashas Yisro,* which speaks of the construction of the Altar. He cites the *Mechilta* that derives from this that the seat of the *Sanhedrin* should be situated in the *Beis HaMikdash,* in proximity to the Altar. [The *Sanhedrin* was not actually situated next to the Altar, but was located in a section of the Temple complex where non-Kohanim were allowed to enter. The *Mechilta* means only that the seat of the *Sanhedrin* was in the *Beis HaMikdash.* It was actually located in the לִשְׁכַּת הַגָּזִית, *the Chamber of Hewn Stone.*]

Now, the statutes that are discussed in the passages of *Mishpatim* include many monetary laws that do not require the adjudication of the *Sanhedrin;* even a lesser court of three judges can rule upon these kinds of cases. These smaller courts could be set up anywhere, not only in the environs of the *Beis HaMikdash.* Thus, we may ask the question: Why does the Torah use this passage to teach us that the *Sanhedrin* must be near the Altar, if this passage applies to *all* judges?

R' Moshe Feinstein explains that in truth, the message of proximity to the Altar is apropos to every judge. A judge must know that whenever he issues a judgment in Torah law, Hashem is with him, as the verse states (*Tehillim* 82:1): אֱלֹהִים נִצָּב בַּעֲדַת אֵל, *HASHEM stands with the congregation of judges.* This will cause him to approach his judgments with the proper deliberation and to exercise his authority with greater care. In a sense, therefore, *every* judge is "before the Altar," and a judge who does not comprehend this should not issue rulings, no matter where he is located. To drive home this message, the Torah requires that the highest court, the *Sanhedrin*, be located in *physical* proximity to the Altar.

Ma'or VaShemesh derives a homiletic teaching from this *Mechilta.* He notes that the Altar is a symbol of *avodah,* service of Hashem, which today, in the absence of the *Beis HaMikdash,* is fulfilled through prayer. And he states that the *Sanhedrin* is a symbol of Jewish scholarship and learning. Thus, the *Mechilta* tells us to "place the *Sanhedrin* near the Altar"; that is, to learn in the same way that we pray.

Ma'or VaShemesh explains that the point of this teaching is to remind us that Torah learning must not be approached simply as analytical

SUNDAY

PARASHAS MISHPATIM

study, but rather with fervor and enthusiasm, and with passion and true *yiras Shamayim* (fear of Heaven). He notes that while people understand that these elements are essential components of truly heartfelt prayer, they often do not realize that they are essential ingredients for true Torah study *lishmah* (Torah learned for its own sake) as well. Hence, the *Mechilta* instructs us to "place the *Sanhedrin* near the Altar"; that is, to learn Torah with passion, emotion and enthusiasm, the same way that we recite our *tefillos.*

MISHNAH OF THE DAY: SHABBOS 20:1

The following Mishnah discusses the permissibility of certain labors involved in the preparation of food on the Sabbath and on Yom Tov: רַבִּי אֱלִיעֶזֶר אוֹמֵר — ***R' Eliezer says:*** תּוֹלִין אֶת הַמְּשַׁמֶּרֶת — ***We may suspend a strainer***[1] בְּיוֹם טוֹב — ***on Yom Tov,*** but not on the Sabbath,[2] וְנוֹתְנִין לַתְּלוּיָה בְּשַׁבָּת — ***and we may pour into a suspended*** strainer even ***on the Sabbath,*** and certainly on Yom Tov.[3]

NOTES

1. I.e., a strainer through which wine is poured to eliminate its dregs. It is attached to the opening of a container and stretched tightly over the entire opening (*Rav; Rashi*). One who stretches a strainer over the opening of a container is thereby making a temporary tent (see above, 17:7), an act that is Rabbinically prohibited even on Yom Tov (*Rav* from Gemara 137b).

2. All labors that the Torah forbids on the Sabbath are also forbidden on Yom Tov, with one general exception: Certain labors that are necessary for the preparation of food are permitted on Yom Tov (*Beitzah* 5:2; *Megillah* 1:5). This exemption applies only to those labors that are *directly* involved in the preparation of the food itself. Activities that are only indirectly involved with the preparation of food (for example, the fashioning of the utensils in which to prepare the food) are termed *preliminaries to the preparation of food.* Their permissibility on Yom Tov is the subject of a dispute between R' Eliezer and the Sages. Here, R' Eliezer permits the performance of a prohibited activity involved in such *preliminaries*, even though it could have been performed before the festival. Nevertheless, even R' Eliezer applies his lenient ruling only to Rabbinically prohibited activities, such as constructing a temporary tent. Biblically forbidden labors are prohibited on Yom Tov even if they are preliminaries to the preparation of food, unless they could not have been performed prior to the festival (*Tosafos* to 137b). Of course, even R' Eliezer agrees that the strainer may not be suspended on the Sabbath, when there is no special dispensation for the preparation of food (*Rav* from Gemara ibid.).

3. When the strainer has already been suspended before the Sabbath, there is no question of construction. However, filtering the wine by pouring it through a strainer would seem to be a violation of the forbidden labor of *selecting* (בּוֹרֵר) or *sifting* (מְרַקֵּד),

וַחֲכָמִים אוֹמְרִים — ***But the Sages say:*** אֵין תּוֹלִין אֶת הַמְּשַׁמֶּרֶת בְּיוֹם טוֹב — ***We may not suspend a strainer*** even ***on Yom Tov,*** and certainly not on the Sabbath,[4] וְאֵין נוֹתְנִין לַתְּלוּיָה בְּשַׁבָּת — ***and we may not pour into a suspended*** strainer ***on the Sabbath.***[5] אֲבָל נוֹתְנִין לַתְּלוּיָה בְּיוֹם טוֹב — ***But we may pour into a suspended*** strainer ***on Yom Tov.***[6]

NOTES

which generally forbid one to sort inedible matter from food (see Mishnah 7:3). Still, R' Eliezer holds that pouring wine through a strainer is permitted, for this is not the usual manner of selecting (*Rav; Rashi*; see *Ritva*).Thus, it is permitted even on the Sabbath to filter wine by pouring it through a strainer constructed *before* the Sabbath.

4. The Sages permit only such preliminaries that could not have been prepared before the festival. No prohibition — even a Rabbinic prohibition, such as the making of a temporary tent — may be violated for the sake of performing a preliminary that could have been prepared before the festival (*Rav*).

5. Moreover, the Sages regard the actual straining as a derivative of a Biblically forbidden labor — either *selecting* or *sifting* (*Rav* from Gemara 138a). Thus, such straining is a Torah prohibition, for which one is liable to a *chatas* (Gemara ibid.).

6. I.e., if the strainer was suspended prior to the festival, we may pour wine into it on the festival. Since the wine is to be consumed on that day, preparing it by straining it is a *direct* preparation of food and is permissible (*Beur Halachah* 510:4). Suspending the strainer, however, is regarded as a *preliminary* to the preparation of the food, and it is therefore prohibited according to the Sages.

GEMS FROM THE GEMARA

In the course of its discussion of our Mishnah, the Gemara (139a) introduces a Baraisa that considers a cause for Jewish suffering:

R' Yose ben Elisha says: If you see a generation upon which many troubles descend, go and examine the [corrupt] judges of Israel, for all misfortune that comes to the world comes only on account of the judges of Israel (who are not fulfilling their judicial responsibilities correctly). As it is stated in the verse (*Michah* 3:9-11): *Hear this now, O heads of the House of Jacob and officers of the House of Israel, who detest justice and twist all that is straight; who build Zion with blood and Jerusalem with iniquity. Her heads judge for bribes and her priests issue rulings for a fee and her prophets divine for money, yet they rely on* H*ASHEM* . . .

The Gemara further demonstrates the negative impact of a corrupt judiciary, stating that the Holy One, Blessed is He, will not rest his Divine Presence on Israel until corrupt judges and officials cease to exist in Israel. As the verse states (*Isaiah* 1:25,26): *I will turn My hand against you, I will clean away your dross as with soap and I will remove all your base metal. And I will restore your judges as in the first place, and your advisers as in the beginning . . . afterward you will be called a city of righteousness, a faithful city.* This implies that the Divine Presence will rest upon Israel only after the corrupt judges are removed and righteous judges are installed in their place.

Having mentioned the elimination of judges, the Gemara elaborates upon this point. Rav Pappa said: . . . If [corrupt] judges disappear, idolatrous court officers will also disappear.

The Gemara cites a Scriptural source for this teaching:

If corrupt judges disappear, idolatrous court officers will [also] disappear, as it is written (*Tzephaniah* 3:15): *HASHEM has removed your judgments; He has turned away your enemy.* The verse is expounded to mean that the "enemy" (the idolatrous officers who had resided in a position of power) will be removed when the incorrect judgments (rendered by the corrupt judges) will cease.

A MUSSAR THOUGHT FOR THE DAY

The question is often asked: Why, immediately after giving the Torah to the Jews, did Hashem begin to teach them *mishpatim,* which means *statutes,* laws that have logical underpinnings, that man himself would have instituted? Seemingly, it would have made more sense to begin with *chukim,* the laws that only Hashem understands. How does teaching logical laws that are self-understood show the majesty of the Torah?

R' Mordechai Gifter, in his *Pirkei Torah,* makes the point that while the *mishpatim seem* to mimic secular law, in fact they are vastly different. Secular laws are based on the decisions of leaders in a given time and place concerning what edicts must be issued so that their society will function — and for this reason, they are not permanent in nature and they are constantly amended, redefined, and overturned. The law of the Torah is not so — it is Divine, timeless and immutable. Indeed, it is precisely for this reason that the Torah begins with *mishpatim* — to teach us that even these laws are Divinely inspired. *Rashi* (to our verse) cites the Gemara in *Gittin* (88b) that teaches that even if a secular court follows the same legal principles with regard to a certain issue as do Jewish laws, we are still forbidden to have cases tried there, for by doing so we imply that Hashem's laws are no different than secular laws, thus desecrating the Name of Hashem.

R' David Feinstein states that we must always remember to approach every situation by attempting to discover the Torah way to react. It is for this reason, he says, that the Torah began here with the so-called "logical" laws. By examining the Torah's *mishpatim,* he says, we can evaluate our own thinking processes; if the laws do not make sense to us, then we know we are not thinking properly, and we must work to adjust our way of viewing things.

An example of this would be the first law taught in our *parashah* — the law of an *eved ivri,* a Jewish servant. The Gemara explains that the servant being discussed is a thief who has no means to make restitution for what he took and is sold as a slave for six years, with the purchase money used to pay back the stolen money. At first glance, this seems somewhat harsh, until we examine the details of the law more closely. The master may not mistreat the servant in any way, nor may he force him to do any degrading work or harsh labor. He must feed and clothe him as one of his household; in fact, the Gemara states that the servant must be treated as well as the master himself! The Gemara goes so far as to say that one who acquires such a servant "has acquired a master for himself." In essence, then, the servant secures for himself guaranteed room and board for half a dozen years. Indeed, many such servants were so happy with their situations that they did not wish to leave at the end of their six-year term — and the Torah even provides a way for them to remain (see *Shemos* 21:5-6). Certainly, this is not the type of "justice" that we would mete out to a thief. However, the Torah provides a plan whereby the needs of the thief and the victim are both satisfied, and the thief is placed in a situation where hopefully he will not repeat his misdeed. This is an example of the wisdom of the Torah.

HALACHAH OF THE DAY

Yesterday, we discussed some of the methods of fastening that are forbidden on Shabbos as part of the *melachah* of *sewing*. Today we will begin discussing permissible types of fastening.

It is permissible to fasten garments by using buttons, zippers or Velcro. To understand the reason for the difference between these methods of closure and the prohibited methods mentioned earlier, we will use buttons as an illustration. When one fastens two articles with a button, it is not the intention to combine the two items into a single entity.

Rather, the intention is to connect separate items by way of fastening a button. It is for this reason that buttoning garments together is not considered *sewing*. The same reasoning holds true for using zippers and Velcro. Moreover, it is even permissible to fasten items on Shabbos with intent to leave them in place for a long time by using one of these methods, since it is not a method of fastening that is generally used for permanent attachment. For example, one is permitted to zipper a lining into a raincoat on Shabbos even if he intends to leave it there for the entire winter. Taping, stapling, or gluing, however, *are* used to permanently fasten items together — thus, they can be considered *sewing*

We will now discuss some of the practical applications of the halachos of *sewing*.

It is permissible to put a Band-aid upon a wound on Shabbos, since the Band-aid definitely will be removed before long. [As we discussed earlier, it is permissible to attach an adhesive item to another surface temporarily — i.e., for less than a twenty-four-hour period, and in case of necessity, for less than seven days.] However, one must be careful to attach the Band-aid directly to the skin, and not on top of another Band-aid. This is due to the fact that attaching a Band-aid is permissible only as long as it is a temporary attachment. If one attaches one Band-aid to another, it is very likely that one will remove the bottom Band-aid from the wound, leaving the upper Band-aid permanently attached to the lower one. In the same vein, when placing a Band-aid upon one's finger, a person should not overlap the ends of the Band-aid, for he may then come to slip it off and discard it without opening it. Rather, the Band-aid should be wound around the finger as a spiral, so that both ends will adhere directly to one's skin. In this way, when the Band-aid is eventually removed, no part of the attachment will remain permanently. [If one did mistakenly fasten one end of the Band-aid to the other end on Shabbos, he should be sure to unfasten the ends when removing it, rather than simply slipping it off.]

QUESTION OF THE DAY:

What lesson can be learned from the fact that the Torah speaks of the prohibition to ascend the Altar with steps immediately before speaking of mishpatim?

For the answer, see page 114.

פרשת משפטים

SUNDAY

PARASHAS MISHPATIM

A CLOSER LOOK AT THE SIDDUR

This week, we will continue our discussion of the eleventh of the Thirteen Fundamental Principles (י"ג עיקרים) enumerated by *Rambam*, which states:

אֲנִי מַאֲמִין בֶּאֱמוּנָה שְׁלֵמָה שֶׁהַבּוֹרֵא יִתְבָּרַךְ שְׁמוֹ גּוֹמֵל טוֹב לְשׁוֹמְרֵי מִצְוֹתָיו וּמַעֲנִישׁ לְעוֹבְרֵי מִצְוֹתָיו.

I believe with complete faith that the Creator, Blessed be His Name, rewards with good those who observe His commandments, and punishes those who violate His commandments.

It should be noted that although we believe that Hashem rewards those who observe His commandments, this does not mean that we should obey them *in order* to receive that reward. In fact, the Mishnah in *Avos* (1:3) states in the name of Antigenos, leader of Socho: אַל תִּהְיוּ כַּעֲבָדִים הַמְשַׁמְּשִׁין אֶת הָרַב עַל מְנָת לְקַבֵּל פְּרָס אֶלָּא הֱווּ כַּעֲבָדִים הַמְשַׁמְּשִׁין אֶת הָרַב שֶׁלֹּא עַל מְנָת לְקַבֵּל פְּרָס, *Do not be as servants who serve their master for the sake of receiving reward; rather, be as servants who serve their master not for the sake of receiving reward.* The proper reason for serving Hashem is not in hope of reward; rather, it is to serve Hashem out of love for Him (see *Tos. Yom Tov* to *Avos* ibid.).

This principle stresses that we must believe that there *is* reward, even if it is not always discernible, and even if it is not given in this world. This is in direct opposition to the erroneous beliefs of the *Tzedokim* (Sadducees) and Boethusians, heretical sects that denied the truth of the Oral Law and the words of the Sages. *Rambam* (to *Avos* ibid.) tells us that the founding of this sect was the result of a misunderstanding of the Mishnah cited above, and a denial of this principle. When Tzaddok and Boethus, two disciples of Antigenos, heard him teach the Mishnah, they understood him to be saying that one should not serve Hashem out of hope for reward because no reward would be forthcoming. They carried this further as meaning that there is neither reward for fulfillment of mitzvos nor punishment for misdeeds, and no afterlife. As a result, they rejected the Torah completely. When they were unable to attract followers to this radical view, they adopted the position that while the Written Torah was Divine, all else was false. Their followers were called *Tzedokim* and Boethusians, after Tzaddok and Boethus. These sects caused the Sages much grief during the era of the Second *Beis HaMikdash*. [According to *Avos D' Rabbi Nassan* (4:2), it was not Tzaddok and Boethus *themselves* who misunderstood the Mishnah, but their disciples, to whom they failed to transmit Antigenos' teaching properly. According to this version of the events, although Tzaddok and Boethus themselves were righteous men, the groups were named after the teachers.]

A TORAH THOUGHT FOR THE DAY

פרשת משפטים

MONDAY

PARASHAS MISHPATIM

וְכִי־יְרִיבֻן אֲנָשִׁים וְהִכָּה־אִישׁ אֶת־רֵעֵהוּ . . .
אִם־יָקוּם וְהִתְהַלֵּךְ בַּחוּץ עַל־מִשְׁעַנְתּוֹ וְנִקָּה
הַמַּכֶּה רַק שִׁבְתּוֹ יִתֵּן וְרַפֹּא יְרַפֵּא

When men will quarrel and one strikes his fellow . . .
If he gets up and goes about outside
on his own power, the one who struck is absolved;
only for his [victim's] sitting idle he shall pay,
and he shall provide for healing (*Shemos* 21:18,19).

Someone who strikes another person and injures him may be liable for any or all of five obligations: (1) נֶזֶק, *damages,* compensation for the value of the limb; (2) צַעַר, compensation for the *pain* caused by the injury; (3) רִיפּוּי, *healing* expenses; (4) שֶׁבֶת, *disability* from work; and (5) בֹּשֶׁת, *embarrassment* caused by this injury. This passage teaches us about two of the above payments — compensation for disability (#4) and healing expenses (#3).

Rav Elchanan Wasserman (in *Kovetz Shiurim* to *Gittin* 12b) notes that the obligation of providing for healing is different than the other four payments. While the four obligations are monetary payments that must be made as compensation for the related loss, once the victim receives the money he is free to spend it as he wishes. Healing expenses, on the other hand, must be used to heal the injured. The money handed to the injured party is not his to use as he sees fit, but must be used only for actual healing.

This is derived from the fact that the Torah uses different phraseology to teach each of the two obligations mentioned in this verse. Regarding the obligation to pay for lost income, the verse says שִׁבְתּוֹ יִתֵּן, *for his [victim's] sitting idle he shall* **pay.** But for medical fees, the verse says וְרַפֹּא יְרַפֵּא, *he shall heal,* implying that what is required is not simply a payment, but the actual healing. Now, obviously the verse does not mean that the damager is required to heal his victim himself. Even if he is a doctor, the Gemara states in *Bava Kamma* (85a) that the victim can refuse his services because he is entitled to feel uncomfortable with using his attacker as a healer. It would seem, though, that if not for this claim, the victim would have to accept the attacker's services to heal him, because that is the essence of this obligation. Thus, the payment of medical expenses is viewed as a fulfillment of the perpetrator's obligation of healing the injured party.

Rav Elchanan proves this from the following halachah. The Gemara in

Gittin (12b) states that if someone strikes a slave [כְּנַעֲנִי] who belongs to his friend, he must pay four of the five monetary payments mentioned earlier to the slave's master, as all income of the slave belongs to the master [מַה שֶּׁקָּנָה עֶבֶד קָנָה רַבּוֹ]. The healing costs, however, are given directly to the slave.

From this Gemara it is clear that medical payments are different because the attacker is obligated to heal the slave — the money to cover the healing expenses is his form of "healing." Thus, this money must go to the slave, so that he can use it for healing himself. The other payments are all considered income, so they go straight to the master.

MISHNAH OF THE DAY: SHABBOS 20:2

The previous Mishnah taught that according to the Sages, using a wine-strainer is prohibited. In contrast, the following Mishnah considers several similar activities that are *permitted* on the Sabbath: **נוֹתְנִין מַיִם** — ***We may pour water***[1] **עַל גַּב הַשְּׁמָרִים** — ***over wine dregs,***[2] **בִּשְׁבִיל שֶׁיִּצּוֹלוּ** — ***so that*** the dregs ***become liquefied.***[3] **וּמְסַנְּנִין אֶת הַיַּיִן בְּסוּדָרִין וּבִכְפִיפָה מִצְרִית** — ***And we may filter wine through cloths,***[4] ***or through a basket made of palm twigs.***[5]

NOTES

1. I.e., even during the Sabbath (*Rav; Rashi*).

2. That is, over wine-dregs that have been placed in a strainer prior to the Sabbath (*Rav; Rashi*).

3. I.e., so that the dregs will release the residue of wine in them (*Rav; Rashi*). Our Mishnah thus teaches that this activity does not entail the forbidden labor of *selecting*. [Although, by pouring water through the dregs that are in the strainer, one is causing the water to mix with the dregs and then separate from them, this is not considered *selecting*, because the water and the dregs come together only in a place where they will not remain together — i.e., in a strainer — and therefore they are never considered mixed.]

4. I.e., we may filter the wine to eliminate the fungus-like mold which can collect therein (*Rav; Rashi*). Our Mishnah refers to [mostly] clear wine that is already drinkable, so that this filtering does not render it potable, and is therefore not prohibited as *selecting.* Wine that contains refuse that renders it undrinkable may not be filtered, since this is indeed considered *selecting* (Gemara 139b as explained by *Ran*).

5. Since the basket is being put into place on the Sabbath, it may be used only if it is *less* than a handbreadth above the floor of the container into which the wine is flowing, so that no temporary tent is formed [see the previous Mishnah] (*Rav* from Gemara 139b).

וְנוֹתְנִין בֵּיצָה בִּמְסַנֶּנֶת שֶׁל חַרְדָּל — *And we may put a* raw *egg into a mustard strainer.*[6] וְעוֹשִׂין אֲנוּמְלִין בְּשַׁבָּת — *And we may make honeyed wine on the Sabbath.*[7] רַבִּי יְהוּדָה אוֹמֵר — *R' Yehudah says:* בְּשַׁבָּת בְּכוֹס — *On the Sabbath,* it may be made *in a cup;*[8] בְּיוֹם טוֹב בְּלָגִין — *on Yom Tov,* it may be made *in a bottle;*[9] וּבַמּוֹעֵד בְּחָבִית — *and on the* intermediate *festival* days, it may be made *in a barrel.*[10] רַבִּי צָדוֹק אוֹמֵר — *R' Tzadok says:* הַכֹּל לְפִי הָאוֹרְחִין — *Everything depends on the* number of *guests.*[11]

NOTES

6. I.e., we may add a raw egg to a strainer in which mustard has been strained. [The Mishnah is referring to mustard that is already lying beneath a strainer from before the Sabbath, for mustard may not be strained on the Sabbath (Gemara 134a).] It was customary to add egg yolk to mustard for coloring by cracking an egg over the mustard strainer. The yolk would drain through the strainer, coloring the mustard below (*Rav; Rashi*). [Although the white of the egg is thicker, and remains in the strainer, the forbidden labor of *selecting* is not violated here, since there is no prohibition against selecting within one food type provided all the components are edible. It is for this reason that one may sort the various pieces of one food type according to size (*Rama* 319:3). Therefore, one may do so even for the purpose of eating one of them separately from the other (*Tur* ibid., as explained by *Magen Avraham* 319:16).]

7. I.e., we may mix wine with honey and pepper in any quantity desired (*Rav* from Gemara 140a). Our Mishnah teaches that it is permitted to make this mixture even though its mixing involves excessive toil (*Tiferes Yisrael*).

8. I.e., on the Sabbath it may be made only one cupful at a time, because of the excessive toil involved in mixing large quantities (*Tiferes Yisrael*).

9. This is larger than a cup but smaller than a barrel (*Rav; Rashi*).

10. During the intermediate days of the festival, even though certain forms of labor are prohibited, one is still permitted to exert himself more than he may on the festival itself.

11. If one has many guests, he may prepare even a large quantity of honeyed wine at one time, whether on the Sabbath, festival, or the intermediate days of a festival (*Rav*).

GEMS FROM THE GEMARA

Our Mishnah teaches that it is permitted to prepare the concoction of honeyed wine on the Sabbath. The Gemara (140a) cites a Baraisa that identifies the ingredients of this beverage; it is comprised of wine mixed with honey and pepper. However, not every beverage can be mixed on the Sabbath. The very same Baraisa that permits the making of honeyed wine forbids the concoction of *aluntis* on the Sabbath.

פרשת משפטים

MONDAY

PARASHAS MISHPATIM

Aluntis is a beverage consisting of old wine mixed with clear water and balsam, and is used to cool off those who use the bathhouse. [This beverage is not drunk primarily to quench one's thirst, but rather to help one recover from the fatiguing effects of the heat of a bathhouse. Since healthy people do not usually partake of this concoction, if one drinks *aluntis* it is apparent that his intention is to benefit from its medicinal (cooling) property. That being the case, the Rabbinic injunction against the making of medications on the Sabbath applies to its preparation (*Rashi;* see *Mishnah Berurah* 321:70).]

The Gemara recounts a related incident: Rav Yosef said: One time I went after Mar Ukva into a bathhouse. When I came out of the bathhouse, he brought me one cup of [*aluntis*] wine to drink, and I felt its cooling effect from the hair on my head down to the nails of my feet. And if he had given me a second cup to drink, I would have been nervous that the Heavenly Court would deduct from the merits that I possessed, which were awaiting reward in the World to Come. [Rav Yosef felt that the wine's chilling effect was severe enough to bring him close to death. Being saved from this fate would require a miracle, and would thus "use up" some of the reward earned through his good deeds, which would otherwise have been reserved for his reward in the World to Come (see *Rashi*).]

The Gemara asks: But there is Mar Ukva who drinks *aluntis* daily! Obviously, then, *aluntis* does not have such a strong chilling effect! The Gemara answers: Mar Ukva is different, for he was accustomed to drinking *aluntis.* Thus, it did not affect him so greatly.

A MUSSAR THOUGHT FOR THE DAY

The *Chofetz Chaim* teaches us a remarkable lesson regarding how we should view all the suffering and pain that may come our way. All pain, hurt, or embarrassment, even when it is inflicted by someone with malicious intent, is carried out only through Heavenly order. [This does not excuse the perpetrator, of course, for he freely chose to be the instrument of harm to another.]

He bases this on the Gemara in *Bava Kamma* (85a) that expounds the words וְרַפֹּא יְרַפֵּא to teach that a doctor has "permission" to heal. Had the Torah not granted this specific permit, one could say: "Hashem inflicted this suffering on the person. What gives a doctor the right to defy the King's orders?!"

Now, the verse is not talking about someone who fell ill from natural causes. Rather, it involves a healthy man who ended up in a quarrel, resulting in an injury. In such a situation, one might think that there is no reason to assume that this injury came about as the result of a Heavenly decree! Here the Torah reveals to us that it is not so — there is **nothing** that befalls a person without Heavenly consent and approval.

This belief, which can ease much hardship in a person's life, was embraced by Dovid HaMelech. The verses in *Shmuel II* (16:7-10) tell us how Shimi ben Geira cursed the king with terrible curses. When one of Dovid HaMelech's servants offered to dispose of Shimi, the king's reaction was: כֹּה יְקַלֵּל כִּי ה׳ אָמַר לוֹ קַלֵּל אֶת־דָּוִד, *Let him curse, for HASHEM has said to him, "Curse David!"* *Sefer HaChinuch* (Mitzvah §231) explains that a person must realize that suffering does not take place unless it was preordained by Hashem. Hashem is sending the person a message to repent of his sins, because they are the real reason for his suffering; the one responsible for causing the pain is only Hashem's agent.

A person should consider such occasions as great opportunities for being cleansed of some of his sins, while at the same time strengthening his *emunah* that everything in this world comes from Above.

Rav Elyah Lopian would often repeat this lesson from the Chofetz Chaim, and would conclude with a sigh: "How far are we from seeing the lesson in the simple interpretation of this *pasuk,* whereas the Chofetz Chaim with his great *emunah* saw it at first glance!"

HALACHAH OF THE DAY

Yesterday, we discussed one practical application of the *melachah* of *sewing*, namely, putting on Band-aids that have their own adhesive backs. We will now discuss the halachah that applies to a cloth or gauze bandage that must be secured onto a wound on Shabbos.

One should not use a Band-aid or tape to secure a cloth or gauze bandage on Shabbos, for this is a type of fastening that will not be undone when the bandage is removed, and it is therefore forbidden. Rather, one should tie the bandage in place with a handkerchief. If, however, one did secure it with tape, one should make sure to unfasten the tape when removing the bandage. If one customarily unfastens the tape whenever he removes a bandage, he is permitted to fasten a bandage with tape on Shabbos.

We will now discuss another common application of the *melachah* of *sewing* — the question of using diaper pins to fasten baby diapers on Shabbos.

It is permissible to fasten a diaper with a safety pin on Shabbos, even if one does so by threading the pin through the diaper twice, since the pin will surely be removed when the diaper gets changed.

It is also permissible to fasten a diaper using adhesive tabs (such as those found on many disposable diapers), but one must be sure to unfasten the tabs when removing the diaper, rather than simply slipping the diaper off. Also, care must be taken when disposing of the diaper not to tape the diaper closed, as that would be a permanent fastening. [If the diaper closes with Velcro strips, this would be permitted, as discussed above.]

It is permissible to fasten a sanitary napkin with adhesive strips to an undergarment on Shabbos, since the napkin will remain attached only for a short period of time.

It is forbidden to insert photos into a photo album on Shabbos if the album has adhesive pages and the photos are being placed there to remain in the album.

It is forbidden to tighten a loose thread of a seam or hem, or to tighten the thread around a loose button on Shabbos.

It is forbidden to tape book covers, or to reattach tape that came loose from the binding of a book on Shabbos.

It is forbidden to fasten adhesive notes to any surface on Shabbos, if they will remain attached for more than twenty-four hours.

It is permissible to attach a brooch pin to a garment on Shabbos, even by threading the pin through the garment twice, since the brooch will be removed at the end of the day, when the garment is taken off.

A CLOSER LOOK AT THE SIDDUR

In the eighth blessing of the weekday *Shemoneh Esrei*, we ask of Hashem: רְפָאֵנוּ ה׳ וְנֵרָפֵא . . . וְהַעֲלֵה רְפוּאָה שְׁלֵמָה לְכָל מַכּוֹתֵינוּ, *Heal us, HASHEM — then we will be healed . . . bring a complete recovery to all of our ailments.*

Only when Hashem Himself heals us are we confident that it is not temporary or partial relief, but a complete recovery. That is why, when we beseech Hashem, the true Healer [as the verse states (*Shemos* 15:26): כִּי אֲנִי ה׳ רֹפְאֶךָ, *for I am* HASHEM, *your Healer*], we ask Him for a רְפוּאָה שְׁלֵמָה, *a complete healing*.

[It is stated in the name of the *Zohar* that while someone who is healed through a messenger of Hashem (e.g., a doctor) may experience the return of the sickness, someone who merits being healed through Hashem's *direct* action will never suffer a relapse. Thus, we pray that Hashem Himself heal us.]

Although we discussed [see *A Mussar Thought for the Day*] that the Torah gave permission to a doctor to practice and to heal, it is important to remember that he is limited in his ability. Many times one doctor suggests a certain remedy, while a more knowledgeable doctor disagrees with that approach. It is unfortunately not uncommon that the entire medical community agrees that a certain practice or medication is healthy, only to learn a few years later, after more facts and information become known, that it is actually dangerous to one's health.

Only Hashem, Who is not limited in time or knowledge, and Who created the human being, knows exactly how a person functions and totally understands his ailments. Thus, it is only Hashem Who can provide a רְפוּאָה שְׁלֵמָה, *a complete healing.*

This *berachah* is not reserved for sick people alone; it concerns healthy people as well. We ask Hashem that those who are healthy should remain healthy. This is indicated by the text of the blessing itself, in which we note that Hashem is the ultimate Healer. Any human doctor, even the greatest in his field, is only a messenger of Hashem, and it is really Hashem Who is healing the patient. This is why the Torah needs to grant a permit to a doctor to heal (see *A Torah Thought for the Day*). Along these lines, the Gemara (*Berachos* 10b; *Pesachim* 56a) states that King Chizkiyahu hid the *Sefer HaRefuos,* a book of medical advice, and the Sages agreed with him in this matter. *Rashi* says that Chizkiyahu was afraid that people would put their trust in this book and forget to pray to Hashem.

Ramban addresses the issue of doctors in *Parashas Bechukosai* (26:11) and states: "What business does a doctor have in the house of those who do the will of Hashem?" He goes on to explain at length that when Bnei Yisrael were on an elevated spiritual level, Hashem was their only healer. If someone did get sick, he did not need to seek medical advice; rather, he went to the prophet to ask him which sin he had committed, so that he could rectify the sin and bring about his own cure. He brings many sources in *Tanach* and in the Talmud to support this.

Ramban also notes that the Gemara cited above, which gives the doctor a permit to heal, does not say that a sick person has permission to seek out the services of the doctor. The *Gra* makes an identical observation, and states that the sick person must first turn to Hashem and trust in Him that his sickness will be cured when he repents of his sins.

Although today we are unfortunately not on this exalted level and we must seek medical advice, we must remember that Hashem is the True Healer, and that only He can send a complete recovery.

QUESTION OF THE DAY:

For what is the payment of* שֶׁבֶת *(disability) given?

For the answer, see page 114.

A TORAH THOUGHT FOR THE DAY

אִם־הִמָּצֵא תִמָּצֵא בְיָדוֹ הַגְּנֵבָה מִשּׁוֹר
עַד־חֲמוֹר עַד־שֶׂה חַיִּים שְׁנַיִם יְשַׁלֵּם

If the theft shall be found in his hand — whether a live ox or donkey or lamb — he shall pay double (Shemos 22:3).

This is the punishment for stealing — the thief must pay back double what he stole. The *Tosefta* in *Bava Kamma* (§7) lists seven forms of stealing that are not the standard stealing of objects that must be returned, but which are nevertheless forbidden. These are known as גּוֹנֵב דַּעַת הַבְּרִיּוֹת, *stealing the mind of other people.* An example is inviting someone to eat in your house, when you know that he will not come. The *Tosefta* even goes on to say that when Bnei Yisrael stood by Har Sinai and proclaimed, "*Naaseh v'nishma,* We will do and we will listen," they were stealing the mind of Hashem, as it were, because shortly thereafter they committed the terrible sin of the Golden Calf.

The *Tosefta* concludes that there is one form of stealing that is not only permitted, but even deserving of sevenfold reward. This is the case of one who hides behind someone who is learning Torah, and listens and absorbs all that is being taught; although he is technically called a "thief," he is deserving of reward. Eventually he will be appointed as a teacher to students.

This brings to mind the famous story of the great sage Hillel. When he could not afford the minimal entrance fee to the great study hall and was not permitted entrance, he climbed up to the skylight in order to listen to the Torah being discussed by the great Torah leaders. He stayed there through a heavy snowstorm, and nearly perished from the cold after being covered by the snow. After he was found and revived, it was predicted that he would one day be a great Torah leader; and indeed, it did not take long for him to attain the office of *Nasi.*

It is noteworthy that such behavior is called "stealing," even thought it is permitted and praiseworthy. The question may be asked: Why does the *Tosefta* give it the derogatory title of stealing? We may answer with the teaching of the *Mesillas Yesharim,* who says that every bad trait or behavior has some purpose in the service of Hashem. Now, although stealing is an evil practice, our Sages looked for an instance where this trait can be used to serve Hashem, and even brings in its wake blessing and reward.

The Gemara in *Bava Metzia* says that before Reish Lakish did *teshuvah*, he was the head of a band of thieves. Rav Yochanan saw his great

potential ability and told him: חֵילָךְ לְאוֹרַיְיתָא, *Your strength is fit to be used for Torah.* Reish Lakish accepted upon himself the yoke of Torah and became a great Torah sage. He said about himself that first he was the head of robbers and then he became the head of the yeshivah. Here, too, we see that Reish Lakish turned around his life and used his abilities in a positive fashion, in the service of Hashem.

There is actually a halachic discussion regarding the issue of whether one may copy someone else's Torah ideas. See *Shach* to *Shulchan Aruch*, *Choshen Mishpat* 292:35 for when this is permitted and when it is not. The *Magen Avraham* (156:2) says clearly that someone who writes Torah ideas that are not his own and does not cite their source is transgressing the sin of stealing. *Maharam Schick* (*Yoreh Deah* §156) disagrees, saying that this cannot be called stealing, since he did not actually take a tangible object. However, he is guilty of the sin of *sheker,* lying, because he is deceiving people, by letting them believe that the ideas are his own original works.

MISHNAH OF THE DAY: SHABBOS 20:3

The following Mishnah continues to consider prohibited and permitted activities performed in food preparation:

אֵין שׁוֹרִין אֶת הַחִילְתִּית — ***We may not soak chiltis***[1] בְּפוֹשְׁרִין — ***in warm water,***[2] אֲבָל נוֹתֵן לְתוֹךְ הַחוֹמֶץ — ***but*** one ***may put it in vinegar.***[3] וְאֵין שׁוֹרִין אֶת הַכַּרְשִׁינִין וְלֹא שָׁפִין אוֹתָן — ***And we may not soak vetches,***[4]

NOTES

1. *Chiltis* is a plant that has a hot, spicy flavor and is therefore popular in cold lands (*Rav*).

2. Soaking *chiltis* in warm water is prohibited because it is reminiscent of a weekday activity (Gemara 140a). This is evidently because the soaked *chiltis* was used as a remedy for heaviness of the heart (see Gemara ibid.). Thus, if one soaks it in warm water, it appears that he is preparing a drug rather than a beverage.

3. I.e., one may add *chiltis* to vinegar and dip his food into it (*Rashi*). Since healthy people partake of *chiltis* in this manner as a condiment, it is not apparent that this person is preparing the mixture for medicinal purposes. Accordingly, it is permissible to do so even if one's intent is for therapeutic purposes (*Beur Halachah* to *Orach Chaim* 321:18).

4. Vetches are species of beans used for cattle fodder. Before feeding them to the cattle, they are soaked in water to soften them (*Meleches Shlomo*; see above, Mishnah 1:4). Since this process also separates the husks (which float to the top) from the beans (that sink to the bottom), doing so is a violation of the forbidden labor of *selecting* (see *Beitzah* 14b).

nor may we rub them;[5] אֲבָל נוֹתֵן לְתוֹךְ הַכְּבָרָה אוֹ לְתוֹךְ הַכַּלְכָּלָה — ***but one may put them into a sieve or into a basket.***[6]

אֵין כּוֹבְרִין אֶת הַתֶּבֶן בִּכְבָרָה — ***We may not sift straw with a sieve,*** וְלֹא יִתְּנֶנּוּ עַל גַּבֵּי מָקוֹם גָּבוֹהַּ בִּשְׁבִיל שֶׁיֵּרֵד הַמּוֹץ — ***nor may we put it on a high place so that the chaff will drop*** from it;[7] אֲבָל נוֹטֵל הוּא בִּכְבָרָה וְנוֹתֵן לְתוֹךְ הָאֵיבוּס — ***but one may take it in a sieve and pour it into the feeding trough.***[8]

NOTES

5. I.e., we may not rub vetches by hand to remove their husks. This too is prohibited as *selecting* (*Rav; Rashi*).

6. I.e., one may put them into a sieve or basket for storage even though the husks will sometimes fall through the holes of the sieve, thereby automatically *selecting* the food (*Rav; Rashi*). Since he has no intention of selecting them, and it is not inevitable that they will be selected, it is permissible (*Mishnah Berurah* 319:30 and *Beur Halachah* there). [To put them into a sieve in order to select is obviously prohibited.]

7. I.e., one may not place a sieve containing straw on a high place, so that the inedible chaff will fall through the holes, leaving behind clean straw that can be used as fodder for livestock. This constitutes sifting, a derivative of the forbidden labor of *selecting* (*Rashi; Rambam, Hil. Shabbos* 21:32).

8. I.e., he may scoop the straw up with a sieve and pour it into an animal's feeding trough. Although some chaff will thereby be eliminated when it falls through the holes in the sieve, it is permissible, since he does not intend to select the straw, and it is not inevitable that selecting will occur. This fits into the category of דָּבָר שֶׁאֵינוֹ מִתְכַּוֵּן, *an unintended labor,* which is permissible according to R' Shimon as long as it is not inevitable (*Rav; Rashi*).

GEMS FROM THE GEMARA

The Gemara to this Mishnah (140b) cites a series of practical suggestions by Rav Chisda. For example, Rav Chisda said: A Torah scholar who buys a bunch of vegetables (such as scallions) should buy a bunch that contains longer vegetables. For one bunch is as thick as the next bunch (and all are sold for the same price); thus, the added length of the longer vegetables represents an automatic benefit over shorter bunches.

Similarly, Rav Chisda also said: A Torah scholar who buys a bundle of sticks should buy a bundle containing longer sticks. For one bundle is as thick (and sells for the same price) as the next bundle, and the added length of one bundle represents an automatic benefit over a shorter bundle.

Another piece of advice given by Rav Chisda was that a Torah scholar

who does not have funds to buy a large quantity of bread should not eat herbs, because they whet one's appetite, and he does not have enough bread to satisfy that appetite.

Rav Chisda added: "I myself never ate herbs, neither when I was poor, nor when I was wealthy. When I was poor I did not eat herbs because they whet one's appetite, and I did not have enough bread to satisfy that appetite. When I was wealthy I did not eat herbs because I said, 'In the place where herbs can enter, let meat and fish enter instead!' " [I.e., why should I eat my fill of plain fare when I can eat delicacies instead.]

Moreover, said Rav Chisda: A Torah scholar who does not have much bread should not divide his bread into many small pieces, and eat many small meals; rather, he should save his bread until he has enough for a satisfying meal. And in a related teaching, Rav Chisda said: A Torah scholar who does not have much bread should not be the one chosen to make the blessing over a communal loaf and give it out to those partaking in a meal together. What is the reason for this? Because there is a possibility that, due to his poverty, he will not apportion the bread generously. Rav Chisda continued, "I myself, originally when I was poor, would not break bread for others . . . unless I had first examined the entire basket of bread with my hand and found that there was enough for my own needs."

In another teaching, Rav Chisda said: Any person who is able to eat inexpensive barley bread without suffering pain from such hard-to-digest fare, and instead eats more expensive bread made of wheat, transgresses the sin of: לֹא תַשְׁחִית, *You shall not destroy* [by wasting money] (*Deuteronomy* 20:19). And similarly Rav Pappa said: Any person who is able to drink beer and instead drinks [the more expensive] wine, transgresses the sin of *You shall not destroy.*

[Rav Chisda's stricture applies only to a poor person. A person who can afford the more expensive wheat bread is certainly entitled to purchase it. Indeed, Rav Chisda himself stated above that once he became wealthy, he would eat fish and meat rather than herbs (see *Megadim Chadashim*). See also *Sfas Emes* for another explanation.]

However, the Gemara rejects Rav Chisda's position. It concludes that there is actually no problem if the poor person buys wheat bread rather than barley bread, for seeking to avoid the sin of *You shall not destroy* with regard to one's body is a greater consideration than the added expense. [Wheat bread and wine are healthier for the body than barley bread and beer. Thus, the added expense incurred by the poor person acquiring them is justified, and cannot be decried as a waste of money.]

A MUSSAR THOUGHT FOR THE DAY

A large section of this *parashah* deals with those who damage or steal someone else's property. The Gemara in *Makkos* 23b tells us that *geneivah,* thievery and robbery, are sins that a man's heart desires [נַפְשׁוֹ שֶׁל אָדָם מְחַמַּדְתָּן]. In fact, the Gemara in *Bava Basra* 165a tells us that רוֹב בְּגָזֵל, most people transgress this sin in some way.

What is the root of this sin, and how can one overcome it? We have mentioned earlier in our studies (see *A Mussar Thought for the Day,* Monday of *Parashas Noach*) that R' Moshe Feinstein would say that thievery has its roots in a lack of *emunah.* One who truly believes that Hashem provides for him and gives him all that he needs will never resort to thievery.

The *Chofetz Chaim* also elaborates on this idea, and explains it with a parable. A person had a huge barrel of wine, filled to the brim, with one spout at its bottom from which to draw the wine. One day, he decided to double the amount of wine he could draw by inserting an additional spout. Of course, this is foolish reasoning, since everyone understands that by adding a spigot, he is not doubling the amount of wine, but rather speeding up the depletion of the wine. The same holds true regarding a person's income. *Chazal* tell us that on Rosh Hashanah it is designated how much income will be allotted to a person that year. By stealing from other people, he is not adding one cent to his income, he is only getting that money more quickly; and in the long run his yearly allocation will be exactly as was designated on Rosh Hashanah, for he will simply fail to receive an amount equal to that which he stole — and he will be punished for his thievery as well.

The punishment for stealing is to pay back double the amount of the item stolen. This drives home the lesson that although the thief may have thought that he would gain by stealing, in truth he does not; for not only must he return the stolen object, he must also pay back an equal amount from his own pocket, losing money that was rightfully his.

The Gemara in *Shabbos* (31a) provides us with a list of six questions that everyone will be asked on the Day of Judgment. The first question will be: נָשָׂאתָ וְנָתַתָּ בֶּאֱמוּנָה. Translated simply, this means: Did you conduct business honestly? Were you careful not to cheat, deceive, etc.? However, some commentators explain that the word אֱמוּנָה should be understood in its usual meaning, *trust in Hashem,* which fits well with the explanation of the root cause of robbery, as explained above. Hashem asks: Did you conduct your business with full trust in Hashem, with the

belief that only He will provide you with all that you need? If someone conducts his business dealings with *emunah* in Hashem, then he will find it easy to overcome all temptation to steal, and will be able to withstand all such tests and challenges. It is only when one's *emunah* is weak that his desire for someone else's money is difficult to overcome.

HALACHAH OF THE DAY

After the *melachah* of *sewing,* we find the *melachah* of קוֹרֵעַ, *tearing*. The curtains used in and around the Mishkan would at times develop small holes, which required repair. In order to repair these small damages in expert fashion, artisans would first tear the fabric surrounding the imperfection, thereby enlarging and shaping the hole. Since tearing was a part of the activity required in the Mishkan, tearing is one of the thirty-nine *melachos* forbidden on Shabbos.

The *melachah* of *tearing* corresponds to the *melachah* of *sewing*. As a general rule, the restrictions against *tearing* apply in the same circumstances as those of *sewing*. For instance, just as it is forbidden to sew together any soft materials (e.g., cloth, leather, paper, plastic, etc.), so too, one may not tear apart any soft materials on Shabbos. The prohibition against tearing does not apply only to items that were initially one piece; it extends to the tearing apart of items that have been glued or sewn together as well.

The prohibition of *tearing* is particularly pertinent to the question of opening packages on Shabbos. We will now begin to examine these laws in detail.

As we have noted several times previously, as a general rule an action is considered a *melachah* on Shabbos only if the action is constructive in nature. Destructive activity, unless it is an act of destruction required for constructive purposes, is not considered a *melachah*. The *melachah* of *tearing* is no exception to this rule. For this reason, only constructive acts of tearing are forbidden under Biblical law. The tearing performed in the Mishkan, as described above, was constructive in nature, because it was a necessary step in an overall constructive process — the repair of the curtains. Indeed, the Mishnah in Shabbos describes forbidden tearing as קוֹרֵעַ עַל מְנָת לִתְפּוֹר, *tearing for the purpose of [proper] sewing.*

Since tearing is inherently a destructive act, there are those *poskim* who are of the opinion that tearing is Biblically forbidden only when it is done for the same purpose it was done in the Mishkan — in order to allow for proper sewing. According to these *poskim,* all other constructive tearing is only Rabbinically forbidden. Most *poskim,* however, maintain that the Biblically forbidden *melachah* includes all forms of constructive tearing. They therefore describe the forbidden activity as קוֹרֵעַ עַל מְנָת לְתַקֵּן, *tearing for the purpose of repairing.* According to these *poskim,* tearing rolled-up sheets of paper into small pieces usable for the drying of one's hands would be an example of a Biblically forbidden act.

The halachah follows the more stringent view; accordingly, all constructive tearing is Biblically forbidden on Shabbos.

A CLOSER LOOK AT THE SIDDUR

There are certain sins that block a person's prayers from being accepted by Hashem. One such sin is thievery. The Midrash on *Parashas Beshalach* (22:3) states: When one's hands are soiled with robbery, he calls out to Hashem and he is not answered. The *Yesod VeShoresh HaAvodah* says that there is no other sin that blocks a person's prayer from going up to Hashem as much as robbery.

Maharam Schick, in his concluding remarks on *Bava Kamma,* brings down from *Kadmonim*: The highlight of all the days of the year are Yamim Tovim, the highlight of all the Yamim Tovim is Yom Kippur, and the highlight of Yom Kippur is the *tefillah* of *Ne'ilah*. And what do we find in the text of that prayer? A request to Hashem to protect us from the sin of stealing. For we know that an evil decree can be signed due to the sin of stealing (as was the case with the Generation of the Flood), and, at the time when the year's decrees are signed, we add one more prayer to protect us from this great sin. (See further, Monday of *Parashas Noach, A Closer Look at the Siddur.*)

The reason why this sin prevents one's prayers from being heard is as we discussed in *A Mussar Thought for the Day*. The root cause of this sin is lack of *emunah.* How can one possibly pray to Hashem earnestly when he is practicing the antithesis of *emunah*?! Prayer is referred to in the Torah as *emunah.* In the end of *Parashas Beshalach* (17:12), the Torah states regarding Moshe: וַיְהִי יָדָיו אֱמוּנָה, which means literally, *he was with his hands in faith.* The *Targum Yonasan* says that this means Moshe's hands were stretched out in prayer.

There is a custom cited in the name of the *Arizal* to give *tzedakah*

when one reaches the words in *Shacharis* in *Vayevarech David*: וְהָעֹשֶׁר וְהַכָּבוֹד מִלְּפָנֶיךָ, וְאַתָּה מוֹשֵׁל בַּכֹּל, *wealth and honor come from You, and You rule over everything* (see *Mishnah Berurah* 92:36). We give money to charity at that point to actively demonstrate that everything one owns is really a present from Hashem. Giving charity prior to prayer strengthens our *emunah*, and reminds us of Who really controls all riches and honor. When one confirms his belief in this principle by taking his own money and giving it to charity, this will allow him to stretch out his own hands to Hashem in prayer with true *emunah.*

QUESTION OF THE DAY:

Why does the verse (22:3) use the double verb הִמָּצֵא תִמָּצֵא?

For the answer, see page 114.

A TORAH THOUGHT FOR THE DAY

פרשת משפטים

WEDNESDAY

PARASHAS MISHPATIM

כִּי־יִתֵּן אִישׁ אֶל־רֵעֵהוּ כֶּסֶף אוֹ־כֵלִים לִשְׁמֹר וְגֻנַּב . . .
וְנִקְרַב בַּעַל־הַבַּיִת אֶל־הָאֱלֹהִים אִם־לֹא שָׁלַח יָדוֹ
בִּמְלֶאכֶת רֵעֵהוּ . . . וְאִם־גָּנֹב יִגָּנֵב מֵעִמּוֹ יְשַׁלֵּם לִבְעָלָיו . . .
וְכִי־יִשְׁאַל אִישׁ מֵעִם רֵעֵהוּ וְנִשְׁבַּר אוֹ־מֵת . . .
אִם־בְּעָלָיו עִמּוֹ לֹא יְשַׁלֵּם אִם־שָׂכִיר הוּא בָּא בִּשְׂכָרוֹ

6 *If a man shall give his fellow money or utensils to safeguard,*
and it is stolen 7 *. . . the householder shall approach the court*
[and state] that he has not laid his hand upon his fellow's property . . .
11 *If it shall be stolen from him, he shall pay to its owner . . .*
13 *If a man shall borrow from his fellow and it shall become*
broken or shall die . . . 14 *If its owner is with him,*
he shall not make restitution. If he was a renter,
it came in return for his rental (*Shemos* 22:6-14).

This Torah passage teaches us the laws of שׁוֹמְרִים (*shomrim*), *guardians.* The Gemara (*Bava Metzia* 94b) observes that verses 6-8 absolve a guardian from responsibility as long as *he has not laid his hand upon his fellow's property,* while the law taught in verse 11 requires a guardian to repay the owner *if it shall be stolen from him.* To resolve this apparent contradiction, the Gemara explains that the laws of several different *shomrim* are being taught in this passage. The *shomer* who must repay the owner if the object is stolen from his care (verse 11) is a שׁוֹמֵר שָׂכָר (*shomer sachar*), *paid guardian,* while a שׁוֹמֵר חִנָּם (*shomer chinam*), *unpaid guardian,* is the subject of discussion in verses 6-8. The Torah is telling us that a person who agrees to watch an object without receiving personal benefit such as payment is held accountable only when he misappropriates the object under his custody. [The Gemara (*Bava Metzia* 36b) teaches that there is another reason why a *shomer chinam,* even when he did not steal the object, is responsible to pay — when negligent in his duties. See *A Taste of Lomdus.*]

Verses 13-14, the Gemara continues, deal with a third type of *shomer* — a שׁוֹאֵל (*sho'el*), *borrower.* The borrower, unlike the other *shomrim* mentioned in the Torah, is allowed to use the object and does not even have to pay rent. Such a *shomer* must pay for the object's loss under almost any circumstance, even when it is the result of an unavoidable accident. [The only time a *sho'el* is absolved from payment, the Torah teaches us in verse 14, is *if its owner is with him, he shall not make restitution.* Briefly, this means that if the lender was in the employ of the borrower at the time the item was borrowed, the borrower is exempted

from responsibility for loss — see *Bava Metzia* ibid. for further details.]

A fourth type of *shomer* — a שׂוֹכֵר (*socher*), *renter,* is also mentioned in this passage: *if he was a renter, it came in return for his rental* (verse 14). However, the Torah does not state the conditions under which such a *shomer* is responsible to pay for loss. The Gemara concludes that a *socher's* responsibilities are the same as that of a *shomer sachar;* he too is responsible for theft, and is absolved from repayment when unable to return the borrowed item because of an unavoidable accident.

The commentaries offer various reasons for the fact that different *shomrim* have different levels of responsibility. *Tosafos* (*Kesuvos* 56b) explain that, although any person who is given an object to watch must of course guard it appropriately, not every *shomer* agrees to be held to the same level of accountability if something beyond his control happens to the object. In this passage, therefore, the Torah is detailing the standards that people in different situations are willing to accept upon themselves. A person who is watching something as a favor does so only on the assumption that he would not have to replace the item if it were stolen. A hired watchman, while understanding that since he is being paid to guard the item, he will be held accountable if it is stolen during his watch, nevertheless does not agree to accept responsibility to pay for an item that is lost due to a circumstance that he was powerless to prevent. A borrower, however, since he is taking the object to use, understands that he is being given the item only on the condition that he return it in the same condition that he received it. When this is impossible, he implicitly agrees that he will pay for a new one, even if he was powerless to prevent the loss.

Rambam, in his *Moreh Nevuchim* (3:42, cited by *Rabbeinu Bachya*), has a different approach. He explains that the degree of benefit that a person receives from an item regulates the level of accountability that he assumes in regard to it. When a *shomer chinam* watches an item as a favor for the owner, and does not gain in any way by doing so, there is no reason why he should pay for the loss if the article is stolen. The only person who loses in cases of theft or conventional loss is the one who benefited from this guarding in the first place, i.e., the owner of the object, who enjoyed free protection of his article. A borrower, explains *Rambam,* is the opposite; his permission to use someone else's item without having to pay for it gives him all of the benefits in this transaction, while the owner, who is doing him a favor, receives nothing. Accordingly, if the object is damaged in any way — even by accident — the owner, who did not gain by giving the borrower his object, need not lose by having done so; it is the borrower — by virtue of his total benefit — who is obligated to make restitution.

A שׁוֹמֵר שָׂכָר, *paid guardian,* and שׂוֹכֵר, *renter, Rambam* concludes, are both considered to be receiving an intermediary level of benefit, for both the owner and *shomer* gain to some degree from the transaction. A paid watchman is compensated for his efforts, and the owner gains from having his object protected. And in the case of a rental, the renter is able to use the article, and the owner profits by receiving rental money. Since both parties benefit from this agreement, it is appropriate that both maintain a level of accountability if the item is damaged, lost or stolen; the *shomer* is therefore responsible to make appropriate restitution in cases of theft or conventional loss, and the owner must suffer the loss in the case of an unavoidable accident.

MISHNAH OF THE DAY: SHABBOS 20:4

The following Mishnah discuss how food for an animal may be moved about on the Sabbath:

גּוֹרְפִין מִלִּפְנֵי הַפְּטָם — ***We may sweep out*** the feeding-trough ***from before an ox that is being fattened*** for slaughter,[1] וּמְסַלְּקִין לַצְּדָדִין מִפְּנֵי הָרְעִי — ***and we may move*** excess fodder ***to the sides*** of its stall ***because of the excrement.***[2] דִּבְרֵי רַבִּי דוֹסָא — These are ***the words of R' Dosa;*** וַחֲכָמִים אוֹסְרִין — ***but the Sages prohibit it.***[3]

NOTES

1. I.e., we may clean out on the Sabbath the cinders and dirt from the ox's feeding-trough, so that they will not become mingled with the ox's food, thereby causing the food to be revolting to him (*Rav; Rashi*).

2. When there is too much straw and fodder before the ox, we may move it aside, lest the ox tread upon the fodder with his feet and soil it with the excrement that is in the stall (*Rav; Rashi*).

3. Both R' Dosa and the Sages agree that one may not sweep out, nor move about, excess feed in a feeding-trough that has an earthen floor. This is prohibited for fear that while doing so one will flatten out any irregularities in the floor. To flatten out the floor of the trough violates the forbidden labor of *building.* The Mishnah, however, is discussing a trough which is a utensil. Since it does not have an earthen floor, R' Dosa sees no reason to prohibit it. The Sages, however, prohibit it for fear that people will fail to distinguish between a utensil and an earthen-floored trough (*Rav* from Gemara 140b).

נוֹטְלִין מִלִּפְנֵי בְּהֵמָה זוֹ וְנוֹתְנִין לִפְנֵי בְּהֵמָה זוֹ בְּשַׁבָּת — ***We may take feed from before this animal and place it before this*** other ***animal on the Sabbath.***[4]

NOTES

4. I.e., we may take away feed from before one animal and place it before another. Since one animal will eat the leftovers of another, moving the feed from one trough to another is a useful activity and therefore permissible (*Rav; Rashi*). It is not considered an excessive exertion, which is sometimes forbidden on the Sabbath. However, one may not take feed from an ox and give it to a donkey. Since an ox drools while eating, he makes the food repugnant to a donkey, who is more fastidious. Moving it is therefore unproductive and is consequently prohibited (*Rav, Rashi* from Gemara ibid.).

GEMS FROM THE GEMARA

The Mishnah stated: *We may take feed from before this animal and place it before this [other] animal on the Sabbath.*

The Gemara (140b) cites a pair of related Baraisos: One Baraisa taught: "We may take feed from before this animal which has a fine mouth and place it before an animal with a poor mouth." And it was taught in another Baraisa: "We may take feed from before this animal which has a poor mouth and place it before an animal with a fine mouth."

Abaye immediately explains these two Baraisos: Both Baraisos mean to teach the same law: that we may take feed from before a donkey to place before an ox, but we may not take feed from before an ox to place before a donkey.

Abaye continues, explaining the phraseology of each Baraisa: When the first Baraisa taught: "We may take feed from before this animal which has a fine mouth," it used this term to refer to a donkey, which does not drool into its feed; it is thus said to have a "fine" mouth. And when the Baraisa taught: "and place it before an animal with a poor mouth," it referred to an ox, which drools into its feed. Its mouth is thus "poor" in that it emits something repulsive. The Baraisa's ruling is thus understood: Since the donkey does not drool into his feed, his leftovers are not *muktzeh* and may be placed before an ox. But an ox's leftovers are ruined by its drool and thus rendered *muktzeh,* and they thus may not be taken to be placed before a donkey.

And when the second Baraisa taught that we may take feed from before this animal which has a poor mouth, it too referred to a donkey, which is not a discriminating eater. Its mouth is referred to as "poor" because it will eat even virtually inedible thorns and thistles. And when that Baraisa taught that we may place the feed before an animal with a fine mouth, it referred to an ox, which is a discriminating eater. Its mouth is referred to as "fine" in that it will take in only unsullied foods.

In the final analysis, then, both Baraisos are teaching the same ruling: We may move the leftovers of a donkey and place them before an ox, but not vice versa.

[The second Baraisa makes the point that an ox will eat a donkey's leftovers, *even though an ox is a discriminating eater,* because the donkey does not drool into its feed. And a donkey will *not* eat an ox's leftovers, *even though a donkey is a less discriminating eater,* since the ox surely drooled into it (see *Ohr HaChamah*).]

A MUSSAR THOUGHT FOR THE DAY

Sfas Emes (5635 and 5636) observes that although much of *Parashas Mishpatim* deals with everyday interpersonal laws, such as the requirement to guard one's animals from damaging the property of others, and the financial obligations of the different types of *shomrim,* the principles and messages stated in these passages may also be seen as metaphors that teach a person how to better serve Hashem. The Torah passage of *shomrim,* when simply understood, describes the obligation of constant responsibility and protection that a person must manifest when he is entrusted with someone else's property. For example, even though a person may choose not to lock the doors to his own car when parking in a safe neighborhood, a *shomer* caring for someone else's car — who must always do all that is possible to protect the item under his guard from theft — does not enjoy this luxury. Failing to take an ordinary precaution such as locking the doors is negligence that would obligate him to pay if the car were stolen. A *shomer's* responsibility of watching something for someone else places him on a constant state of alert that he is unable to ignore.

Sfas Emes explains that this lesson of constant vigilance must be applied to a person's own life. A watchman must keep the property entrusted to him safe and return it unharmed. Now, Hashem gives each person a lofty *neshamah* that, after a lifetime, will be returned to Hashem. The way that a person protects his *neshamah* is, of course, by living a life that follows the Torah's guidelines. Performing mitzvos and refraining from sin ensures that the *neshamah* will not be damaged by the taint of the physical world, so that when it is time, the *neshamah* will return to its Master in perfect condition.

Sfas Emes continues, explaining that many of the specific laws of *shomrim* also provide direction and motivation in the proper service of Hashem. One such lesson is illustrated by the law of *shlichus yad,* literally, *sending one's hand* to improperly use an item that one is watching. If a *shomer* uses an item in his care when he is not entitled to do so, then he becomes liable for any misfortunes that befall the item, even if the item is lost in a way that would not normally render him liable. [For example, if an unpaid guardian uses an object in his care and then it is stolen after he replaces it, he is liable.] This lesson is also true, explains *Sfas Emes,* in regard to serving Hashem. A person must always keep in mind that his body and talents were given to him only to be used for carrying out Hashem's mitzvos. Someone who uses these gifts for improper purposes is, like any *shomer* who improperly benefited from the item placed under his watch, liable for misappropriation. Moreover, properly caring for these gifts — by using them for the purposes that they were given — has another benefit as well; just as a guardian (other than a borrower) who properly executes his duties is exempt from paying for damage caused by circumstances that he was unable to prevent, a person who "guards the gifts that he was given" — by using his talents only for the proper purposes — will not be held accountable if he sins by accident. Since this person's only focus in life is serving Hashem, and he in fact does so whenever possible, it is evident that his sin was due to circumstances that were beyond his control.

HALACHAH OF THE DAY

We learned yesterday that only constructive tearing is forbidden under the Biblical restriction against *tearing.* While this is true, the Sages were concerned that if destructive tearing would be completely unrestricted on Shabbos, a situation might arise where one would tear an item and then come to mend the item that he has torn — which would be a transgression of the *melachah* of *sewing.* The Sages therefore decreed that even destructive tearing is forbidden on Shabbos. However, since this decree was enacted for the sole purpose of protecting against possible violation of the *melachah* of *sewing,* the Sages applied their decree only to materials that are subject to the restrictions against *sewing.*

Now, as we learned previously in our discussions of sewing, included in the *melachah* of *sewing* are other methods of fastening such as gluing, stapling, and taping. Accordingly, it is forbidden by Rabbinic decree to tear in a destructive manner any material that may be mended through the employment of any of these methods. It is, however, permissible to tear in a destructive manner any material that cannot be mended through an act of "sewing." Thus, one may, for example, tear or cut string in a destructive manner. String is repaired through tying, an act that, while forbidden in its own right, is not forbidden as part of the *melachah* of *sewing.* To illustrate this point: if one desires to open a package on Shabbos and it is tied with string in a knot that may not be untied on Shabbos, he may cut or tear the string in order to open the package. If, however, the package is glued shut, or it is sealed in cellophane, one may not tear it open — even in a destructive manner — except under the conditions that will be set forth below.

The Sages did not enact their decree in cases where it would impede the honor or enjoyment of Shabbos. For this reason, one may open a package in order to procure food, medicine, or some other item for Shabbos use, provided that the package is torn in a destructive manner.

For example: If one desires to open a box of breakfast cereal on Shabbos, he may not tear open the glued box top in the usual way, since doing so would be an act of constructive tearing on Shabbos. This form of tearing is viewed as constructive because by tearing open the box top he creates a closure which can be opened and resealed, allowing for the efficient storage and use of the cereal. One may, however, cut the box open in a manner that spoils its usefulness and leaves it unfit for storage (e.g., cutting open the sides of the box). Similarly, when opening a sealed plastic bag containing food, one may not simply pull apart the top of the bag. Rather, he must tear or cut the bag in a way that renders the bag unusable for future use.

QUESTION OF THE DAY:

For what type of loss is even a borrower not liable?

For the answer, see page 114.

A CLOSER LOOK AT THE SIDDUR

As we explained in *A Torah Thought for the Day,* the Torah tells us the laws of three different types of *shomrim* — a שׁוֹמֵר חִנָּם, *unpaid guardian,* a שׁוֹמֵר שָׂכָר, *paid guardian,* and a שׁוֹאֵל, *borrower.* The *Imrei Emes* (cited in *Likkutei Yehudah, Shemos*) observes that, in essence, the Torah is telling us that there are several different reasons why a person is motivated to care for someone else's property. Sometimes one accepting this responsibility is altruistic, and driven only by a genuine desire to do for the other person. Other times, a person agrees to do something for another person only because of the reward or payment that he will be given for doing so. Finally, there are times when even the promise of a future payment is not enough to motivate a person to accept responsibility; he will agree to help another person only when he also gains during the time that he is actually helping.

Continuing the lesson of his father the *Sfas Emes,* the *Imrei Emes* observes that a person who realizes that Hashem has made him a *shomer* over the talents that he was given can act like any one of the three *shomrim* described by the Torah. These three ways to serve Hashem, continues the *Imrei Emes,* are the subjects of the three chapters of *Krias Shema.*

The first passage of *Krias Shema* — which contains the verse: וְאָהַבְתָּ אֵת ה׳, *You shall love* H*ASHEM,* is speaking of the loftiest level of service of Hashem. Like a *shomer chinam* who watches an object based purely on the desire to help another person, a person who serves Hashem out of love does not think of the reward that he will be given for performing mitzvos; the only thing on his mind is how much Hashem desires that this action be done. The total lack of self-interest when it comes to *avodas Hashem* allows a person who loves Hashem to carry out His will at all times, even to the extent of בְּכָל־לְבָבְךָ וּבְכָל־נַפְשְׁךָ וּבְכָל־מְאֹדֶךָ, *with all your heart and with all your soul and with all your resources.*

The second passage of *Krias Shema,* which promises great rewards for performing mitzvos: וְנָתַתִּי מְטַר־אַרְצְכֶם בְּעִתּוֹ יוֹרֶה וּמַלְקוֹשׁ וגו׳, *then I shall provide rain for your Land in its proper time, the early and the late rains etc.,* tells a person who is unable to carry out Hashem's commandments for totally altruistic reasons that he should perform mitzvos nonetheless. For like a *shomer sachar* who is paid for his watch, he too will ultimately gain by doing so.

The third chapter of *Krias Shema* focuses on the mitzvah of *tzitzis.* The advantage that performing the mitzvah of *tzitzis* brings a person, explains the *Imrei Emes,* is best understood by looking at a *sho'el,* a borrower, whose benefit from accepting responsibility to guard his friend's article does not come with payment that will be received at a later time. Rather, a borrower gains from his actual use of the object. Additionally, a *sho'el* inherently benefits (by not having to pay while with the owner) by maintaining an ongoing relationship with the one who gave him the object. These benefits also exist with regard to *tzitzis.* Since *tzitzis* are worn constantly, one has the ability to see them, which results in: וּזְכַרְתֶּם אֶת־כָּל־מִצְוֹת ה׳ וַעֲשִׂיתֶם אֹתָם, *and you shall remember all of the commandments of* Hashem *and perform them.* The Torah tells us in the third passage of *Krias Shema* that properly performing the mitzvah of *tzitzis* reminds a person to always perform mitzvos, thereby bringing him closer to Hashem. Thus, this passage carries the message that there is immediate benefit gained from performing a mitzvah; a person's life, through his now closer connection with Hashem, is enriched through his actions. It is for this reason, concludes *Imrei Emes,* that it is written concerning the Torah: עֵץ־חַיִּים הִיא לַמַּחֲזִיקִים בָּהּ, *It is a tree of life to those who grasp it* (*Mishlei* 3:18). Simply studying Torah and fulfilling mitzvos immediately and immeasurably enhances a person's life.

A TASTE OF LOMDUS

We explained in *A Torah Thought for the Day* that the Torah, in our passage, details varying responsibilities for different types of *shomrim.* The Gemara (see also *Rambam, Hil. Sechirus* 2:3) points out that a closer reading of the Torah passage makes it clear that the laws of *shomrim* taught in this passage do not apply every time a *shomer* assumes responsibility to watch something. In describing a *shomer's* responsibilities, the Torah begins: כִּי־יִתֵּן אִישׁ אֶל־רֵעֵהוּ כֶּסֶף אוֹ־כֵלִים לִשְׁמֹר, *If a man shall give his fellow money or utensils to safeguard* (verse 6) and: כִּי־יִתֵּן אִישׁ אֶל־רֵעֵהוּ חֲמוֹר אוֹ־שׁוֹר אוֹ־שֶׂה וְכָל־בְּהֵמָה לִשְׁמֹר, *If a man shall give his fellow a donkey or an ox or a lamb or any animal to safeguard* (verse 9). Thus the Torah limits the laws of *shomrim* to these categories of items: money, utensils and animals. A person who assumes responsibility to guard an object that is not included in these categories, such as land, or documents which do not have intrinsic value, would not be liable if the object were stolen or destroyed. The Biblical guidelines of *shemirah* do not include these circumstances, and thus these rules do not apply.

Rambam remarks that although these categories are in fact excluded from the laws of *shomrim,* these exceptions are limited to liability for conventional loss (*geneivah v'aveidah*) and accidents. That is, a *shomer* whose responsibility would ordinarily obligate him for these occurrences would not be liable when watching an item not included in the laws of *shomrim.* Loss caused by negligence, however, must always be paid for, even if one is watching properties or documents that are excluded from the regular laws of *shomrim.* Explaining his ruling, *Rambam* states that a *shomer* must always pay when negligent, because improperly caring for an item for which he assumed responsibility is viewed as equivalent to actively destroying the item.

One may ask: What is the difference how the item was destroyed? Why should the fact that the damage was caused by the *shomer*'s negligence make him liable, when the Torah clearly says that the laws of *shomrim* apply only to movable items of intrinsic value?

Shach (*Choshen Mishpat* 66:126) answers this question by pointing out that a close reading of the Torah passage of *shomrim* reveals something surprising: the Torah never mentions a *shomer's* obligation to pay for an item that broke because of his negligence. The reason for this, he explains (see also *Kehillos Yaakov* to *Bava Kamma* §2:5 and to *Bava Metzia* §34), is that the Torah does not need to teach this obligation, since, as *Rambam* explained, it is obvious that loss caused by negligence must be paid for. In this sense, a *shomer's* need to pay for an object under his guard that was destroyed through his negligence is a different type of accountability than his other responsibilities, such as the need to pay for theft or other loss. The Torah's directive to pay the owner for the object when it was stolen or broken through an accident is one of financial responsibility. Although the *shomer* did not cause the theft or accident, the Torah, in this passage, teaches that a person who borrows, rents, or accepts payment to guard an object does so with the understanding that he will pay for it if it is lost or stolen. A *shomer* who is negligent, however, is responsible because he is viewed as a damager, whose negligence caused the loss of the item. This *shomer,* like any other person who damages another's possessions, must make restitution for the damage that he caused. [Of course, the failure to properly protect someone else's item only obligates a person who accepted responsibility to guard it, for otherwise the owner had no right to assume that this person would protect his possessions, and should have taken proper precautions on his own to prevent loss.]

It is for this reason, conclude *Shach* and *Kehillos Yaakov,* that *Rambam* holds even a *shomer* of documents and land liable for damage caused through negligence. Although the laws of *shomrim* do not apply to these items, the *shomer* is still not supposed to damage them. And since negligence is tantamount to damaging, the *shomer* is liable for any loss that results from the negligence.

A TORAH THOUGHT FOR THE DAY

כָּל־אַלְמָנָה וְיָתוֹם לֹא תְעַנּוּן. אִם־עַנֵּה תְעַנֶּה אֹתוֹ
כִּי אִם־צָעֹק יִצְעַק אֵלַי שָׁמֹעַ אֶשְׁמַע צַעֲקָתוֹ

You shall not torment any widow or orphan.
If you will torment him . . . for if he will cry out to me,
I shall surely hear his cry (Shemos 22:21-22).

There seems to be a strange pattern in the wording of these verses. Three verbs are written in duplicate fashion: (1) עַנֵּה תְעַנֶּה, (2) צָעֹק יִצְעַק, and (3) שָׁמֹעַ אֶשְׁמַע. Why does the verse speak of double persecution, double crying out, and Hashem's double hearkening to the cries? Also, the punishment for making the widow or orphan cry seems unusually severe: וְהָרַגְתִּי אֶתְכֶם בֶּחָרֶב וְהָיוּ נְשֵׁיכֶם אַלְמָנוֹת וּבְנֵיכֶם יְתֹמִים, *I will kill you by the sword, your wives will be widows and your children orphans.* Certainly, one should be punished for causing pain to an orphan, as it is a very cruel act, but why does he deserve death? We know that Hashem metes out punishment מִדָּה כְּנֶגֶד מִדָּה, *measure for measure.* How does this punishment fit into that guideline?

Rabbeinu Bachya addresses the fact that the Torah uses a double verb when speaking of the pain being caused. He explains that widows and orphans are downtrodden and weak, and are therefore very vulnerable to being tormented. The verse "doubles" its mention of their pain to tell us, "Beware, it is very easy to cause them pain."

The *Kli Yakar* explains that when one causes pain to an orphan with no father (*if you will torment **him***), the mother is also pained, for she must watch her dear son being hurt with no one there to protect and shield him. Therefore, the verse makes a double reference, since by one act one can cause pain to both the orphan and the widow.

Matnos Moshe explains further, citing the words of *Rashi* in *Shabbos* 11a: Orphans and widows, their tears come easily. The reason for this is that most people do not cry over minimally upsetting things, because they realize how insignificant they are. They find true happiness in other areas of life, such as a wholesome family, etc. Not so the widows and orphans, whose lives have been broken and robbed of true happiness. Any minute or seemingly insignificant pleasure is therefore very important to them, and trampling on these "small" things awakens their original pain. They therefore cry out doubly: once for this insignificant pain, but even more so, for being reminded how empty their lives really are.

The Torah therefore tells us: Beware not to cause pain to the widow or orphan, because every pain of theirs is a double pain. When they cry out, they are crying out with double agony: one for the present pain, and then again for the loss of their loved one. And Hashem listens doubly — that is, to both cries — as they are two independent outcries caused by the persecution of the tormentor.

Now we understand the "measure for measure" in this punishment. Because causing widows or orphans pain and making them cry awakens their old wounds, and they relive the pain of losing their close ones, "measure for measure" dictates that the tormentor's family will feel the same pain that he brought upon them.

MISHNAH OF THE DAY: SHABBOS 20:5

The following Mishnah deals with the proper methods of moving *muktzeh* items when it is permitted to do so:

הַקַּשׁ שֶׁעַל גַּבֵּי הַמִּטָּה — ***Straw that is on a bed,*** [1] **לֹא יְנַעְנְעֶנּוּ בְיָדוֹ** — ***one may not move it with his hand,*** [2] **אֶלָּא מְנַעְנְעוֹ בְגוּפוֹ** — ***but he may move it with his body.*** [3] **וְאִם הָיָה מַאֲכַל בְּהֵמָה** — ***And if*** the straw ***was*** fit for ***animal feed,*** [4] **אוֹ שֶׁהָיָה עָלָיו כַּר אוֹ סָדִין** — ***or if there was a pillow or sheet on it*** from before the beginning of the Sabbath, **מְנַעְנְעוֹ בְּיָדוֹ** — ***he may move [the straw],*** even ***with his hand.*** [5]

NOTES

1. Straw is usually used for kindling; since on the Sabbath it may not be used for that purpose, it is therefore *muktzeh* (*Rav; Rashi*). In this case, a person wishes to move straw in order to be able to lie down on the bed. *Rosh* (3:19) explains that he wishes to move the straw around the bed in order to make it comfortable to lie on, while *Ran* (to Gemara 43b) explains that he wishes to remove the straw from the bed entirely.

2. Since it is *muktzeh,* one may not move it with his hand (*Rav; Rashi*).

3. I.e., while lying down on the bed, he may shift his shoulders, causing the straw to move. Moving the straw in an unusual fashion (viz., with his body rather than his hands) is categorized as טִלְטוּל מִן הַצַּד, *indirect movement of muktzeh,* which is permissible (*Rav; Rashi*).

4. I.e., if the straw had been designated for use as animal fodder prior to the Sabbath, it is not *muktzeh.*

5. By placing a pillow or a sheet over the straw, the person indicates his intention to use it as a mattress. Thus, it is no longer considered to be designated for kindling. Rather, it acquires the status of a utensil (e.g., a mattress), and it is not *muktzeh* (*Rav; Rashi*). [This special designation is required only in places where straw is usually used for kindling. In our countries, however, straw is usually used for fodder or bedding. It is therefore not *muktzeh* even if it was not specifically designated as such (*Magen Avraham* 308:53).]

The Mishnah now deals with an unrelated Sabbath law:

מַכְבֵּשׁ שֶׁל בַּעֲלֵי בָתִּים מַתִּירִין — ***We may release a householder's press***[6] to remove a garment held therein,[7] אֲבָל לֹא כוֹבְשִׁין — ***but we may not*** initially ***press it down*** on a garment on the Sabbath.[8] וְשֶׁל כּוֹבְסִין לֹא יִגַּע בּוֹ — ***And we may not touch a launderer's*** press, even to release it.[9] רַבִּי יְהוּדָה אוֹמֵר — ***R' Yehudah says:*** אִם הָיָה מוּתָּר מֵעֶרֶב שַׁבָּת — ***If it was*** partially ***released from before the Sabbath,*** מַתִּיר אֶת כּוּלּוֹ וְשׁוֹמְטוֹ — ***one may release it completely*** on the Sabbath ***and remove*** the garment held therein.[10]

NOTES

6. The press was composed of two long, heavy boards. Garments were laid out on the lower board, and the upper one was then lowered upon them to press them. To secure the press, four posts were set at the four corners of the lower boards. The posts passed through four corresponding holes in the upper boards, and the upper boards would move up and down along these posts. When the upper board was pressed down into place, pegs were inserted into specially placed holes in the posts, and they would hold the upper boards down (*Rashi*).

7. I.e., we may release the press (by removing the holding pegs) to remove the garments to wear on the Sabbath (*Rav; Rashi*).

8. Since they would not be ready for use on the Sabbath, in pressing the garments one is preparing them for use after the Sabbath, and it is forbidden to prepare on the Sabbath for after the Sabbath (*Rav; Rashi*).

9. I.e., one may not undo this particular type of press. Since it is made to shape clothing, it is pressed together very tightly. Undoing it is therefore similar to the Biblically forbidden labor of destroying [סוֹתֵר], and hence prohibited by Rabbinic decree (*Rav; Rashi*).

10. I.e., if it was partially undone before the Sabbath, even though it was still partially fastened, one may finish undoing it on the Sabbath (*Tiferes Yisrael*).

GEMS FROM THE GEMARA

The Gemara to our Mishnah (141b) relates a series of rulings concerning the wearing of shoes on the Sabbath.

The Gemara first cites a Baraisa that teaches that a person should not go out into a public domain wearing a shoe that is too large for him. [This is because it will likely slip off his foot, and he may come to carry it four *amos* in a public domain (*Rashi*).] But he may go out wearing a shirt that is too large for him. [This is because it is unlikely that the shirt will slip off his body. Moreover, he is not likely to remove it (even due to its ill fit), since he surely will not leave himself unclothed in the public domain (*Rashi*).]

The Baraisa then rules that a woman should not go out into the public domain wearing a torn shoe. [This is because she may be embarrassed to be seen wearing such a shoe, and she may therefore remove it and carry it home through the public domain (*Rashi*).]

The Baraisa's final ruling is that one may not go out with a new shoe on the Sabbath.

The Gemara clarifies this last ruling by stating that it concerns only a woman's shoe. [A woman is very particular that her shoe fit her foot precisely. Hence, we are concerned that if she finds that it is too large or too small, she may come to remove it and carry it home through the public domain (*Rashi*).]

This ruling itself is then qualified by a Baraisa in which Bar Kappara taught that this ruling applies only if the woman did not go out wearing the new shoe for a while before the onset of the Sabbath. However, if she went out wearing it for a while before the Sabbath, it is permitted for her to wear the new shoe outside on the Sabbath. [If she wore the new shoes for a while before the Sabbath, she has already determined that they fit well enough to wear; there is then no concern that she will be particular about their fit and remove them on the Sabbath (*Rashi; see Yerushalmi*).]

A MUSSAR THOUGHT FOR THE DAY

Rashi tells us that the prohibition of causing pain to orphans and widows does not speak exclusively of them; the same law prohibits persecuting any man. The Torah, however, speaks of that which is prevalent, for orphans and widows are weak, and persecuting them is a common occurrence.

To illustrate the extent of this sin, the *Ramban* (in *Shaar HaGemul*) brings down a fascinating story from *Maseches Semachos*. When Rabban Shimon ben Gamliel and R' Yishmael Kohen Gadol were sentenced to be killed, R' Yishmael was crying. Rabban Shimon asked him, "Why are you crying? In just a few moments you will be sitting with the greatest *tzaddikim*!" He replied, "I am sad over the way we are being led to our death — like criminals who desecrated the Sabbath, or idol worshipers." Rabban Shimon asked, "Perhaps once while you were eating or sleeping, a woman came to your door to ask a halachic inquiry, and you caused her to wait until you had finished eating or sleeping?" The Torah prohibits this, as the verse states: *You shall not torment a widow, for if you do . . . I will kill you by the sword, and your wives will be widows.*

The exacting nature of Heavenly punishment is extremely awesome, especially regarding *tzaddikim.* Rabban Shimon ben Gamliel and R' Yishmael Kohen Gadol were two of the Ten Martyrs (*Asarah Harugei Malchus*), regarding whom the Gemara (*Bava Basra* 10b) says: "No other creatures can stand in their chambers in the World to Come." Each of them was killed with a cruel death in an extremely painful manner. And the "sin" that is mentioned as the possible reason for their deserving such a death was that perhaps one of them kept a widow waiting unnecessarily while he was concluding his meal.

A story is told of an incident that occurred in the Chofetz Chaim's hometown when he was a young man. A widow lived in a rented house, and one winter her meager income did not allow her to pay the rent. She faced the threat of eviction. People tried to intercede on her behalf but to no avail. First the landlord removed the roof of the house. People begged him to at least allow the widow to remain until the end of the winter. He would not relent, and threw her out into the cold. Years passed and the Chofetz Chaim would wonder aloud: "The Torah says specifically, *You shall not torment any widow or orphan. If you will ... I shall surely hear his cry.* Why is this man not getting punished?" About ten years after this occurred, the man was bitten by a wild dog and suffered a painful death.

The Chofetz Chaim was known for his love of every Jew, and surely did not receive any pleasure or satisfaction from hearing of someone being punished. Why, then, did he anticipate the punishment of this man? The *sefer Beis HaAv* explains that since the Torah clearly stresses a severe punishment for this sin, it is a "mitzvah" to watch how Hashem Himself gets involved to protect these humble and sensitive people, and to inflict punishment when they are wronged.

HALACHAH OF THE DAY

We learned yesterday that the Sages allowed tearing in a destructive manner when the tearing is necessary in order to access an item necessary for the enjoyment of Shabbos. However, it must be noted that this dispensation applies only to items such as foodstuffs or medicines. One may not tear — even in a destructive manner — in order to acquire items of mere convenience. For example, one may not tear open an envelope in order to read a letter on Shabbos. Additionally, even when tearing is permitted, one must take great care not to tear apart any letters, numbers, or pictures on the package, so as not to violate the prohibition against *erasing* (a *melachah* that we will study in coming lessons).

We mentioned previously that the prohibition against tearing extends to items that have been glued or sewn together. However, this applies only to items that have been attached intentionally. If two items become attached to one another inadvertently, they may be separated on Shabbos.

Now that we have discussed the basic rules that govern the *melachah* of *tearing,* we will consider some common practical applications.

We have already laid out the basic premise that governs the opening of food packaging on Shabbos. Tearing may be done in a destructive manner in order to access food. However, how this rule is applied varies greatly depending on the specific form of packaging and must be judged on a case-by-case basis. Furthermore, opening packages may involve the violation of more than one *melachah.* Our discussion at this time will focus on the prohibition of *tearing.*

It should be stressed that as a general rule, it is preferable to open all food packages and containers before Shabbos.

The opening of sealed paper or plastic bags on Shabbos is a matter of dispute among the *poskim.* According to some, it is forbidden to unseal or unglue a paper or plastic bag. This prohibition would apply to both snack bags such as potato chip bags which are heat-sealed, as well as to bags of sugar and the like which are glued shut. According to these *poskim,* if the contents of such packages are necessary on Shabbos, the bags must be torn open in a destructive manner while exercising care not to tear characters, pictures or symbols.

There are other *poskim* who rule that a bag that can be opened easily may be opened in the usual manner. These *poskim* reason that if the bag can be opened easily, the closure is too weak to constitute a halachically significant seal. If the closure is not recognized by halachah as being a seal, opening it cannot be proscribed by the prohibition against *tearing* on Shabbos.

On a practical level, it is best to act stringently in this regard and to open all bags in a destructive manner.

QUESTION OF THE DAY:

Why does the Torah stress that one may not oppress "any" widow or orphan?

For the answer, see page 114.

A CLOSER LOOK AT THE SIDDUR

In the *Pesukei D'Zimrah* that we recite during *Shacharis* of Shabbos morning, we add several chapters of *Tehillim* that are not recited every day. In one of them we find the verse (*Tehillim* 34:19): קָרוֹב ה׳ לְנִשְׁבְּרֵי־לֵב וְאֶת־דַּכְּאֵי־רוּחַ יוֹשִׁיעַ, *HASHEM is close to the brokenhearted, and those crushed in spirit He saves.*

This verse reveals to us how one can ensure that Hashem listens to him. Although we say three times each day in *Ashrei*: קָרוֹב ה׳ לְכָל־קֹרְאָיו לְכֹל אֲשֶׁר יִקְרָאֻהוּ בֶאֱמֶת, *HASHEM is close to all who call upon Him — to all who call upon Him sincerely,* it is clear that there are different levels of closeness to Hashem, and they affect how one's prayers will be answered.

The Torah tells us (*Shemos* 23:9) not to abuse and oppress a stranger (this refers to a convert), *because you were strangers in the land of Egypt. Ramban* explains that Hashem is reminding us of the helpless feeling of a stranger. Hashem says, "I saw the pain that you suffered at the hands of the Egyptians, and I took revenge upon them, because I look out for the tears of the exploited who do not have the strength nor the morale to stand up for themselves. The same is true with the widows and orphans — do not hurt them, because I will listen to their cries. All of these people do not have trust in themselves, only in Me, and they cry out with a humble heart." *Ramban* goes on to say that it was in this merit that Hashem had mercy on Bnei Yisrael in Egypt, because they cried out with pure trust in Him.

The verse says in *Tehillim* (51:19): לֵב־נִשְׁבָּר וְנִדְכֶּה אֱלֹהִים לֹא תִבְזֶה, *a broken and crushed heart, HASHEM does not turn away.* If we internalize this attitude and feeling when we come to daven, we are guaranteed that our prayers will be heard.

The *Shaarei Teshuvah* in *Shulchan Aruch (Orach Chaim* §98) cites from the disciples of the Arizal that when one recites the blessing following *Krias Shema,* while saying the words, וְעוֹזֵר דַּלִּים, וְעוֹנֶה לְעַמּוֹ יִשְׂרָאֵל בְּעֵת שַׁוְּעָם אֵלָיו, *He Who helps the poor, and Who responds to His people Israel when they cry out to Him,* he should have in mind the following: He should consider himself a poor man even if he is financially secure, because nothing is guaranteed for life.

This echoes what we have said above: In order to ensure that Hashem hearkens to our prayers, we must prepare ourselves to pray with the mind-set of someone who feels totally dependent upon Hashem's help. This is the connection with the next words of the blessing: *Who responds to His people Israel when they cry out to Him.* When it is clear to us that only Hashem can help us, we will pray to Him properly, and He will respond.

A TORAH THOUGHT FOR THE DAY

בְּכוֹר בָּנֶיךָ תִּתֶּן־לִי. כֵּן־תַּעֲשֶׂה לְשֹׁרְךָ . . .
וְאַנְשֵׁי־קֹדֶשׁ תִּהְיוּן לִי

The firstborn of your sons you shall present to Me.
So shall you do to your ox . . .
People of holiness shall you be to Me (*Shemos* 22:28-30).

Sforno expounds upon the role of the firstborn, and the connection between these laws and the statement that the Jews will be a holy people. He explains that the firstborn was designated for all holy work, whether serving in the Mikdash or teaching Torah. [Originally, this was the role of the firstborn, but it was later given to the Kohanim (after the sin of the Golden Calf). Scripture indeed tells us that the Kohen is the source of Torah learning, for it is stated (*Malachi* 2:7): כִּי שִׂפְתֵי כֹהֵן יִשְׁמְרוּ־דַעַת וְתוֹרָה יְבַקְשׁוּ מִפִּיהוּ, *For the lips of the Kohen should safeguard knowledge, and people should seek teaching from his mouth.*]

We may ask: Why was it that the firstborn children were originally chosen to be the ones to transmit the Torah to the next generation? Why was it not enough for the sons to learn it from their fathers?

Maharal explains that a firstborn plays a double role. Since he is closest in age to the parents and is also one of the siblings, he becomes the bridge for transmission of the Torah, acting to minimize any generation gap that may exist. He is the first recipient of knowledge from the previous generation, but at the same time he is the father's assistant to help transmit all the father's teachings to the other siblings.

This is why the firstborn were chosen to be the ones to transmit our *mesorah* to the next generation. They are the ones who have the best understanding of the recipients' way of thinking, and they can relate to them in some ways better than the father can. However, *Sforno* explains that since they are not natural authority figures as fathers are, it takes acts of recognition to establish them as teachers. For this reason, a firstborn receives a double portion of the father's estate. This show of appreciation for their work will help to make their guidance welcome, giving them the ability to help the Jews become a holy people. [*Sforno* explains that this same idea applies to the Kohanim as well; if the nation treats the Kohanim with respect and honor, by giving them the *matnos Kehunah* (priestly gifts), then they will be able to teach Torah to the nation, and the Jews will become holy men.]

MISHNAH OF THE DAY: SHABBOS 21:1

The following Mishnah deals with exceptions to the ban against moving *muktzeh*:

נוֹטֵל אָדָם אֶת בְּנוֹ וְהָאֶבֶן בְּיָדוֹ — ***A person may take his son*** in his arms even ***when there is a stone in his*** son's ***hand,***[1] **וְכַלְכָּלָה וְהָאֶבֶן בְּתוֹכָהּ** — ***or take a basket*** even ***when there is a stone in it.***[2] **וּמְטַלְטְלִין תְּרוּמָה טְמֵאָה עִם הַטְּהוֹרָה** — ***Similarly, we may move terumah that is tamei together with that which is tahor,*** **וְעִם הַחוּלִּין** — ***or together with ordinary food*** that is not *terumah.*[3]

רַבִּי יְהוּדָה אוֹמֵר — ***R' Yehudah says:*** **אַף מַעֲלִין אֶת הַמְדוּמָּע בְּאֶחָד וּמֵאָה** — ***We may also remove*** one measure ***from a mixture of one*** measure of *terumah* ***and one hundred*** measures of unconsecrated food.[4]

NOTES

1. I.e., he may pick him up if he is in a house or a yard in which one is permitted to carry on the Sabbath (*Rav; Rashi; Tiferes Yisrael*). Even though the child is holding a stone which he refuses to drop, and even though the stone is *muktzeh,* the father is not regarded as handling the stone itself and is therefore permitted to pick up the child (*Rav; Tiferes Yisrael*).

2. The Gemara explains that this stone is being used to fill a hole in the basket; consequently, the stone becomes part of the structure of the basket and is no longer *muktzeh* (*Tos. Yom Tov; Tiferes Yisrael* from Gemara 142a; see *Rav*). [This is similar to the rule stated above, Mishnah 17:6.]

3. *Terumah* that is *tamei* may not be eaten even by a Kohen. Since the only purpose for which it may be used is kindling — which is forbidden on the Sabbath — it is completely unusable on the Sabbath and is consequently *muktzeh.* Our Mishnah teaches, however, that one may carry such *terumah* in a container that also contains *terumah* that is *tahor* or ordinary, non-*terumah* food (*Rav; Rashi*). Although this container is a base to both *muktzeh* (*terumah* that is *tamei*) and non-*muktzeh* (*terumah* that is *tahor,* or ordinary food), since the non-*muktzeh* is the more valuable, the base may be moved.

4. When one measure of *terumah* is nullified because it became mixed with 100 measures (i.e., 100 times as much) of unconsecrated food, it loses its sanctity. Nevertheless, one is required to remove one measure of the mixture and give it to a Kohen, and the law treats that one measure as if it is the original part of *terumah* that became mixed in — even though no logical basis exists for such a presumption. R' Yehudah further maintains that since the part removed is treated as the original *terumah,* it is treated as if it were never truly mixed into the other produce. Rather, we regard this "mixture" as two distinct piles of produce — one of *terumah* and another of ordinary food. Consequently, R' Yehudah does not consider the removal of the *"terumah"* to be a form of fixing the produce (which would be forbidden on the Sabbath), and he therefore permits it (*Rav; Rambam Commentary*). [The Sages disagree and forbid the removal of the part of *terumah* as a form of fixing the produce.]

GEMS FROM THE GEMARA

We saw in our Mishnah that a father may pick up and carry his young son while his son is holding a rock. Even though the child is holding a rock which he refuses to drop, and even though the rock is *muktzeh,* the father is not regarded as handling the rock itself, and he is therefore permitted to pick up the child (*Rav; Tiferes Yisrael*).

The Gemara (141b) qualifies the Mishnah as referring only to a child who is so attached to his father that if his father does not pick him up, he may become ill. In such a case, the Rabbis permitted the father to pick him up (even though the child's life is not in danger), since he is not handling the rock directly (*Rashi*). The Rabbis did not require the father to force the child to drop the rock, since this would add to the child's distress (*Tosafos* to 142a).

Others explain that the Rabbis permitted the father to pick his son up despite the rock in his hand even where there is no danger that the child will become ill, as long as parting with his father causes him anguish (*Meiri*).

In any event, our Mishnah's dispensation is granted only if the child was holding a *rock.* Should the child be holding a coin, however, no leniency is granted. This is because the coin is valuable to the father as well, and the Rabbis therefore feared that if child were to drop the coin, the father would be tempted to pick it up (Gemara 142a). Consequently, even if the child walks with the coin in his hand, the father may not hold his hand, lest the child drop the coin and the father be tempted to pick it up (*Rashi* to Gemara ibid.). [*Ramban,* however, disagrees, asserting that the Gemara means only to prohibit *carrying* a child with a coin in his hand. Walking with him, however, is permitted (see *Ran*). He explains that just as we do not ordinarily prohibit someone from standing next to a child who is holding a coin, so too, we do not prohibit his walking next to him. The Rabbis forbade the father only to *carry* the coin indirectly (by carrying the child), lest he come to carry the coin directly.]

QUESTION OF THE DAY:

Why does the Torah mention the law of the firstborn son here* (22:28-30)*, when its laws were taught earlier?

For the answer, see page 115.

פרשת משפטים

FRIDAY

PARASHAS MISHPATIM

A MUSSAR THOUGHT FOR THE DAY

The *Rashbam* says that the Torah puts a special emphasis on things called רֵאשִׁית (*reishis*), *first.* Two examples of this are *bikkurim* and *terumah,* which are both referred to in the Torah as רֵאשִׁית, *first.*

In *A Torah Thought for the Day,* we discussed the advantages of a firstborn and his role; now we will see what is so special about all things that are called "firsts."

The *Imros Chaim* (Rav Chaim Wisoker) speaks about the concept of רֵאשִׁית with respect to the first *Rashi* in *Chumash,* which lists certain things that are רֵאשִׁית. Rav Wisoker explains that רֵאשִׁית does not mean "first" as in "number one," because this would not be a cause for greatness. Rather, it means that these items of רֵאשִׁית are the beginnings of everything that will follow them. All potential, and everything that will eventually grow, have their origin in these "beginnings." The more one concentrates on how perfect the beginning is, the more perfect the end result will be.

Take, for example, the firstborn. The toil and labor that parents invest in their firstborn child will set the tone for the growth of all subsequent children. The Torah gives a special pass from military obligations to a young man in his first year of marriage, to allow him to invest his best efforts, together with his wife, in establishing their home properly. The Torah is telling us that if we want to see good results in whatever we do, we must see to it that the הַתְחָלָה, *beginning,* should be done to its greatest perfection.

The verse says in *Koheles* (7:8): טוֹב אַחֲרִית דָּבָר מֵרֵאשִׁיתוֹ, *The end of a matter is better than its beginning;* some commentators explain it as meaning that the goodness and quality of the end of something is dependent on its beginning.

The *Eliyahu Rabbah* in *Orach Chaim* 625:1 says that the reason the Yom Tov of Succos is celebrated after the summer and not in what would seem to be its proper time (after Pesach, when the miracle of the *succos* occurred), is because Hashem wanted the beginning of each of the main two seasons of the year to be holy times. The summer season begins with the Yom Tov of Pesach (when we stop asking for rain), and the beginning of the rainy season begins with Succos. [The rainy season really begins with the first day of Succos; we refrain from requesting the rain only because it is a bad sign if it rains on Succos.] Hashem wants those all-important beginning days to be holy and filled with mitzvos, so the days that follow will continue that same pattern.

HALACHAH OF THE DAY

We spoke yesterday about opening plastic bags on Shabbos. Today we will discuss opening other types of containers.

It is forbidden to unglue the top of a cardboard box. When an item in a sealed cardboard box is a Shabbos necessity, one must cut the box open in a destructive manner, taking care not to tear any words, pictures or symbols.

It is forbidden to peel apart the sealed top of a cardboard milk or juice carton, as this is constructive tearing. It is certainly forbidden to fashion a spout out of the top of the carton (as one will do when opening certain milk and juice cartons). If one needs milk or juice from a sealed cardboard milk or juice carton on Shabbos, he must puncture a hole on the bottom of the carton (taking care not to tear any words), thereby ruining the carton.

According to some *poskim,* it is permitted to tear off the plastic ring with which the cap of a plastic milk carton is sealed. However, other *poskim* prohibit this; thus, it is preferable to open plastic milk cartons before Shabbos. If one forgot to do so, he may rely upon the lenient opinion and open the plastic ring. [It should be noted that one can often avoid this problem entirely by inserting a fork or a similar implement under the ring and lifting it up; in this way the cap can usually be removed without tearing the ring at all.]

Bottle caps that can be lifted or screwed off without breaking (i.e., without leaving a ring around the bottle) may be removed on Shabbos. Those that have ring-seals attached that break upon opening may not be opened on Shabbos according to many *poskim;* thus, the bottle should be opened in a destructive manner.

It is forbidden to tear any label from a bottle on Shabbos, even destructively, since this does not fall into the category of tearing in order to access an item that is necessary for the enjoyment of Shabbos.

It is permitted to push a straw into the small piece of foil on the top of a "box-drink," as the opening thus created is too small to be considered a halachically significant "opening," and thus no *tearing* is deemed to have taken place. It is also permissible to peel a seal off the top of a container (of the type commonly found beneath the jar lids of peanut butter and the like) on Shabbos (again, taking care not to tear any words or symbols).

A CLOSER LOOK AT THE SIDDUR

After the prayer of *Vayechulu* is repeated following the *Maariv Shemoneh Esrei* of Friday night, we find a section of the *Maariv* prayer known as the בְּרָכָה מֵעֵין שֶׁבַע, *The blessing that is like seven.* It consists of three parts: a blessing, recited by the *shliach tzibbur,* that is very similar to the beginning of the opening blessing of *Shemoneh Esrei;* a paragraph, recited by the congregation and repeated by the *shliach tzibbur,* that contains a brief mention of the main theme of each of the seven blessings of the Sabbath *Shemoneh Esrei;* and a second paragraph, recited by the *shliach tzibbur,* that is a repetition of the central blessing of the *Shemoneh Esrei.*

The Gemara in *Berachos* (24b) explains the reason for these additions to the prayers. The synagogues of those times were usually located outside of the cities, and the Sages were concerned that people who arrived late for *Maariv* would not finish with the congregation, and would be left alone to make their way home in the darkness. To avoid this problem, they instituted these additions after the *Shemoneh Esrei,* so the latecomers would have a chance to finish their prayers.

The name of this prayer is derived from its middle paragraph, which has seven phrases that correspond to the seven blessings in the *Shemoneh Esrei*: (1) מָגֵן אָבוֹת, *Shield of our fathers,* corresponds to the opening blessing of *Avos;* (2) מְחַיֵּה מֵתִים, *He Who brings the dead back to life,* corresponds to the second blessing; (3) הָאֵל הַקָּדוֹשׁ, *The holy God,* corresponds to the third blessing; (4) הַמֵּנִיחַ לְעַמּוֹ, *He Who grants rest to His people,* corresponds to the central blessing, which speaks of the Sabbath as a holy day of rest; (5) לְפָנָיו נַעֲבֹד, *Before Him we will serve,* corresponds to the blessing of *Avodah,* which speaks of Hashem's acceptance of our service; (6) וְנוֹדֶה לִשְׁמוֹ, *And we will give thanks to His Name,* corresponds to the blessing of *Modim* (thanksgiving); and (7) אֲדוֹן הַשָּׁלוֹם, *Master of peace,* corresponds to the closing blessing of peace.

Interestingly, when Succos or Shavuos fall on Friday night, these prayers are recited, but when Pesach falls on a Friday night, they are not. This is because the night of Pesach is a לֵיל שִׁמּוּרִים, *a night of protection,* on which the Jews enjoy extra Divine safeguarding, and there was no need to add prayers to protect any stragglers.

These paragraphs are omitted when an individual prays alone or when a *minyan* is held in a place where prayers are not usually said (such as a *minyan* held in the house of a mourner). However, the central paragraph may be recited, if one wishes to do so.

A TORAH THOUGHT FOR THE DAY

פרשת משפטים

SHABBOS

PARASHAS MISHPATIM

הִנֵּה אָנֹכִי שֹׁלֵחַ מַלְאָךְ לְפָנֶיךָ לִשְׁמָרְךָ בַּדָּרֶךְ וְלַהֲבִיאֲךָ אֶל־הַמָּקוֹם אֲשֶׁר הֲכִנֹתִי

Behold! I send an angel before you to protect you on the way, and to bring you to the lace that I have prepared (*Shemos* 23:20).

Rashi says: Here they were informed that they were destined to sin at the incident of the Golden Calf, and that the *Shechinah* (Divine Presence) would then say, "I will not ascend in your midst." [As a result, it would be an angel, and not Hashem's Presence, that would lead the Jews into Eretz Yisrael.]

The *Ramban* notes that this prophecy never came to pass, because later, when the Jews sinned, Moshe nullified this decree with his prayer. We find that Moshe said to Hashem: *If Your Presence does not go along, do not bring us onward from here* (*Shemos* 33:15). Hashem answered his request favorably, as the verse states (ibid. v. 17): *Even this thing of which you spoke I shall do. Ramban* explains that in truth Moshe did not annul the decree entirely; he was capable only of delaying its fulfillment during his lifetime. It was fulfilled, however, in the times of Yehoshua after the death of Moshe (see *Yehoshua* 5:13-15).

The *Netziv* raises several difficulties with this interpretation of *Rashi* and *Ramban.* One of the questions he asks is: Why did Hashem see fit to discuss the future sins of the Jews at this point? The Gemara (*Berachos* 9b) tells us: דַּיָּהּ לְצָרָה בְּשַׁעְתָּהּ, *It is sufficient to deal with a problem in its time,* and *Rashi* in *Parashas Shemos* (3:14) says similarly. Why bring up future problems and troubles, when the Jews had not yet sinned and the *Shechinah* was still guiding them? Furthermore, the *Tzror HaMor* asks: If Moshe was aware that this decree was looming over the Jews, why did he not attempt to have it nullified immediately, instead of waiting until after the sin of the Golden Calf, when it would be much harder to find merit for the Jews?

Tzror HaMor answers this question by offering a different explanation. He suggests that the angel spoken of in this verse was not the same angel that Hashem wished to appoint to accompany the Jews after the sin of the Golden Calf. Rather, this angel was a messenger from the *Shechinah,* sent to hasten their passage into Eretz Yisrael, who was appointed specifically to destroy the other nations that were then occupying Eretz Yisrael. The *malach* proposed by Hashem later, however, was indeed a punishment, as it represented rejection and disapproval. For this reason, Moshe had no reason to try and nullify the decree regarding the angel spoken of in our *pasuk*. It was only later, when Moshe heard that the Jews were to suffer the severe punishment of losing the *Shechinah* to guide them, that he cried out in prayer.

Rav Elyah Lopian explains why Moshe saw the possibility of losing Hashem's direct involvement with the Jews as such a terrible punishment that he was willing to jeopardize the continuation of Bnei Yisrael's journey to Eretz Yisrael to have this decree annulled. The verse (*Yeshayah* 4:4) refers to Hashem forgiving Bnei Yisrael with the words: אִם רָחַץ ה׳ אֵת צֹאַת בְּנוֹת־צִיּוֹן, *When HASHEM will have washed away the excrement of the children of Tziyon.* When a child soils his clothing and an unpleasant odor is discharged, bystanders will all leave the area. The only one who can deal with the mess with loving care is the child's mother. Because of her overwhelming love and affection for her child, she does not even notice the terrible smell.

A sin, too, creates the spiritual equivalent of a foul odor, chasing away even good angels. Only Hashem, with His unconditional love, will cleanse the sinner. This was the danger Moshe envisioned in handing over the Jews to the angel. If the Jews would sin further, the angel would be repelled; the only One Who could be counted upon to cleanse the Jews was Hashem Himself.

MISHNAH OF THE DAY: SHABBOS 21:2

The following Mishnah considers indirect movement of *muktzeh*: הָאֶבֶן שֶׁעַל פִּי הֶחָבִית — ***A stone that is*** resting ***upon the opening of a cask,*** מַטָּה עַל צִדָּהּ וְהִיא נוֹפֶלֶת — ***he may tilt*** the cask ***on its side so that*** the stone ***falls off.***[1] הָיְתָה בֵּין הֶחָבִיוֹת — ***If*** the cask ***was among other casks*** that might break if the stone would fall against them, מַגְבִּיהָהּ וּמַטָּהּ עַל צִדָּהּ וְהִיא נוֹפֶלֶת — ***one may lift*** the cask as is, remove it to a safe area, ***and*** there ***tilt it on its side so that*** the stone ***falls off.***[2]

NOTES

1. I.e., if a stone is covering the mouth of a cask from which one wishes to draw wine, one may not remove the *muktzeh* stone with his hands, but he may tilt the cask so that the stone falls off (*Rav; Rashi*). [However, this indirect movement of *muktzeh* is permissible only when it is done for the sake of a non-*muktzeh* object — e.g., to enable one to draw wine from the cask. If the purpose of moving the stone is to protect the stone (or, in the Mishnah's next case, the money) from theft or the like, even tilting the cask to move the *muktzeh* would be prohibited (see *Mishnah Berurah* 309:14).]

2. I.e., upon reaching an area where he can slide the stone off the cask without causing any damage, he must do so (*Rav; Rashi*). [He may not continue to carry the cask any further without first removing the stone, since such movement is unnecessary.]

פרשת משפטים

SHABBOS

PARASHAS MISHPATIM

מָעוֹת שֶׁעַל הַכַּר — ***Money that is on a pillow,*** **מְנַעֵר אֶת הַכַּר וְהֵן נוֹפְלוֹת** — ***one may shake the pillow so that it falls off.***[3]

Having mentioned a law concerning a pillow, the Mishnah digresses to discuss other Sabbath laws concerning pillows:

הָיְתָה עָלָיו לִשְׁלֶשֶׁת — ***If there was filth on*** the pillow, and one wishes to clean it on the Sabbath,[4] **מְקַנְּחָהּ בִּסְמַרְטוּט** — ***he may wipe it off with a rag,*** but may not rinse it with water.[5] **הָיְתָה שֶׁל עוֹר** — But ***if*** the dirty pillow ***was*** made ***of leather,*** **נוֹתְנִין עָלֶיהָ מַיִם עַד שֶׁתִּכְלֶה** — ***we may pour water on it until*** the filth ***disappears.***[6]

NOTES

3. I.e., if money, which is *muktzeh,* is lying on a pillow, and one wishes to use that pillow, one may shake the pillow so that the money falls off, just as in the previous case of the stone on the cask. On the other hand, if he wishes to use the place being occupied by the pillow, he may pick up the pillow with the money still on it and carry it away (*Rav* from Gemara 142b). [Since shaking the money off the pillow onto the bed will in any case prevent him from using the space, the Rabbis permitted him to carry everything away (via the pillow) since this is an indirect movement of *muktzeh.*] This ruling applies also to the case of the cask upon which a stone is lying (*Tur* 309; *Tos. Yom Tov*).

These two cases refer only to a *muktzeh* article *forgotten* atop a permissible article. Should one *intentionally* leave the *muktzeh* article there, the permissible article becomes a *base for a forbidden article* (בָּסִיס לְדָבָר הָאָסוּר), thus becoming *muktzeh* in its own right. This being the case, even tilting the cask or shaking the pillow would be forbidden (*Rav* from Gemara ibid.).

4. I.e., if there was filth, such as spittle, excretum (*Rav; Rashi*), or bird droppings (*Aruch*) on the pillow.

5. He may wipe the pillow off with a rag, but he may not apply water, since the pillow is made of cloth. Soaking cloth in water is tantamount to washing it — an act prohibited on the Sabbath as a derivative of the forbidden labor of *whitening* (*Rav; Rashi;* see above, Mishnah 7:2).

6. The rule that soaking is tantamount to washing applies only to absorbent fabric, not to leather. Thus, one may rinse the leather pillow with water. Nevertheless, since a pillow is made of soft leather, one may not *scrub* it to remove the stain, for that would be a violation of the prohibition against laundering (*Rav; Rashi* from *Zevachim* 94b).

QUESTION OF THE DAY:

What does the verse (23:20) refer to when it states that the angel would bring the Jews to "the place that I have prepared"?

For the answer, see page 115.

GEMS FROM THE GEMARA

Our Mishnah considered the moving of *muktzeh* indirectly. The Gemara (142b) introduces another means by which *muktzeh* may be moved. The Gemara cites R' Oshaya, who says that a person who forgets a purse containing money in a courtyard where it is unprotected, may place a loaf of bread or a young child upon it, and then he may move it to a protected area.

[The purse is a *base for a forbidden article* (בָּסִיס לְדָבָר הָאָסוּר) and is therefore itself *muktzeh.* Nevertheless, in order to prevent the loss of the money inside the purse, the Rabbis granted a dispensation allowing one to move the purse while a loaf of bread or infant is on it (*Rashi*). The basis for this dispensation is that whenever a non-*muktzeh* item is carried upon a *muktzeh* item, the *muktzeh* is regarded as an accessory (like a tray or base) to the non-*muktzeh.* Thus, the *muktzeh* purse is rendered secondary to the non-*muktzeh* bread or infant that is resting upon it, and may be moved together with the primary item — e.g., the bread or infant. Moreover, the loaf of bread and the infant are mentioned merely as examples — presumably because they are lightweight and usually available. Any other non-*muktzeh* item will do equally well (*Ritva*).]

The Gemara then cites similar rulings issued by R' Yitzchak and by R' Yehudah bar Shila in the name of R' Assi. These rulings are then qualified by Mar Zutra, who says that the halachah follows all these teachings only when the *muktzeh* object was *forgotten* in the unprotected area. If it was left there intentionally, this stratagem may not be utilized to move it (as the one who left it there intentionally was obviously not concerned that it would be lost).

Finally, however, the Gemara cites the dissenting opinion of Rav Ashi, who rules that even if one forgot the *muktzeh* object in an unprotected area, he may not utilize this stratagem to move it. Rav Ashi maintains that the Rabbis instituted the dispensation for moving *muktzeh* by placing a loaf of bread or a young child upon it only for the purpose of moving a corpse (which will otherwise decay), and may not be employed in any other circumstances.

[According to Rav Ashi, this mode of transporting *muktzeh* represents a special leniency declared by the Sages expressly for the purpose of preserving human dignity. It applies only in cases where the physical integrity of a corpse is threatened if it should remain in the same place throughout the Sabbath, such as if it is outside and exposed to the sun (*Rashi*).]

A MUSSAR THOUGHT FOR THE DAY

There is a fundamental question that may be asked regarding the creation of angels. We know that everything in this world is created for a purpose — to honor Hashem's Name, as it says in *Avos* (6:11): כָּל מַה שֶּׁבָּרָא הַקָּדוֹשׁ בָּרוּךְ הוּא בְּעוֹלָמוֹ לֹא בְרָאוֹ אֶלָּא לִכְבוֹדוֹ, *Everything that the Holy One, Blessed is He, created in this world was created solely for the purpose of honoring Him.* Of course, Hashem does not need the honor for His sake. It is for our sake that Hashem tells us to honor Him, to find ways to serve Him and to spread the glory of His rule and His kingdom as much as possible. A man who has free choice and chooses to bring honor to Hashem and stands fast in the face of all temptations, provides through his actions honor to Hashem. Angels, however, are created without free choice. Thus, what purpose was there in creating them? After all, their adherence to Hashem's will proves nothing; that is what they were programmed to do!

Rav Avigdor Miller in his *sefer Toras Avigdor* offers the following explanation. He notes that in our introduction to the *Kedushah,* we say as a preface: נְקַדֵּשׁ אֶת שִׁמְךָ בָּעוֹלָם כְּשֵׁם שֶׁמַּקְדִּישִׁים אוֹתוֹ בִּשְׁמֵי מָרוֹם, *We will sanctify Your Name in this world, just as they (the angels) sanctify Him in Heaven.* This means that the sole purpose of the creation of angels is that they serve as examples, and teach us how to praise Hashem. In fact, in the blessings that precede *Krias Shema,* we designate a large portion of our prayers to reporting how the angels give praise to Hashem in unity, with purity, with clear articulation, etc., and then we repeat their words. What is the reason for all this elaboration, and why is it important for us to know how the angels praise Hashem?

The answer is that humans do not even know where to begin to glorify, sanctify, and exalt the King of kings. We need guidance of a spiritual nature from spiritual beings, who understand the concept of *kedushah.* They can teach us how to properly sanctify the Name of Hashem, Who is the essence of holiness. Every detail that is revealed to us is important, for it provides us with something to emulate. Indeed, this is evident from several laws that we learn in connection with *Kedushah.* For example, *Kedushah* must be recited standing, with the feet together, in unity. This is learned from the way the angels say *Kedushah.*

It emerges that the creation of the angels was for the purpose of mankind — to teach us how to serve Hashem. This is why although an angel is holier than a human, a human who serves Hashem with all his ability can achieve higher levels of greatness than an angel, as discussed at length in the *sefer Nefesh HaChaim.*

פרשת משפטים

SHABBOS

PARASHAS MISHPATIM

HALACHAH OF THE DAY

Yesterday, we discussed some of the common practical applications of the *melachah* of *tearing,* as it applies to opening packages on Shabbos. Today we will continue discussing various types of packages, and what may or may not be done on Shabbos.

Any sealed paper or plastic food wrapper may be removed only by destroying the wrapper, taking care not to tear any words or symbols. This applies to items such as candy bar wrappers and small packets of sugar or coffee. It also applies to tearing the paper wrapper of an ice-cream bar or popsicle. On weekdays, people often peel back the wrapper of an ice-cream bar, and then use the wrapper to hold the bar and also catch any melting ice cream. This is a constructive use of the wrapper, and thus one may not tear open a wrapper and then use it in this way on Shabbos. Rather, on Shabbos, one must destroy the wrapper when opening it, taking care not to rip any words or symbols.

If metal cans must be opened on Shabbos, they should be opened in a destructive manner. This can be accomplished in the following manner: The can should be opened halfway, its contents removed immediately, and then the can must be discarded.

It is permissible to tear open, in a destructive manner, a package of napkins or paper towels needed for the Shabbos meal, as this is considered a Shabbos necessity.

It is also permissible to use paper napkins, towels or tissues, even though they may tear during use. It is absolutely forbidden, however, to rip a paper towel from a roll. This is a violation of the *melachah* of *tearing.* If one tears along the perforations, he is also violating the *melachah* of מְחַתֵּךְ, *cutting* to a specific size. Similarly, many tissue boxes have tissues that are fastened to each other. Pulling a tissue out of this type of tissue box (and thus tearing one tissue away from its attachment to the next tissue) is prohibited on Shabbos. [It should be noted that this problem is also found with respect to many types of baby wipes that are packed in pop-up canisters. If the wipes are torn from each other as they are pulled out of the container, they may not be used on Shabbos.]

A CLOSER LOOK AT THE SIDDUR

In *A Mussar Thought for the Day,* we discussed the role of angels. Let us now take a closer look at a subject we have discussed before — the interaction between angels and our prayers.

We know that angels play an active role in bringing our *tefillos* to the appropriate places. *Siddur HaGra* (*Avnei Eliyahu*) states that there are over 180,000 angels that are in charge of bringing the *tefillos* to Hashem; they separate the prayers that are not eligible to be brought to *HaKadosh Baruch Hu.* There are some prayers that we purposely say in Aramaic (a language that angels do not comprehend) so that the angels should not understand them, e.g., *Yehei Sh'mei Rabbah* in *Kaddish* (see *Tosafos* to *Berachos* 3b). Some prayers we recite quietly so as not to draw attention from the angels and possibly incite jealousy (e.g., בָּרוּךְ שֵׁם, which is recited silently after the first verse of *Krias Shema*).

The *poskim* grapple with the question of whether one may pray directly to the angels, asking them to intercede on our behalf. One of the Thirteen Principles of Faith (אֲנִי מַאֲמִין) is that we must pray to Hashem alone, and that it is not proper to pray to any other. There are several areas of *tefillah* where this issue arises:

(1) In *Selichos,* there is a *piyut* called מַכְנִיסֵי רַחֲמִים. In it, we request that the angels should have mercy on us and bring our *tefillos* to their proper places. Also, in *Selichos* we find a stanza that reads: מִדַּת הָרַחֲמִים עָלֵינוּ הִתְגַּלְגְּלִי וְלִפְנֵי קוֹנֵךְ תְּפִלָּתֵנוּ הַפִּילִי, *Attribute of Mercy, overflow upon us, and before Your Creator cast our supplication.*

(2) The *Mishnah Berurah* in *Hilchos Rosh Hashanah* says that when a person goes to a grave of a *tzaddik* to pray, he should not direct his *tefillos* to the *tzaddik,* because we do not *daven* to dead people. Rather, he should *daven* to Hashem in the merit of the *tzaddik* who is buried there. This explanation would not work for the *Selichos* mentioned above, because we are not asking Hashem to answer us in the merit of the angels.

Some *poskim* are of the opinion that it is forbidden only to pray directly to an angel and ask him that he should grant our wishes; asking an angel to forward *tefillos* to Hashem, however, is permitted, just as it is permitted to go to a *tzaddik* and request that he pray on one's behalf.

(3) When we welcome the angels on Friday night, we say: בָּרְכוּנִי לְשָׁלוֹם מַלְאֲכֵי הַשָּׁלוֹם, *Bless me for peace, O angels of peace.* Some omit this stanza because of the above problem, while others maintain that we are not really asking the angels for a blessing. Rather, we are making

reference to the Gemara in *Shabbos* that states that if the escorting angels are pleased with the Shabbos preparations that they find, they extend the blessing that this shall continue in succeeding weeks.

The *Chasam Sofer* (168) would not recite the *Selichah* of מַכְנִיסֵי רַחֲמִים; he prolonged the recitation of *Tachanun* that immediately precedes it, so as not to make it obvious that he was omitting the prayer.

The *Shibbolei HaLeket* in *Hilchos Rosh Hashanah* (182) brings a Midrash in *Shir HaShirim* (2:7) that states: Klal Yisrael beseech the angels that guard the gates of prayer and ask each of them to be a מֵלִיץ, *defender,* for us and help our *tefillos* enter those gates. It would seem from this Midrash that to ask angels to help our prayers reach their intended destination does not involve a problem of prayer to any other than Hashem.

ANSWERS TO QUESTIONS OF THE DAY

Sunday:

The Gemara in *Sanhedrin* (7b) derives from here that a judge must be deliberate in judgment, and not come to hasty decisions.

Monday:

Rashi explains that it is given for the victim's disability while he recovers from the attack. [The payment for the fact that he will no longer be able to work at the job he originally held (e.g., if the attack caused him to lose a limb) is included in the context of נֶזֶק, *damages.*]

Tuesday:

The Gemara (*Gittin* 77a et al.) derives from this that one is liable even if the stolen object is not physically in his hand, as long as it is within his property.

Wednesday:

When the borrowed item breaks (or dies) in the course of its normal use (מֵתָה מֵחֲמַת מְלָאכָה), the borrower is not liable.

Thursday:

This comes to include even a wealthy widow who lives comfortably (*Ramban*).

Friday:

This verse teaches that the firstborn animal should be cared for by its mother's owner for thirty days, before it is given to the Kohen, just as a firstborn son is redeemed after thirty days (*Rashi*).

Shabbos:

This refers either to Eretz Yisrael (which was prepared for the Jews) or the *Beis HaMikdash* (see *Rashi* and *Sifsei Chachamim*).

פרשת תרומה

Parashas Terumah

A TORAH THOUGHT FOR THE DAY

וְזֹאת הַתְּרוּמָה אֲשֶׁר תִּקְחוּ מֵאִתָּם
זָהָב וָכֶסֶף וּנְחֹשֶׁת . . . וְאַבְנֵי מִלֻּאִים

This is the portion that you shall take from them: gold, silver, copper . . . and stones for the settings (*Shemos* 25:3-7).

Rashi states that there were thirteen varieties of materials called for, to be used either for the Mishkan and its activities, or for the vestments of the Kohanim. This is problematic, however, for the count of the items listed in the verses appears to be fifteen. Two possible answers are offered by *Sifsei Chachamim*: (1) Three of the items listed, *techeiles, argaman* and *tolaas shani* are all wool, and differ only in the color that they are dyed. Therefore, they may be counted as one item. (2) The *shoham* stones and the stones for settings of the *ephod* (an apronlike garment worn by the Kohen Gadol) and the *choshen* (the breastplate worn by the Kohen Gadol) were donated by the *Nesiim,* and *Rashi* lists only the items contributed by the general public. In *Mizrachi* we find a third possibility: that the hides of the *techashim* were not counted, since this animal was created by Hashem specifically for the use of its hide in the Mishkan; and the *shittim* wood was not counted, because Yaakov prepared it in Egypt and ordered that it be taken with the Jews during the Exodus. These two items were unlike the other materials, which were personal possessions that people contributed for the sake of the Mishkan.

Olelos Ephraim corroborates *Rashi's* position, in a discussion of the significance of age 13 for a Bar Mitzvah. He says that the three pillars upon which the world stands — Torah, *avodah* (service of Hashem), and *gemillas chasadim* (acts of lovingkindness) — all have direct links to the number 13. Many laws of the Torah are derived through the thirteen methods of exegesis (also known as the י״ג מִדּוֹת שֶׁהַתּוֹרָה נִדְרֶשֶׁת בָּהֶן, The Thirteen Laws of Hermeneutics, listed in the Baraisa that we recite at the end of the *korbanos* section of *Shacharis*). *Milah* (circumcision), a symbol of our willingness to be a servant of Hashem and serve Him through our *avodah,* was established through thirteen covenants. And *gemillas chasadim* is manifested through Hashem's Thirteen Attributes of Mercy.

Expanding on the last point, he cites a *Midrash Tanchuma.* Hashem said to the Jews: Do not think that you have been overly generous with your donations. The thirteen items that you designated for Me were merely replacement (payment) for the thirteen forms of sustenance that

I provided for you in Egypt, as enumerated in *Yechezkel* (Ch. 16). [Nevertheless,] I will treat them as generous contributions, and in the World to Come I will pay you back in kind with thirteen gifts, as enumerated in *Yeshayahu* (Ch. 5). Referring to this, King David said: אָשִׁירָה לַה׳ כִּי גָמַל עָלָי, *I will sing to HASHEM for He has dealt kindly with me* (*Tehillim* 13:6). That is, He promised me exceptional rewards, though they were not deserved.

Olelos Ephraim concludes that the age of 13, therefore, is a fitting and symbolic time for a young man who, until this point possessed only a *yetzer hara,* evil inclination, to be aided by the gift of a *yetzer hatov,* good inclination. This will allow him to take his place in upholding the three pillars of the world.

MISHNAH OF THE DAY: SHABBOS 21:3

The following Mishnah cites a dispute concerning the permissibility of removing *muktzeh* remnants from a table:

בֵּית שַׁמַּאי אוֹמְרִים מַגְבִּיהִין מִן הַשֻּׁלְחָן עֲצָמוֹת וּקְלִפִּין — ***Beis Shammai say: We may pick up bones and husks from the table.***[1] וּבֵית הִלֵּל אוֹמְרִים — ***But Beis Hillel say:*** מְסַלֵּק אֶת הַטַּבְלָא כּוּלָּהּ — ***One must remove the entire table board,***[2] וּמְנַעֲרָהּ — ***and shake it*** clean, and not handle the bones and husks directly.[3]

NOTES

1. The Mishnah refers to bones that are fit for a dog or husks fit for cattle fodder. These may be removed from the table by hand. Since such bones and husks still qualify as animal food, they are not *muktzeh.* Bones and shells that are not fit for animals, and hence useless, are intrinsically *muktzeh* like sticks and stones, and may not be moved (*Rav; Tosafos; Rif; Rambam*).

2. This is a large board that was placed upon the table; the modern-day equivalent would be a tablecloth (see *Mishnah Berurah* 308:115; cf. *Rambam Commentary*).

3. Beis Hillel rule that the bones and husks may not be handled because they are *muktzeh,* under the category of *nolad.* Since before the Sabbath they were still part of the meat or produce, and thus deemed human food, and they have now become animal food, their change of status is sufficient to deem them *nolad,* i.e., in a newly created state (*Mishnah Berurah* 495:17; see above, Mishnah 2:3). [Beis Shammai, however, consider such a change insufficient for the article to be deemed *nolad.*] On the other hand, the table or board is not *muktzeh* because it is a utensil, and it may therefore be lifted on the Sabbath (*Rav; Rashi*).

[Although by lifting and shaking the board one is also moving the *muktzeh* (bones and husks), this is permitted because it is *indirect* movement of *muktzeh* (as in the previous Mishnah).]

The Mishnah continues:
מַעֲבִירִין מִלִּפְנֵי הַשֻּׁלְחָן — ***We may remove from upon the table***[4] **פֵּירוּרִין פָּחוֹת מִכְּזַיִת** — ***crumbs*** that are ***smaller than the size of an olive,***[5] **וְשֶׂעָר שֶׁל אֲפוּנִין וְשֶׂעָר שֶׁל עֲדָשִׁים מִפְּנֵי שֶׁהוּא מַאֲכַל בְּהֵמָה** — ***as well as the pods of chickpeas and the pods of lentils, because they are animal food.***[6]

Having set forth several *muktzeh* laws related to clearing off a table, the Mishnah continues with another law concerning this subject:
סְפוֹג — ***A sponge,***[7] **אִם יֵשׁ לוֹ עוֹר בֵּית אֲחִיזָה מְקַנְּחִין בּוֹ** — ***if it has a leather handle, we may wipe*** a table ***with it*** even when it is damp,[8] **וְאִם לָאו אֵין מְקַנְּחִין בּוֹ** — ***but if not, we may not wipe*** a table ***with it*** when it is damp.[9] **וַחֲכָמִים אוֹמְרִים בֵּין כָּךְ וּבֵין כָּךְ נִיטָּל בְּשַׁבָּת** — ***The Sages, however, say: In either case, it may be moved on the Sabbath*** when it is dry,[10] **וְאֵינוֹ מְקַבֵּל טוּמְאָה** — ***and it is not susceptible to tumah.***[11]

NOTES

4. Other editions read: מַעֲבִירִין מֵעַל הַשֻּׁלְחָן, *we may remove from upon the table* (*Rav; Rashi; Rif; Rosh*). [This is the meaning of the phrase in any event.]

5. Although people do not generally eat such small crumbs, these are still not *muktzeh* because they are animal fodder, as the Mishnah goes on to explain (*Rav*).

6. This ruling follows the view of Beis Shammai, who do not consider such a change in status (from human fare to animal fodder) to be *nolad.* According to Beis Hillel, however, since prior to the Sabbath these pods were part of the food and were not yet designated for animal fodder, they are *nolad* and therefore *muktzeh* (*Rashi* to Gemara 143a).

7. It was customary to dip a sponge in water and use it to wipe the table (*Meiri*). However, wringing water out of a wet sponge is a derivative of the forbidden labor of whitening (*Rambam, Hil. Shabbos* 22:15). When one grasps a wet sponge with his bare hand, water is likely to be squeezed out between his fingers.

8. Since by gripping the sponge by its handle it is possible to wipe the table board without squeezing the water out of the sponge, it may be used. This fits into the category of דָּבָר שֶׁאֵינוֹ מִתְכַּוֵּן, *an unintentional act.* The Mishnah thus reflects the view of R' Shimon, who permits performing a permissible act even though it may unintentionally lead to a prohibited one (Gemara 143a).

9. I.e., if the sponge does not have a leather handle, when one takes it into his hand he will inevitably squeeze out some of the water. In this case, even R' Shimon prohibits performing the permissible act (*Rashi; Rambam, Hil. Shabbos* 22:15).

10. I.e., whether or not the sponge has a leather handle, since it is a utensil, it may be moved about on the Sabbath when it is dry and no problem of squeezing exists (*Rav; Rashi*). However, since the primary function of a bare sponge (e.g., wiping a table while wet) is prohibited on the Sabbath, the sponge is classified as a כְּלִי שֶׁמְּלַאכְתּוֹ לְאִסּוּר, *a forbidden-use utensil,* that may be moved only for the sake of its use in a permissible capacity or for the sake of its place (*Ritva*).

11. *Tumah* contamination of utensils is limited by the Torah to garments, metal utensils, leather goods, and wooden utensils (*Numbers* 31:20). Since a sponge does not fit into any of these categories, it is not susceptible to *tumah* (*Rav; Rashi*).

GEMS FROM THE GEMARA

The Gemara (143a) states that the proper reading of our Mishnah should reverse the positions of Beis Shammai and Beis Hillel — viz., that it is Beis Shammai's view that the bones and husks not be directly handled, while Beis Hillel permit this. This revised reading of the Mishnah is substantiated by the *Tosefta* (17:4), as well as by the series of Mishnahs in *Eduyos* (5:1-5), where the instances in which Beis Hillel's rulings are more stringent than those of Beis Shammai are enumerated. Our Mishnah is conspicuously absent, implying that here, too, Beis Hillel rule leniently regarding *muktzeh,* while Beis Shammai rule stringently, as is true in the vast majority of cases (see *Tosafos*).

[The importance of this revision is that the halachah, with few exceptions, follows the opinion of Beis Hillel over Beis Shammai.]

Although Beis Hillel rule leniently regarding *muktzeh,* they nevertheless require that the scraps be fit for animal fodder. Otherwise, they are *muktzeh* even according to Beis Hillel. Consequently, Beis Hillel permit only the moving of soft bones that are fit to be fed to dogs, and of such husks that are fit for cattle fodder. Hard bones that are unfit even for dogs, and nutshells that are unfit even for cattle, may not be picked up from the table, even according to Beis Hillel. [This is borne out by the Mishnah's ruling regarding pods of chickpeas and pods of lentils. The Mishnah states that they may be moved only on account of their status as animal fodder. The Gemara attributes this ruling to R' Shimon, who is always cited by the Gemara as possessing the most lenient of all Tannaic opinions with regard to the laws of *muktzeh.* This indicates that remnants that are unfit for cattle fodder are indeed *muktzeh* even according to R' Shimon (*Tosafos*).] This view is shared by *Rambam* (in his *Commentary* and in *Hil. Shabbos* 26:16), *Rif* and *Rav.*

Indeed, the halachah is that one may directly remove any bones or husks which are fit for animal consumption. Those that are not suitable for animals may be removed only by lifting the table board (or tablecloth) and shaking them off (*Shulchan Aruch* 308.27), or by scraping them off with a knife or other utensil, as long as one does not touch them directly. This constitutes an *indirect movement of muktzeh,* which is permitted to facilitate the use of a non-*muktzeh* object — e.g., the table (*Mishnah Berurah* 308:115).

פרשת תרומה

SUNDAY

PARASHAS TERUMAH

A MUSSAR THOUGHT FOR THE DAY

Mesillas Yesharim (Ch. 6) discusses the importance of the quality of זְרִיזוּת, *alacrity* and zeal, in the performance of mitzvos, and the harmful consequences of עַצְלוּת, *laziness* and procrastination. One of the major points that he highlights is a unique characteristic of laziness, the fact that it does not appear to be intrinsically evil. Because of this, one does not take notice of its corrosive nature, and slowly but surely one's service to Hashem, whether in prayer, study or mitzvah performance, declines, until this trend is almost impossible to reverse. In this way laziness is similar to a poison which, if left to work its harm unchecked, will eventually kill a person.

What is particularly insidious about this negative character trait is that it can affect even someone who understands his obligations to Hashem and wants to lead a righteous and proper life. But his evil inclination can produce a seemingly infinite number of excuses as to why he should procrastinate, and his power of rationalization will elaborate upon the propriety, and even desirability, of deliberation and cautious behavior.

Therefore, concludes *Mesillas Yesharim,* one must harness extraordinary strength and perform mitzvos with alacrity and enthusiasm, to throw off the yoke of עַצְלוּת that weighs him down. And even though the quality of זְרִיזוּת is an exalted trait that describes the enthusiastic and instantaneous obedience displayed by angels, it behooves every person to strive toward attaining it to the greatest degree possible.

R' Chaim Shmulevitz (*Sichos Mussar* 32:22) utilizes this *Mesillas Yesharim* to elucidate a Midrash cited by *Ohr HaChaim* and *Rashi.*

Ohr HaChaim asks why the *shoham* stones and the stones for settings are the last ones listed among the materials needed for the Mishkan. Since they were the most precious objects needed, they should have been mentioned first! Among his answers, he alludes to the Midrash (*Bamidbar Rabbah* 12:16) that is cited by *Rashi* (*Shemos* 35:27). The Midrash states that the *Nesiim,* the heads of each tribe, said, "Let the people donate whatever they will, and whatever is missing, we will supply." [Although their intent was good, this was a miscalculation on their part, for the people brought their donation with such selflessness that all that was needed was donated.] After the completion of the people's donations, which more than fulfilled the Mishkan's needs, the *Nesiim* declared, "What is left for us to do?" As a result, they brought only the *shoham* stones and the stones for the settings. Because they were lazy at the beginning, a letter was removed from their name. [When the verse (ibid.) says that the *Nesiim* brought the precious stones, the word is spelled הַנְּשִׂאִם, without the *yud* that would normally appear between the א and the ם.] For this same reason, Hashem showed displeasure by listing the precious stones last.

R' Chaim Shmulevitz points out that the intention of the *Nesiim* was admirable, for they wished to ensure that all of the requested material for the Mishkan would be available. It is quite possible that the *Nesiim* were not even aware that their pledge had a semblance of laziness or lack of zeal. Nevertheless, they are taken to task for not being at the forefront of the donors, and allowing their behavior to exhibit a modicum of laziness.

HALACHAH OF THE DAY

We will now continue our discussion of common applications of the *melachah* of *tearing.*

One may tear open, in a destructive fashion, the wrapper of a bandage that is needed for use on Shabbos. Since a bandage is a necessary item rather than a mere convenience, it is exempt from the restriction against destructive tearing. Once again, one must exercise caution when opening the package not to tear any lettering that may be on it. [It should be noted that prior to tearing open the wrapper of the bandage, one should first carefully examine it (time permitting). There are some brands of Band-aids which may be removed from their packaging without any tearing at all. These Band-aids may be slipped out by simply unfolding the end of the wrapper.]

We mentioned previously, in our discussions of the *melachah* of *sewing,* that using glue in order to attach two pieces of fabric or paper may be a form of *sewing* and thus prohibited. As we have noted above, any attachment prohibited under the *melachah* of *sewing* is similarly prohibited to be separated, because such separation would be restricted by the *melachah* of *tearing.* For this reason, there are those *poskim* who forbid the removal on Shabbos of the plastic tabs glued to the adhesive parts of brand new Band-aids. These tabs are fastened to the Band-aids in the factory and are intended to remain in place until such time as the Band-aid is required for use. Since, according to many *poskim,* this attachment constitutes a violation of the *melachah* of *sewing,* it follows that removing them would constitute a violation of the *melachah* of *tearing.* According to these *poskim,* one must remove the tabs before

Shabbos, and then he may reattach them until he uses them on Shabbos. Since he has now reattached them only temporarily, they may be removed on Shabbos.

HaRav Moshe Feinstein ruled that one may remove these tabs on Shabbos. According to Rav Moshe, such attachment does not constitute a violation of *sewing,* because an attachment is viewed as sewing only if tearing is required in order to separate the attachment. Since the tabs are easily removed without any tearing at all, they may be removed on Shabbos.

Harav Chaim Pinchas Scheinberg also permits removal of these tabs on Shabbos. He reasons that the tabs are placed on the Band-aids in the factory with the intent that they be removed whenever the Band-aids are required for use. If there were someone in the factory who required a Band-aid, the tabs would be removed immediately. He therefore rules that this attachment can be viewed as being only temporary in nature, and that it may therefore be separated on Shabbos.

Tomorrow we will discuss another possible ramification of this dispute.

A CLOSER LOOK AT THE SIDDUR

The first blessing of every *Shemoneh Esrei* is known as אָבוֹת, *Patriarchs,* because it recalls the greatness and devotion of our forefathers, in whose merit we ask Hashem to sustain and help us, though we may be undeserving (*Abudraham*). [We have discussed in earlier studies that each of the *Avos* embodied and represented an outstanding quality — Avraham represented *chesed* (generosity), Yitzchak represented *gevurah* (strength), and Yaakov represented *emes* (truth) — and that their varied attributes in combination laid the foundation for the making of the Jewish nation.]

Rav Pam (*Atarah LaMelech*) adds that we invoke the forefathers at the beginning of *Shemoneh Esrei* as an introduction to our *tefillah,* carrying the following intent: "We are simple people, and we cannot fathom even a fraction of Your blessed Essence, or properly comprehend before Whom we are standing in supplication. But we have no other thought than pouring out our words to the Lord of our forefathers; and may the One Who accepted their devotions and heeded their prayers accept and heed ours as well."

Yet another interpretation might be suggested by *Rav Shimon Schwab's* explanation of a seemingly difficult Midrash. The *Midrash*

Rabbah states (49:2): "Gold symbolizes Avraham, who was tested in the furnace that was fiery, like gold; Yitzchak was purified like silver [by his elevation] on the altar during the *Akeidah;* and copper refers to Yaakov, of whom Lavan said (*Bereishis* 30:27): נִחַשְׁתִּי וַיְבָרְכֵנִי ה׳ בִּגְלָלֶךָ, *I have learned by divination that HASHEM has blessed me on account of you.*" [The word נְחֹשֶׁת, *copper,* has the same root as נִחַשְׁתִּי, *learned by divination.*]

There are several points in this Midrash that need elucidation. First, what is the point of the comparison of the *Avos* to metals? Furthermore, it would appear that the *Avos* are graded in terms of decreasing greatness or importance, similar to the metals. This descending scale is not found in other parables or writings that refer to the *Avos.* If anything, Yaakov is usually referred to as the בְּחִיר הָאָבוֹת, the chosen of the *Avos,* and yet in this Midrash he seems to be cast as the least worthy.

Rav Shimon Schwab explains that these three metals have different characteristics. Gold has intrinsic shine and beauty, and is found in nuggets, largely devoid of impurities. Silver, on the other hand, is generally found in impure form, and must be cleansed and purified to bring out its full beauty. Copper in its natural state does not appear to be precious at all. But with repeated burnishing and buffing, its appearance is completely altered and approaches that of gold in its luster and beauty.

The parable of the *Avos,* explains Rav Schwab, is not referring to each forefather's level of greatness, but rather to the ease with which their greatness was recognized. Thus, Avraham's exalted, gleaming personality was obvious to all who came in contact with him. After the episode of the furnace, his reputation spread to the degree that all kings of his period flocked to him for advice. Yitzchak, however, did not merit such recognition immediately. The entourage that journeyed to the *Akeidah* included not only Avraham and Yitzchak, but the two "young men" as well. These were Eliezer, who, the Sages tell us, was a complete *tzaddik* and a disseminator of Avraham's values and beliefs, and Yishmael, who at that time was a *baal teshuvah,* having renounced his sinful past. It was not yet clear, argues Rav Schwab, who would in fact be the "chosen" among them. It became obvious only after Yitzchak saw the cloud hovering on the mountain, which Eliezer and Yishmael did not see, and when Avraham told them to remain behind with the donkey. It was clarified at this time that only Yitzchak and his offspring would have the status of intrinsic holiness, and like silver, their beauty would be perceptible. Yaakov, however, who had to suffer exile and difficulties for most of his life, was like copper, unappreciated until late in life (when the

Egyptians wanted to deify him). This is borne out by Lavan who, despite the bounty that he accumulated in Yaakov's merit, attributed it to "divination" — that is, Yaakov's auspicious astrological fortune, and not his righteousness.

The intent of incorporating these three metals into the building of the Mishkan was to mirror the trials of the *Avos* in gaining recognition of their exalted status, and to highlight that these trials were part of the historical journey of the nation.

In his commentary to *Parashas Lech Lecha,* Rav Schwab mirrors this theme as it relates to *tefillah,* maintaining that there are two ideas present in the blessing of *Avos.* First is the concept of *mesorah,* the recognition that the roots of our holiness are found in the *Avos,* who passed down the precepts of our belief system to their descendants, generation to generation. Second, as indicated by the closing phrase of the blessing, "the shield of Avraham," we learn that just as each of the *Avos* had a unique personality and strove in his unique way to be a servant to Hashem, each succeeding generation and individual must do the same.

QUESTION OF THE DAY:

Why does the Torah mention gold as the first item that was given as a donation for the Mishkan?

For the answer, see page 176.

A TORAH THOUGHT FOR THE DAY

וְעָשׂוּ לִי מִקְדָּשׁ וְשָׁכַנְתִּי בְּתוֹכָם

And they shall make for Me a Sanctuary — so that I may dwell among them (*Shemos* 25:8).

The commentators offer several interpretations of the word מִקְדָּשׁ, *Sanctuary*, and the message that it conveys. *Rashi* says that the Sanctuary was to be a "house of holiness" (קְדֻשָּׁה), constructed specifically for the sake of Hashem. *Abarbanel* also understands the word מִקְדָּשׁ to be indicative of the intrinsic holiness of the Sanctuary. He notes that because of the Sanctuary's holy status, one who is an עָרֵל, *uncircumcised*, or טָמֵא, *ritually impure*, may not enter its confines. *Rashbam* and *Rambam* suggest that the name מִקְדָּשׁ implies that which has been **separated** and **consecrated** for a particular task; thus, the Sanctuary was set aside and designated as a meeting place between Hashem and Bnei Yisrael. Indeed, it was from between the Cherubim in the Holy of Holies that Moshe heard God's voice and commandments.

One might wonder why this verse initially commands the Jews to make a מִקְדָּשׁ, and then the next verse describes the building as a מִשְׁכָּן. Indeed, the topic of the whole *parashah* is the building of the Mishkan and its utensils.

Ohr HaChaim posits that this verse is the basis for the mitzvah of building a Sanctuary, not only in the Wilderness, where it is referred to as a מִשְׁכָּן, but even upon entering Eretz Yisrael, and in the generations that follow. He suggests that this command would apply even to Jews living in exile, if it were not for the specific prohibition against building a Temple and offering sacrifices outside the *Beis HaMikdash* once it is built. Had the verse begun by simply commanding the Jews to make a "Mishkan," it would have been understood as a command that applied only during their sojourn in the Wilderness.

The most pressing difficulty with this verse is the implication that God can reside in a particular place, as if He possesses some physical form that can be confined. This is of course not the case. Indeed, it is one of the Thirteen Fundamental Principles that He has no physical characteristics, nor is He subject to any boundaries of the physical world. As Hashem declares (*Yeshayahu* 66:1): הַשָּׁמַיִם כִּסְאִי וְהָאָרֶץ הֲדֹם רַגְלָי אֵי־זֶה בַיִת אֲשֶׁר תִּבְנוּ־לִי וְאֵי־זֶה מָקוֹם מְנוּחָתִי, *The Heaven is My throne, and the earth is My footstool; what house could you build for Me, and what place could be My resting place?*

Ramban explains that the building of the Mishkan was meant to

parallel the Revelation of Hashem's Presence that the Jews experienced at Har Sinai. Just as at Har Sinai, Hashem openly revealed His Glory, as stated in the verses: וַיִּשְׁכֹּן כְּבוֹד־ה׳ עַל־הַר סִינַי, *The Glory of HASHEM rested upon Mt. Sinai* (*Shemos* 24:16), and: הֵן הֶרְאָנוּ ה׳ אֱלֹהֵינוּ אֶת־כְּבֹדוֹ וְאֶת־גָּדְלוֹ, *Behold! HASHEM, our God, has shown us His Glory and His greatness* (*Devarim* 5:21), so too, does it state (twice) regarding the Mishkan: וּכְבוֹד ה׳ מָלֵא אֶת־הַמִּשְׁכָּן, *the Glory of HASHEM filled the Tabernacle* (*Shemos* 40:34,35). Thus, the glory of Har Sinai resided in the Mishkan, but in a hidden state (as opposed to Har Sinai, where it was openly revealed). After citing additional corresponding features between Hashem's revelation at Har Sinai and in the Mishkan, *Ramban* says that certainly Hashem cannot physically reside in the Mishkan, as Shlomo HaMelech states (*I Melachim* 8:27): כִּי הַאֻמְנָם יֵשֵׁב אֱלֹהִים עַל־הָאָרֶץ הִנֵּה הַשָּׁמַיִם וּשְׁמֵי הַשָּׁמַיִם לֹא יְכַלְכְּלוּךָ אַף כִּי־הַבַּיִת הַזֶּה אֲשֶׁר בָּנִיתִי, *Would God truly dwell on earth [with man]? Behold, the heavens and the highest heavens cannot contain You, and surely not this Temple that I have built.* However, the *Beis HaMikdash,* and specifically the place between the Cherubim that sit atop the Holy Ark, provide a place for Bnei Yisrael to pray and "converse" with Hashem, and act as a conduit for His Providential care for them.

Abarbanel, whose approach is similar to *Ramban's,* adds an additional thought. He says that Hashem did not want the Bnei Yisrael to feel abandoned in the Wilderness, with the belief that Hashem resides on High, far from the "real," physical world with all its trials and tribulations, with which He does not involve Himself. [This is actually the position of many of the nations of the world, who believe that it is left completely to man to manage his own affairs.] Hashem wanted the Jews to have a place where they could feel close to Him, and be imbued with the feeling and recognition that Hashem is constantly protecting them, and that they are dependent on His Divine care and intervention.

MISHNAH OF THE DAY: SHABBOS 22:1

The following Mishnah deals with the prohibition of extracting liquids from solids. When such extraction is Biblically forbidden (see below, note 4), it is defined as מְפָרֵק, *extracting,* or, as *Rashi* (95a) explains it, *unloading* (i.e., unloading the food from the place in which it was concealed), which is a derivative of the forbidden labor of דָּשׁ, *threshing* (*Rav; Rashi*). [Just as one threshes grain to extract the kernels that lie hidden within the husk, so one presses fruit in order to extract the juice that is within it (*Aruch HaShulchan* 320:3).]

חָבִית שֶׁנִּשְׁבְּרָה — ***A*** wine ***cask that broke*** on the Sabbath, **מַצִּילִין הֵימֶנָּה מְזוֹן שָׁלֹשׁ סְעוּדוֹת** — ***we may save from it*** enough ***sustenance*** [i.e., drink] ***for three meals.***[1] **וְאוֹמֵר לַאֲחֵרִים בֹּאוּ וְהַצִּילוּ לָכֶם** — ***And one may say to others, "Come and save*** some of the wine ***for yourselves";***[2] **וּבִלְבַד שֶׁלֹּא יִסְפּוֹג** — ***but only provided that one does not sponge up*** the spilled wine, since one may be led to squeeze it from the sponge, which is forbidden.[3]

The Mishnah records a related law:

אֵין סוֹחֲטִין אֶת הַפֵּירוֹת לְהוֹצִיא מֵהֶן מַשְׁקִין — ***We may not squeeze fruits*** on the Sabbath ***to extract liquid from them.***[4] **וְאִם יָצְאוּ מֵעַצְמָן אֲסוּרִין** — ***And*** even ***if*** the liquids ***seeped*** from the fruits on the Sabbath ***of their own accord, they are prohibited*** for consumption on that Sabbath by Rabbinic decree.[5] **רַבִּי יְהוּדָה אוֹמֵר** — But ***R' Yehudah says:*** **אִם לְאוֹכָלִין הַיּוֹצֵא מֵהֶן מוּתָּר** — ***If*** one originally stored the fruit ***for***

NOTES

1. This applies only if the cask broke in the evening before the first Sabbath meal. If, however, it broke after the first meal, one may save only enough for the two remaining meals (*Meiri; Rambam, Hil. Shabbos* 22:16). This law was discussed above (Mishnahs 16:2-3), but is repeated here as a preface to the discussion concerning the extraction of liquids. [Above (16:3), we learned that: "We may save one basket full of loaves, even if it contains enough for a hundred meals." That ruling applies here, as well. Hence, as long as one catches the wine in one large container, he may salvage even enough for a hundred meals. If, however, he requires more than one utensil, he may salvage only enough for the number of Sabbath meals he has not yet eaten (*Rav; Rashi; Shulchan Aruch* 335:1).]

2. I.e., each one may save the requirements for those of the three meals he has not yet eaten (*Rashi; Tiferes Yisrael;* see above, 16:2).

3. I.e., provided that one does not lay a sponge upon the wine to soak it up, and then let the sponge drip into a vessel — lest he come to squeeze the wine from the sponge into the vessel (*Rashi*). [Moreover, one may not even put his palm into spilled oil so that it will stick to his palm, and then wipe the oil off on the edge of a vessel — even though no extraction of liquid is occurring. This is forbidden as עוּבְדָא דְחוֹל, a *weekday activity,* that will detract from the aura of the Sabbath (*Rav; Rashi* from Gemara 143b).]

4. Literally, the Mishnah reads: "We may not press *the* fruits." The definite article alludes to the fact that this law applies to fruits customarily designated for pressing — viz., olives and grapes. As will be explained below, it is only the pressing of these fruits on the Sabbath that is forbidden by the Torah (Gemara 145a). Pressing other fruits is Rabbinically prohibited (*Kol HaSofer*).

5. For the Rabbis feared that permitting this liquid might lead one to violate the prohibition against extraction (*Rashi*).

food (i.e., for eating), the liquid ***that seeps from them is permitted.***[6] וְאִם לְמַשְׁקִין הַיּוֹצֵא מֵהֶן אָסוּר — ***But if*** one originally stored the fruits ***for liquid*** (i.e., for squeezing), then the liquid ***that seeps from them is prohibited.***[7]

A similar case:

חַלּוֹת דְּבַשׁ שֶׁרִיסְּקָן מֵעֶרֶב שַׁבָּת וְיָצְאוּ מֵעַצְמָן אֲסוּרִין — ***Honeycombs that one crushed before the Sabbath, and*** then honey ***seeped*** from them on the Sabbath ***on their own accord, they*** [i.e., the honey from the combs] ***are prohibited*** for consumption on that Sabbath. וְרַבִּי [אֶלְעָזָר] (אליעזר) מַתִּיר — ***But R' Elazar permits*** consumption of the honey.[8]

NOTES

6. I.e., one may drink the juice that flowed out by itself on the Sabbath. Since the fruits are stored to be eaten, one does not want the juice to flow out of them. There is, therefore, no reason to fear that one will forget and press them (*Rav; Rashi*).

7. I.e., one may not even drink the juice that flowed on its own on the Sabbath. Since these fruits are intended for juice, one is pleased that the juice has flowed from them. We fear, therefore, that he may come to squeeze them on the Sabbath. To prevent this, the Sages prohibited their consumption on the Sabbath (*Rav; Rashi*).

8. [Since one does not customarily press honeycombs to extract honey, the initial crushing being sufficient for the task, we need not fear that one will actually come to squeeze the honeycombs (*Rashi; Rav*). Although R' Elazar permits consumption of the honey, he does agree that one may not actually press honeycombs on the Sabbath (*Tiferes Yisrael;* see *Magen Avraham* 320:16).]

GEMS FROM THE GEMARA

We learned in our Mishnah that in the case of fruits that are earmarked for juicing, one may not drink the juices that flowed from them on the Sabbath even if they flowed from the fruit on their own, without the fruits having been pressed. This is because in such a case, one is pleased with the juice that has flowed from the fruits. We fear, therefore, that a person may come to squeeze the fruits on the Sabbath, which is Biblically prohibited. To prevent this, the Rabbis prohibited these juices on the Sabbath (*Rav; Rashi*).

Moreover, the Gemara (143b) explains that olive oil and grape juice are forbidden even if one has earmarked the olives and grapes for eating rather than for pressing. This is because the primary usage of olives and grapes is to obtain their respective juices. Hence, the owner is satisfied with the flow of their juice, despite his original intention to eat the fruit. Consequently, this precautionary injunction is needed even according to R' Yehudah. The Gemara explains that the dispute between R' Yehudah and the Sages concerns mulberries and pomegranates, which were only occasionally used for their juice. R' Yehudah's view is that since these are not primarily valued for their juice, if one has gathered them to eat, he will certainly not be content to have the juice seep from them. Therefore, we need not fear that he will come to press them. On the other hand, the Sages hold that since these fruits are also occasionally used for their juice, the owner may in fact be satisfied to use them for that purpose, and therefore juice that flows from them is prohibited.

However, concerning fruits that are rarely pressed for their juice, such as plums, quinces and sorb-apples, even the Sages agree that any juice that flows from them may be used (*Rav*).

[The leniency of R' Yehudah applies only in regard to juice that flows on its own without the fruit having been pressed. One may not, however, actually press mulberries or pomegranates. This is a Rabbinic prohibition. The Biblical prohibition to press fruits applies only to olives and grapes. Any other fruits which are customarily pressed for their juice are considered like mulberries and pomegranates, and pressing them is Rabbinically prohibited (*Rama, Orach Chaim* 320:1).]

A MUSSAR THOUGHT FOR THE DAY

Many commentators ask why the Torah writes concerning the Mishkan (*Shemos* 25:8): וְשָׁכַנְתִּי בְּתוֹכָם, *so that I may dwell among* ***them,*** rather than וְשָׁכַנְתִּי בְּתוֹכוֹ, *and I will dwell in* ***it,*** which would seem to be the main point of building the Mishkan.

R' Chaim Volozhin (*Nefesh HaChaim* 1:4) explains that the wording of the verse is teaching us that the ultimate purpose of the Mishkan is for the betterment of man. The Mishkan was erected to teach us a lesson — that the *Shechinah* resides in a place of holiness. If an individual sanctifies himself properly, and performs all the mitzvos, then **he** becomes a "Sanctuary," and Hashem resides within **him.** Furthermore, says R' Chaim, the phrase, וְכֵן תַּעֲשׂוּ, *and so shall you do* (v. 9), which seems superfluous, also teaches us that the outer (physical) aspects of the Mishkan are not its fundamental value. The underlying purpose of the Mishkan and its utensils is to guide one toward proper behavior and understanding, through their Divine design, applications and messages. By absorbing these messages, one will become prepared and worthy of having the *Shechinah*

reside in him. Thus, the verses should be understood as conveying the message: "You shall make yourselves into a Sanctuary, so that I can dwell within you . . . you shall make yourselves like everything I have shown you."

Expounding on this theme, *R' Aharon Kotler* (*Mishnas R' Aharon* 1:152) maintains that the phrase *I will dwell in them* (the individual) is not merely a hope, but a fact. The *Shechinah does* dwell within each of us, to a greater or lesser extent, based on our actions. The Gemara in *Taanis* (11b) states, "Let man always regard himself as if the Holy One (see *Tosafos* there) dwells within him." Imagine, says R' Aharon, if you were in the presence of a truly great man, such as R' Yisrael Salanter. Would it dawn on you to slight him or upset him in any way, let alone to actually do him any harm or cause him to leave? Obviously not! How, then, can one engage in thoughts and deeds so insulting and rebellious to the Holy One Who resides in him? The answer, says R' Aharon, is that a person is unaware of his own true value, and of the intrinsic holiness of his being.

Recognition of this is, in fact, the lesson of R' Shimon in *Pirkei Avos* (2:18), who says: אַל תְּהִי רָשָׁע בִּפְנֵי עַצְמֶךָ, *Do not judge yourself to be a wicked person.* A person should never view himself as lowly and unworthy, for this is the greatest hindrance to the improvement and elevation of one's behavior. Rather, each person should consider himself worthy and important, in the company of holiness.

R' Aharon concludes with an assurance that a true understanding of one's worthiness and importance will not cause a person to become arrogant. If he attributes his status to the presence of God, his heightened spirituality will actually enhance his quality of humility.

HALACHAH OF THE DAY

According to some authorities, yesterday's discussion concerning the removal of tabs found on Band-aids pertains as well to the adhesive tabs often found on disposable diapers. These authorities state that one should unstick the tabs and refasten them before Shabbos, so that they may be opened on Shabbos without violating the prohibition of *tearing.* According to the ruling of HaRav Moshe Feinstein and HaRav Scheinberg that we discussed yesterday, however, this would be unnecessary.

Often, the ends of disposable diapers are fused together in the factory, and must be torn apart in order for the diaper to be used. This attachment, however, is not intentional; the diapers become fused together either as a result of the cutting or as a result of the packaging process. Since the *melachah* of *tearing* does not apply to items that have become attached unintentionally, one may peel open the diapers on Shabbos.

One may not cut or tear apart the pages of a book that remained attached during the printing and binding process. One who separates these pages may be in violation of three different *melachos*: the *melachah* of *tearing,* the *melachah* of מְחַתֵּךְ, *cutting to specification* (since one would normally be cutting the page to size), and the *melachah* of מַכֶּה בְּפַטִּישׁ, *completing the formation of an item,* since through the cutting one completes the formation of a readable book. It is immaterial whether the book is new or has been previously read; as long as pages remain attached one may not separate them.

If pages became attached inadvertently — for example, if food fell between two pages and the pages have now become fused together — one may separate the pages, providing that he does not rip the paper as a result of the separation. Furthermore, one must be certain that no erasing will take place through the removal of anything stuck to the paper.

It is forbidden to open a sealed envelope on Shabbos. Since reading a letter is not a genuine necessity, this is forbidden even if the envelope is opened in a destructive manner. If, however, someone receives an urgent letter whose contents must be known on Shabbos, he may open the envelope in a destructive way.

It is forbidden to tear toilet paper on Shabbos. One who tears the paper off in a random way (not along the perforations) transgresses the prohibition of *tearing.* Tearing the paper along the perforations further transgresses the *melachah* of *cutting to specification.* If one finds himself in a situation where he does not have cut paper to use, he may tear the paper off the roll in an unusual fashion. This may be accomplished by tearing the paper with one's teeth or elbows. When doing so, one should tear the paper off in a random way. The reason this is permissible is because tearing in an unusual way is only Rabbinically prohibited, and the Sages provided a dispensation for the sake of maintaining human dignity.

This concludes our discussion of the *melachah* of *tearing.*

QUESTION OF THE DAY:

What obligation is derived from the verse, "And they shall make for Me a Sanctuary"?

For the answer, see page 176.

A CLOSER LOOK AT THE SIDDUR

The magnitude of the greatness that we ascribe to the *Beis HaMikdash* (as the permanent Mishkan) is alluded to metaphorically in אָז יָשִׁיר, *The Song at the Sea* (*Shemos* 15:1-18), which we recite each morning as the culmination of *Pesukei D'Zimrah,* prior to the final blessing of יִשְׁתַּבַּח, *May Your Name be praised.* The final two verses read as follows: תְּבִאֵמוֹ וְתִטָּעֵמוֹ בְּהַר נַחֲלָתְךָ מָכוֹן לְשִׁבְתְּךָ פָּעַלְתָּ ה׳ מִקְּדָשׁ ה׳ כּוֹנְנוּ יָדֶיךָ. ה׳ יִמְלֹךְ לְעֹלָם וָעֶד, *You shall bring them and implant them on the mount of Your heritage, the foundation of Your dwelling-place which You,* HASHEM, *have made, the Sanctuary, my Lord, that Your Hands established.* HASHEM *shall reign for all eternity.*

Rashi, citing the Midrash, explains that there is a prophetic message in these verses. "The *Beis HaMikdash* is more beloved than Creation itself, for the world was created with one hand, as it says (*Yeshayahu* 48:13): אַף־יָדִי יָסְדָה אֶרֶץ, *My hand has laid the foundation of the earth,* whereas the Mikdash was fashioned with two hands (a sign of special love and care)." *Rashi* concludes by saying that the Mikdash referred to here is the *Beis HaMikdash* of the future, which will be built at a time when the entire world will acknowledge God's kingship and declare, "Hashem shall reign forever."

Although we no longer have a *Beis HaMikdash,* it is a fundamental belief of Jews that God Himself will rebuild an everlasting *Beis HaMikdash* in the future. We express our deep yearning that Hashem hasten that day in the prayer beginning וּמִפְּנֵי חֲטָאֵינוּ, *It is because of our sins*, that we recite during the *Mussaf Shemoneh Esrei* of every Yom Tov. In that prayer, after acknowledging that our exile was the result of our own sins, we mourn the fact that we are not able to serve and worship Hashem in the great and holy House upon which His Name was proclaimed (the *Beis HaMikdash*). We then beseech God that it be His will, as a merciful king, to once more have compassion on us, and on His Sanctuary, to rebuild it soon and magnify its glory, thus revealing the true glory of His Kingship.

The *Vilna Gaon* presents a beautiful homiletic interpretation of the phrase גַּלֵּה כְּבוֹד מַלְכוּתְךָ, *reveal the glory of Your Kingdom,* which appears in this prayer, by elucidating a passage in *Chagigah* (13b). The Gemara notes a paradox between two verses relating to angels. The Gemara wonders why in one verse (*Yeshayahu* 6:2,3) the prophet Yeshayahu says that each angel had six wings [two to cover its face, two to cover its legs and two with which to fly, after which the angels would call to each other and say in unison: "Holy, Holy, Holy . . ."], while in another verse

(*Yechezkel* 1:6), the prophet Yechezkel reports that each angel had only *four* wings! The Gemara answers that Yeshayahu saw his vision when the *Beis HaMikdash* still stood [in its full glory], but Yechezkel saw his vision when the *Beis HaMikdash* no longer stood [in its original glory, as the Divine Presence was already leaving it, in anticipation of its destruction], and the wings of the angels were therefore reduced. The Gemara establishes that it was the two wings used for flying that were removed prior to the destruction of the *Beis HaMikdash.*

The *Vilna Gaon* cites the *Zohar* that states that one of the six words: בָּרוּךְ שֵׁם כְּבוֹד מַלְכוּתוֹ לְעוֹלָם וָעֶד, *Blessed is the Name of His glorious Kingdom for all eternity* (the ultimate acknowledgment of acceptance and devotion to Hashem's kingship), was written on each of the wings of the angels; בָּרוּךְ שֵׁם on the upper wings, לְעוֹלָם וָעֶד on the lower wings, and כְּבוֹד מַלְכוּתוֹ on the middle wings, which were the ones used for flying. Therefore, says the Gaon, when the middle wings were removed, the words כְּבוֹד מַלְכוּתוֹ were also removed. We therefore pray in the *Mussaf* Service of festivals that Hashem should reveal the glory of His Kingdom (כְּבוֹד מַלְכוּתוֹ) upon us, through gathering the exiles and rebuilding the Temple, so that the wings of the angels that contain the words כְּבוֹד מַלְכוּתוֹ will be restored.

A TORAH THOUGHT FOR THE DAY

בְּטַבְּעֹת הָאָרֹן יִהְיוּ הַבַּדִּים לֹא יָסֻרוּ מִמֶּנּוּ
The poles shall remain in the rings of the Ark; they may not be removed from it (*Shemos* 25:15).

Many commentators discuss the significance of the command that the *badim* (the poles by which the *Aron* [Ark] was carried) had to remain permanently inserted into the rings of the *Aron*, whereas the poles of the Inner Altar and *Shulchan* were inserted in the rings only when they were needed to carry those items. Interestingly, the *Sefer HaChinuch* points out that this command is a מִצְוָה לְדוֹרוֹת, *a commandment for all generations;* that is to say, at any time that the Jews have an *Aron*, it must have carrying poles, which may not be removed on pain of receiving lashes.

The *Chinuch* explains that the *Aron*, as the repository of the Torah, represents our greatest importance and honor, and we must therefore treat it with the utmost respect and reverence possible. If the *Aron* should have to be moved quickly for some reason, the haste and commotion might cause us to lift it without investigating if the poles being used to do so are strong enough to withstand the weight. If they should not be strong enough, and the *Aron* would God forbid fall, it would be a serious breach of the honor of the Torah. However, if properly engineered poles are inserted permanently, this possibility is eliminated.

Based on the same idea of protecting the honor of the *Aron*, *Abarbanel* adds that the permanent insertion of the poles would allow the Leviim to place their shoulders under the poles and lift the *Aron* without ever having to touch the *Aron* itself, as a sign of respect and honor.

R' Shamshon Raphael Hirsch, expounding on the symbolism of having the poles permanently attached to the *Aron*, makes another point. The Gemara calculates that the space allotted for the *Aron* in the Holy of Holies was too small to contain the *Aron* with the poles attached, and consequently the front ends of these poles pushed the curtain outward, and their outlines were visible. To anyone in the Sanctuary, they were the sole evidence of the presence of the *Aron* behind the curtain. R' Hirsch maintains that one must constantly be aware of the presence and centrality of the *Aron*. Moreover, it was necessary that the *Aron* always be in a state of immediate preparedness for transport, should it ever be necessary to move it, so that it would not be defiled or endangered. He stresses the concept that from the very beginning it was made clear that Torah and its mission are in no way bound or confined either to the place or to the existence of the Sanctuary or Temple. In contrast to the *Shulchan* and *Menorah* (which respectively represent Israel's material life in its full completeness, and its spiritual and intellectual life in complete clarity and brightness) that are bound to the soil of the Holy Land, Israel's Torah is not.

Rabbi Moshe Feinstein adds that those who undertook the transport of yeshivos from entrenched Torah communities in Europe to new regions of settlement are worthy of exceptional praise, for they engaged in לָשֵׂאת אֶת־הָאָרֹן, carrying the Torah and its burdens, to ensure the continuation of the time-tested and successful methods of Torah study. The lesson of "the poles shall not be removed" teaches that Torah must be carried everywhere, even nowadays when the *Aron* is not in evidence.

MISHNAH OF THE DAY: SHABBOS 22:2

The following Mishnah is based on the principle of אֵין בִּשּׁוּל אַחַר בִּשּׁוּל, *there is no cooking after cooking,* i.e., once a food has been thoroughly cooked, there is no Torah prohibition on recooking it. [Throughout this Mishnah, the term *hot water* refers to water that is *yad soledes bo* — lit., *the hand draws back from it* — i.e., heated to a degree that one's hand recoils when it comes into contact with it (see *Mishnah Berurah* 318:3).] כֹּל שֶׁבָּא בְּחַמִּין מֵעֶרֶב שַׁבָּת — ***Anything that was placed into hot water*** [i.e., that was cooked] ***before the Sabbath,*** שׁוֹרִין אוֹתוֹ בְּחַמִּין בְּשַׁבָּת — ***we may soak in hot water on the Sabbath.***[1] וְכֹל שֶׁלֹּא בָא בְּחַמִּין מֵעֶרֶב שַׁבָּת — ***But anything that was not placed into hot water before the Sabbath,***[2] מְדִיחִין אוֹתוֹ בְּחַמִּין בְּשַׁבָּת — ***we may*** only ***rinse with hot water on the Sabbath,***[3] חוּץ מִן הַמָּלִיחַ הַיָּשָׁן וְדָגִים מְלוּחִים קְטַנִּים —

NOTES

1. In order that it will become soft and dissolve (*Rashi*). [One may even soak the item in hot water that is in its כְּלִי רִאשׁוֹן, *primary vessel* (the vessel in which it was heated). For although water in a primary vessel will generally cook food that is placed into it, since this item is completely cooked, additional heating will not cook it further. One may not, however, place the item into a pot that is upon a fire, since *chazarah* (*returning* a food to the fire) is prohibited by Rabbinic decree (*Tiferes Yisrael;* see *Mishnah Berurah* 318:32).]

2. E.g., dry meat, that can be eaten raw in case of emergency (*Rashi*).

3. I.e., we may pour hot water onto it from a כְּלִי שֵׁנִי, *secondary vessel,* i.e., a vessel that was not itself on the fire, but into which hot water has been poured from a *kli rishon.* [Soaking in a *secondary vessel* is, however, Rabbinically prohibited, since it looks like cooking (*Magen Avraham* 318:15).]

except for aged salted fish[4] ***and small salted fish,*** וְקוֹלְיֵיס הָאִיסְפָּנִין — ***or a*** salted ***Spanish mackerel,***[5] which we may not even rinse with hot water on the Sabbath, שֶׁהֲדָחָתָן זוֹ הִיא גְּמַר מְלַאכְתָּן — ***for their rinsing*** in hot water ***completes their preparation.***[6]

NOTES

4. I.e., fish that was salted a year before (*Rav; Rashi*).

5. A type of tuna of the *Scombridae* family (*Rashi* 39a). Since its skin is thin, it becomes cooked by merely rinsing it with hot water (*Rav; Tiferes Yisrael*).

6. I.e., since even the low degree of heat available in a secondary vessel suffices to make them edible, this too is considered cooking (see *Mishnah Berurah* 318:36). [This law applies not only to these salted fish, but to any sort of food that requires only rinsing in hot water to render it edible. The rinsing of any such food is deemed to be cooking and is therefore prohibited (*Mishnah Berurah* 318:39).]

GEMS FROM THE GEMARA

Since our Mishnah mentions a ruling concerning the Spanish mackerel, the Gemara (145b) wishes to teach us something further regarding this fish. It therefore relates an incident in which Spanish mackerel are mentioned:

R' Chiya bar Abba and R' Assi were sitting before R' Yochanan, who was dozing. R' Chiya bar Abba asked R' Assi four questions: (1) Why are the birds in Babylonia fatter than those in Eretz Yisrael? (2) Why are the Jews of Babylonia more joyful on the festivals than the Jews of Eretz Yisrael? (3) Why do the Torah scholars of Babylonia adorn themselves with beautiful clothing, while those of Eretz Yisrael do not? (4) Why are idolaters considered impure?

After R' Assi gave answers (that are recorded in the Gemara) to these questions, R' Yochanan awoke and rebuked R' Chiya bar Abba and R' Assi for speaking of these matters, of which they had no actual knowledge. Thereupon, R' Chiya bar Abba and R' Assi asked R' Yochanan to answer these questions, and he did so:

(1) Why are the birds in Babylonia fatter than those in Eretz Yisrael? Because unlike the birds of Eretz Yisrael, they were not exiled. Exile weakens those who must suffer through it. Thus, the birds of Eretz Yisrael, who suffered exile, are not as fat as those of Babylonia, who did not (see *Jeremiah* 48:11). In support of this understanding, the Gemara cites R' Yehudah's teaching in a Baraisa, that for fifty-two years of the Babylonian exile even the birds and animals — and even fish — also went into exile (see *Jeremiah* 9:9).

R' Yaakov in the name of R' Yochanan qualifies this: All the living creatures returned to Eretz Yisrael except for the Spanish mackerel. For, as Rav said, the backbone of the Spanish mackerel is not firm enough to enable it to swim upstream. Therefore, it could not ascend from Babylonia to Eretz Yisrael.

(2) Why are the Jews of Babylonia more joyful on the festivals than the Jews of Eretz Yisrael? Because the Babylonians were not included in the curse that lessened the joy of the festivals, which was addressed to the Jews in Eretz Yisrael (see *Hoshea* 2:13; *Yeshayahu* 1:14) The Babylonian Jews, therefore, experienced the full joy of the festivals.

(3) Why do the Torah scholars of Babylonia adorn themselves with beautiful clothing, while those of Eretz Yisrael do not? Since the Babylonians are not native to their locale, they find it necessary to distinguish themselves through their garments. For, as people say: "When in my own city, my name is enough; when in a city not my own, I must rely on my clothing."

(4) Why are idolaters considered impure? Because they did not stand at Mount Sinai to accept the Torah. When the Jews stood at Mount Sinai to accept the Torah, any impurity in them was cleansed. Idolaters, however, did not stand at Mount Sinai, and hence their impurities were not cleansed.

A MUSSAR THOUGHT FOR THE DAY

Virtually all of the commentators tell us that the construction of the Mishkan and its utensils are meant to symbolize concepts and principles of Jewish life, and that they hint at lessons that should be learned. The *Kli Yakar* points out that three utensils were adorned with the filigree design called a זֵר, literally, *a crown*: the *Aron* (Ark), the *Shulchan* (Table), and the Inner Altar. He notes further that each of the three had different types of dimensions. All of the Ark's three dimensions were fractional ($2^1/_2$ x $1^1/_2$ x $1^1/_2$ *amos*), whereas those of the Inner Alter were all whole (1 x 2 x 2 *amos*) [as were those of the Outer Altar]. The dimensions of the *Shulchan* were also unique, as some of its dimensions were fractional and some were whole (2 x 1 x $1^1/_2$ *amos*). He explains that this variation is based on the dictum of the Sages: "One who prays should cast his eyes downward and his heart upward."

Thus, when one is assessing his spiritual standing (as represented by

the *Aron*), he should look upward, to those of high spiritual standing, whose accomplishments in scholarship, piety or generosity surpass his own. In this way he will feel that his own level is wanting, and he will be motivated to emulate them and improve. He must realize that his general understanding and appreciation of Hashem (on high) is limited by the vastness (length) of Torah and wisdom, the narrowness (width) of his own knowledge, and the shallowness (depth) of his intellect to fathom this subject. It is only with the feeling that he is lacking (represented by the fractional measurements of the *Aron*) that he can be spurred to attain a greater spiritual status. When seeking physical or material success (as represented by the *Shulchan*) however, one should cast his eyes downward, be cognizant of the bounty he has compared to others less fortunate, and be thankful and content with what Hashem has bestowed on him. This is the symbolism of the two full dimensions of the *Shulchan,* which signify the completeness of the gifts that Hashem has bestowed. Complementing this thought, the third, fractional dimension of the *Shulchan* should remind him that he should limit his physical desires to those items that are needed for the service of Hashem.

Both the Inner Altar and the Outer Altar have whole dimensions, for their purpose is to return the person from a state of deficiency (due to his sins) to a state of wholeness. The goal of both the offering of animal sacrifices on the Outer Altar and the burning of the incense on the Inner Altar is to reestablish the wholeness of the individual and the nation.

HALACHAH OF THE DAY

T*rapping* is another of the thirty-nine activities performed in the Mishkan. In preparing for the construction of the Mishkan, it was necessary to trap the multicolored animal known as the *tachash,* whose hide was used to make a leather roof-covering for the Mishkan. Additionally, it was necessary to trap the sea creature known as the *chilazon,* from whose body they would extract the bluish *techeiles* dye used to color many of the cloth items in the Mishkan.

The definition of *trapping* is the capturing of a living creature by confining it, so that it is easily brought into one's possession and control.

There are several common activities that are forbidden due to the prohibition against *trapping.* These include capturing an animal by hand, setting a trap, confining an animal to a small room, and using a hunting animal to trap another animal. We will now elaborate on these activities.

A person is forbidden under the *melachah* of *trapping* to capture a living creature on Shabbos by seizing it in his hand.

It is forbidden for one to set a trap on Shabbos. If an animal will be trapped immediately after the setting of the trap (for example, if the animal is waiting there and will seize the bait as soon as the trap is put out), setting the trap is a violation of Biblical law. If some time will elapse between when the trap is placed and when the animal is captured, one has transgressed a Rabbinic law by setting the trap. The Rabbis enacted this law because they were concerned that if it were permitted to set a trap in a situation where an animal is not immediately captured, one might inadvertently violate the Shabbos by setting a trap in a case where the animal will be captured immediately.

It is forbidden to close the door to a small room or enclosure that contains an animal, if closing the door prevents the animal from leaving.

It is forbidden to send out a hunting animal on Shabbos. If one sends out a hunting hound to catch a deer, for instance, he violates the melachah of *trapping.* If he aids in the hunting, e.g., he stands in front of the deer in order to block it from escaping, thereby enabling the hound to catch it, he has violated the Biblical prohibition. If he simply sent out the hound and did not himself participate in the hunt, he has violated only a Rabbinic decree.

A CLOSER LOOK AT THE SIDDUR

Many commentators interpret the prohibition against removing the poles from the *Aron* as signifying that they are an intrinsic part of the *Aron,* and that their removal would damage the completeness, authenticity or viability of the Torah.

One of the themes presented is that the *Aron* itself symbolizes the study of Torah, and everyone can and should partake of it. However, the Sages and scholars must have material help to be able to properly engage in its study. Those who aid them, supporting the study of Torah and ensuring the welfare of the scholars, are the poles that uphold the *Aron,* and the Torah's success is dependent on them as well (*Meshech Chochmah; Kli Yakar*).

The *Kli Yakar* references this concept to the verse in *Mishlei* (3:18) that states: עֵץ־חַיִּים הִיא לַמַּחֲזִיקִים בָּהּ וְתֹמְכֶיהָ מְאֻשָּׁר, *It is a tree of life to those who*

grasp it, and its supporters are praiseworthy. This verse is part of the prayer וּבְנֻחֹה יֹאמַר, which we say before replacing the Torah in the ark after its public reading.

Expanding on this idea, *Kli Yakar* explains that another question is thereby answered. Why is it, he asks, that the verse instructs that the *Aron* itself had to be gilded with זָהָב טָהוֹר, *pure gold,* while it was sufficient for the poles to be gilded with ordinary gold? He explains that it is only those directly engaged in Torah study (symbolized by the *Aron* itself) to whom we can apply the phrase "pure gold," as they can achieve the greatest spiritual heights. Nevertheless, supporters of Torah can also participate in its safekeeping and flowering, and be worthy of being referred to as "gold."

The *Chofetz Chaim* adds an important dimension to this idea. He says that the philanthropist will participate in the sublime joy of the World to Come as if he, in fact, learned the Torah for which he provided support during his lifetime. As proof to this thought, he cites the *Chazal* that interprets the verse: שְׂמַח זְבוּלֻן בְּצֵאתֶךָ וְיִשָּׂשכָר בְּאֹהָלֶיךָ, *Rejoice, Zevulun, in your excursions and Yissachar in your tents* (*Devarim* 33:18), as: "Rejoice, Zevulun (who symbolizes the supporter of Torah), when you leave this world, for in the World to Come, Yissachar will be with you in your tent."

[This means, says the Chofetz Chaim, that even an unlearned person, who cannot interact with scholars discussing a point of Torah, will be a full participant in those discussions in the World to Come, because he supported Torah.]

Among other interpretations of the verse from *Mishlei,* is that of the *Vilna Gaon.* He notes that the first half of the verse uses the verb מַחֲזִיקִים, which implies holding fast with both hands, and refers to those who unswervingly obey all the mitzvos, both positive and negative. The second half of the verse, however, speaks of תֹמְכֶיהָ, *supporters,* a somewhat lesser form of holding. Nevertheless, even they are praiseworthy. The Gaon adds that the plural form used for each category indicates that there are two methods of support. One can promote the study of Torah with one's wealth; but he can also aid it with his body, by serving and helping scholars.

QUESTION OF THE DAY:

Why was the Aron not constructed of pure gold?

For the answer, see page 176.

A TORAH THOUGHT FOR THE DAY

וְנָתַתָּ עַל־הַשֻּׁלְחָן לֶחֶם פָּנִים לְפָנַי תָּמִיד

And you shall place upon the Table show-bread before Me, always (*Shemos* 25:30).

R*amban* explains that the show-bread, or *lechem hapanim* (literally, *bread that is in front of*), was called by this name because, as this verse commands, this bread must *always* be *before* Hashem. The *lechem hapanim* remained on the *Shulchan* (Table) from the Shabbos that it was placed there until the following Shabbos, when a new set of loaves was substituted for the old. [The loaves, which miraculously remained hot and fresh although they had been baked a week earlier, were then eaten by the Kohanim.] The *Shulchan* remained full, explains the Gemara (*Menachos* 99b), even during the few moments that it took to transfer the loaves. For, instead of removing the old loaves from the *Shulchan* and then replacing them with the new ones, each new loaf was slid onto its tray on the *Shulchan* so that the new loaf pushed the old one off the tray; thus, there was not even one moment when the *Shulchan* was empty of *lechem hapanim.*

Lekach Daas offers a deeper understanding of the instruction to make sure that *lechem hapanim* always remained on the *Shulchan. Ramban* (to v. 24) explains that although the world that Hashem created is of course equipped with the mechanism called nature that, for example, allows a seed to develop and become wheat, the natural world cannot provide the impetus that *begins* this process of growth. [Perhaps a telling reminder of this truth is *R' Shlomo Ganzfried's* observation in his *Apirion* (to *Parashas Toldos*), that only a small percentage of each bushel of seed that is placed into the ground actually takes root, sprouts, and develops into wheat.] Although the entire bushel receives the same water and nutrients from the soil, it is evident from the fact that many seeds simply spoil without germinating that there is something greater than these natural elements that causes — or does not allow — a seed to grow. Similarly, some surgeries are successful and some are not. As is true with any area of *berachah,* only Hashem is able to initiate the process that causes things to multiply. Thus, a connection with Hashem is needed to successfully commence the world's natural processes. The need for this ongoing relationship, explains *Ramban,* was the deeper purpose of the commandment to build and use a *Shulchan* as part of the Temple service. Hashem wished to establish the link between bread, the basis of the world's food supply, and Hashem's *berachah.* Once this *berachah* of sustenance entered the world in the place that Hashem's

connection to humanity is the most clearly felt — the *Beis HaMikdash* — all the bread of the world would be affected as well, allowing it to sustain the Jewish people and mankind at large.

R' Shamshon Raphael Hirsch and *Rabbeinu Bachya* point out that this is in fact alluded to in the name שֻׁלְחָן (*Shulchan*), for שֻׁלְחָן comes from the root שלח, *to send;* thus, the שֻׁלְחָן is the thing *that sends* blessing forth to the world.

Ramban explains that the *Shulchan's* quality of providing the blessing of sustenance to the entire world was also the reason for another miracle that involved the *lechem hapanim.* The Gemara (*Pesachim* 3b and *Yoma* 39a) states that when the Kohanim ate the *lechem hapanim* (which, as stated above, miraculously remained fresh and hot), each Kohen was fully satiated after eating only a very small amount (the size of a bean), and felt no need to eat any more. [See *A Taste of Lomdus.*] Hashem's blessing of sustenance that the *lechem hapanim* brought to the world, explains *Ramban,* was thus evident in the *lechem hapanim* itself.

Hashem's desire that the world should never lack sustenance was also the reason why He commanded that the *lechem hapanim* always be present on the *Shulchan.* The world requires פַּרְנָסָה (*parnassah*), *sustenance,* every moment of every day. Since the source of the world's sustenance is the flow of blessing from Hashem that is signified by the *lechem hapanim,* Hashem, in His commitment to constantly sustain all of His creations, commanded that this connection never — even for the few seconds that it would take to switch the loaves — be severed.

MISHNAH OF THE DAY: SHABBOS 22:3

The following Mishnah considers certain destructive acts that are permitted on the Sabbath:

שׁוֹבֵר אָדָם אֶת הֶחָבִית לֶאֱכוֹל הֵימֶנָּה גְּרוֹגְרוֹת — ***A person may break*** open ***a cask*** in order ***to eat dried figs from it,***[1] **וּבִלְבַד שֶׁלֹּא יִתְכַּוֵּין לַעֲשׂוֹת**

NOTES

1. Although in getting to the figs one is demolishing the barrel, since this is a destructive act, it is permissible (*Rav; Rashi*). Now, the Mishnah above (13:3) states: *Those who destroy are exempt.* And, according to the rule (see Gemara 3a) that wherever the Mishnah in this tractate declares some activity *exempt,* this means that one is *exempt* from liability to a *chatas* but the act is Rabbinically prohibited, destructive acts are at least Rabbinically prohibited on the Sabbath. Thus, destroying the cask should seemingly be prohibited by Rabbinic decree. *Ran* explains, however, that although destructive acts are usually Rabbinically prohibited on the Sabbath, where they are necessary

כְּלִי — *but only provided that he does not intend to make a vessel;*[2] וְאֵין נוֹקְבִין מְגוּפָה שֶׁל חָבִית — *and we may not perforate the bung of a cask.*[3] דִּבְרֵי רַבִּי יְהוּדָה — These are *the words of R' Yehudah;* וַחֲכָמִים מַתִּירִין — *but the Sages permit it.*[4] וְלֹא יִקְבֶנָּה מִצִּדָּהּ — *But one may not perforate it in its side;*[5] וְאִם הָיְתָה נְקוּבָה לֹא יִתֵּן עָלֶיהָ שַׁעֲוָה מִפְּנֵי שֶׁהוּא מְמָרֵחַ — *and if it was perforated, one may not place wax upon it, because he is smoothing* it.[6] אָמַר רַבִּי יְהוּדָה מַעֲשֶׂה בָא לִפְנֵי רַבָּן יוֹחָנָן בֶּן זַכַּאי בַּעֲרָב — *R' Yehudah said: An incident came before Rabban Yochanan ben Zakkai in Arav,*[7] וְאָמַר חוֹשְׁשַׁנִי לוֹ מֵחַטָּאת — *and he said: "I fear on his account that he may be liable to a chatas."*[8]

NOTES

for the Sabbath — as, for example, to reach food for use on the Sabbath — the Rabbis permitted them (see *Tos. Yom Tov*).

2. I.e., provided he does not aim to make a proper opening for the cask (*Rav; Rashi*). *Meiri* adds: He should not make the hole with a measure, similar to a hole that would be made in a utensil. [Making a new opening in a container is considered putting the finishing touch on a utensil, and is therefore a violation of the forbidden labor of מַכֶּה בְּפַטִּישׁ, *striking the final blow* (*Rashi,* 48a; *Rambam, Hil. Shabbos* 23:1; *Ran,* however, writes that it is a violation of the forbidden labor of בּוֹנֶה, *building*).]

3. I.e., we may not perforate the bung (a clay stopper molded to the top of the cask) at the mouth of the cask. We must instead remove the entire bung. Perforating the bung is forbidden because this is considered making a proper opening (*Rav; Rashi*).

4. Since it is not customary to make a hole in the *top* of the bung [so that dust and pebbles do not fall in (*Tiferes Yisrael*)], one who does so is obviously not intending to fashion a proper opening for the cask. Since this is not considered fashioning a utensil, the Sages permit it.

5. I.e., even the Sages permit perforating the bung only on its top, since as explained before, it is unusual to perforate it there. [When it is necessary to open the top, the entire bung is removed.] To perforate the bung on its side, however, *is* customary. It is, therefore, regarded as fashioning a utensil, and even the Sages regard the fashioning of a vessel as a derivative of the forbidden labor of striking the final blow (*Rav* from Gemara 146a; *Rambam, Hil. Shabbos* 23:1,2).

6. In order to make the wax fill the hole and adhere properly to the cask, one must smooth the wax. מְמָרֵחַ, *smoothing,* is a forbidden labor on the Sabbath, a derivative of מְמַחֵק, *smoothing hides* (*Rashi*).

7. A certain town in the Galilee region. The Jerusalem Talmud (*Shabbos* 16:8) records that R' Yochanan resided there for eighteen years.

8. I.e., when Rabban Yochanan ben Zakkai was in Arav, a case came before him of a person who had placed wax over a hole in a cask (see above, Mishnah 16:7). Rabban Yochanan ben Zakkai said he feared that perhaps the person had smoothed out the wax and was therefore liable to a *chatas* (*Rav; Rashi; Ran; Rambam Commentary; Meiri*).

GEMS FROM THE GEMARA

We explained above (see note 1) in the name of *Ran* that although destructive acts are usually prohibited on the Sabbath by Rabbinic decree, the Rabbis permitted such acts when they are necessary for the Sabbath — as, for example, to obtain food for Sabbath use.

However, it is evident from *Eruvin* 3:3 that not all containers may be broken even for the purpose of removing food from within them. *Ran* therefore qualifies this permit and states that our Mishnah refers only to small casks. Large ones — e.g., containers that can hold at least 40 *se'ah,* which is equivalent to the volume of 3 cubic *amos* — may not be broken. On the other hand, *Tosafos* (to 146a) and *Rosh* qualify that our Mishnah refers only to casks that had been previously broken and then glued back together. A perfectly good cask, however, may not be broken open, for fear that one will take care while doing so to form a proper opening for the barrel.

The basis for these distinctions is the statement of the Gemara (122b) that the forbidden labors of *building* and *demolishing* do not apply to utensils to the same degree that they apply to structures built into (or otherwise attached to) the ground. For example, while adding even the smallest refinements to a permanent structure violates the Scripturally forbidden labor of *building,* with regard to utensils one violates the Scripturally forbidden labor only if one crafts a complete utensil (*Tosafos* and *Ran* to 102b). Hence, the Rabbis allowed certain leniencies when the breaking of a vessel is necessary for the Sabbath.

Rama, Orach Chaim 314:1, adopting the stringencies of both *Ran* and *Rosh,* permits breaking open a container only when it is both "small" and "inferior" (i.e., previously broken and fixed).

This, however, applies only to the making of a hole in the body of the cask. Breaking off the bung of the cask is permissible even on a good cask. Since the bung is not considered an integral part of the cask, one is not making a new opening, but merely uncovering the old one (*Mishnah Berurah* 314:23).

QUESTION OF THE DAY:

What was kept on the Shulchan in addition to the lechem hapanim?

For the answer, see page 176.

A MUSSAR THOUGHT FOR THE DAY

Like *Ramban* (see *A Torah Thought for the Day*), *Sefer HaChinuch* (Mitzvah 97) also explains that the deeper function of the *Shulchan* and the *lechem hapanim* was to bring Hashem's sustenance to the entire world. However, *Sefer HaChinuch* adds a reason through which we may better understand this relationship between *lechem hapanim* and sustenance. He states that using an item for a mitzvah actively brings Hashem's blessing into the world with respect to that item. Since the mitzvah of placing *lechem hapanim* upon the *Shulchan* is performed with bread, it is specifically the bread (i.e., grains) of the world that gains as a result. Continuing, *Sefer HaChinuch* points out that the Gemara in *Rosh Hashanah* (16a) in fact gives other examples of the relationship between a mitzvah and prosperity in that specific area of mitzvah involvement. Hashem commanded the Bnei Yisrael to offer the *korban omer* (a sacrifice of wheat) on Pesach, so that crops would flourish in their earliest stages of growth. Water libations are performed in the *Beis HaMikdash* on Succos, immediately preceding the rainy season, in order that the rains be sufficient. And a ram's horn is blown on Rosh Hashanah, to invoke the merit of *Akeidas Yitzchak* (in whose stead a ram was offered) for the well-being of the Jewish people.

Minchas Yitzchak (to *Parshas Bechukosai*) asks a fundamental question on this Gemara: Are we allowed to perform these mitzvos in order to realize these material benefits? We know that, ideally, a mitzvah should be performed *lishmah,* for the singular purpose of fulfilling Hashem's command. While it is true that many — if not all — of us are far from performing mitzvos on this lofty level, how can the Gemara state that these tangible benefits — such as rain and crops — are the reasons that these mitzvos are to be done?

He answers by reminding us of an important principle. In His great desire to perform *chesed,* Hashem wishes to benefit man. Now, it is true that as a rule, a person who carries out a mitzvah in order to achieve personal benefit is not acting in the ideal way. However, this is only a fault when a person does a mitzvah seeking tangible benefit because *he* wants the benefit. If, however, the person is seeking the benefit only because *Hashem* wants him to have it, there is nothing wrong with this action. On the contrary, enthusiastically performing the mitzvah to realize this tangible gain is in fact what Hashem wants him to do. Since Hashem loves the Jewish people and desires that we prosper, he gave us certain mitzvos that allow us to benefit in the areas that we so desperately need

His blessing. Thus, He gave us the mitzvah of *korban omer* — where we offer grains — because He desires that our crops flourish; the commandment to pour water onto the Altar since He wishes that we become worthy to receive abundant rain; and He told us to blow the *shofar* because He wants us to survive the judgment on Rosh Hashanah. Similarly, He granted us the constant mitzvah of *lechem hapanim* to ensure that our bread will always remain connected to His *berachah.*

Even nowadays, when (with the exception of *shofar*) these mitzvos do not apply, the message of fulfilling mitzvos that bring benefit because *Hashem* desires that we will gain from these actions is one that we can internalize in many areas of our lives. One example of benefiting from a mitzvah because Hashem wants to give us pleasure is the mitzvah of *oneg Shabbos* — enjoying Shabbos by eating tasty foods. A person, directed by the Torah to eat delicacies on Shabbos, can easily do so and enjoy himself. However, a person can also enjoy the food motivated by a different, more elevated, reason — because Hashem, Who loves every Jew, wishes him to enjoy the blessings of tasty food on Shabbos, and gave him this mitzvah to allow him this pleasure. Although the pleasure that comes from eating is ostensibly the same in both scenarios, the second person, by thinking of Hashem's interest in his eating instead of only his own, is consciously serving Hashem through his eating.

HALACHAH OF THE DAY

There are several criteria that must be met in order for one to violate the Biblical prohibition against *trapping* on Shabbos. The creature being captured must be healthy and entirely free. The person capturing the animal must intend to use the animal he is going to trap, and it must be a creature that is commonly trapped. Furthermore, the creature must be confined to a small area in order to be considered "trapped."

We will now examine each of these criteria in greater detail.

A basic requirement of the *melachah* of *trapping* is that the animal being trapped must be free and capable of fleeing capture. A creature that is old or injured cannot flee, and is thus considered to be in a constant state of "capture." Thus, one who traps such an animal has not accomplished anything. This act is therefore not considered to be a Biblical violation of the *melachah* of *trapping.* Nonetheless, it is still prohibited by Rabbinic law.

According to Biblical law, one violates the prohibition against *trapping* only if he intends to make use of the animal he traps. For instance, if one traps a deer in order to use its meat or hide, he violates the Biblical prohibition against *trapping.* If, on the other hand, one traps a deer so that it will not damage his vegetable garden, he has not violated the Biblical prohibition. However, even this trapping is forbidden by Rabbinic law.

The Biblical prohibition against *trapping* applies only to creatures that are commonly trapped for some use, such as a rabbit, a parrot or a deer. If one captures a fly, for instance, he has not violated the Biblical *melachah* of *trapping,* even if he intends to use the fly for some purpose other than to prevent it from doing harm. [We will discuss the capturing of insects in greater detail below.] Nevertheless, trapping a creature not commonly trapped is still considered a violation of Rabbinic law.

According to the Biblical law, one transgresses the *melachah* of *trapping* only if the creature is confined to a small area, so that when one wishes to take hold of the animal he can do so easily. This means that one can capture the animal when he wishes to do so without having to rest between attempts. The Rabbis prohibited capturing an animal even when it is not confined to a small place.

A CLOSER LOOK AT THE SIDDUR

We explained in *A Torah Thought for the Day* that the bread placed on the *Shulchan* — the *lechem hapanim* — acted as a conduit bringing Divine *berachah* to the entire world. *Yalkut Yitzchak* (Mitzvah 97) observes that the place where this connection with Hashem took place was of course in the *Beis HaMikdash,* for this is where Hashem promised: וְהָיוּ עֵינַי וְלִבִּי שָׁם כָּל־הַיָּמִים, *My eyes and My heart shall be there forever!* (*I Melachim* 9:3). My relationship with mankind in the *Beis HaMikdash,* says Hashem, is one that is more open and direct than My often concealed administration of the rest of the world. However, points out *Yalkut Yitzchak,* even though the unique, direct relationship with Hashem necessary to *begin* a new area of *berachah* was possible only in the *Beis HaMikdash,* once this *berachah* of sustenance was initiated through the Temple service, the surge of blessing affected other breads as well. Thus, the entire world prospered from the Divine connection that was maintained through the *lechem hapanim.*

A similar channeling of *berachah* from Hashem through the conduit of a particular area is identified in the *Vilna Gaon's* explanation of the *berachah* of *Barech Aleinu,* the ninth blessing of the weekday *Shemoneh Esrei.* In this *berachah,* where we ask Hashem *to bless us with a year of good crops etc.,* there is a difference of opinion as to the proper text to be used. Some authorities, including *Rosh*, rule that וְשַׂבְּעֵנוּ מִטּוּבֶךָ, *satiate us with* ***Your*** *good,* should be recited, while others, such as the Vilna Gaon, maintain that וְשַׂבְּעֵנוּ מִטּוּבָהּ, *satiate us with* ***its*** *good,* is the preferred text. The first reading — וְשַׂבְּעֵנוּ מִטּוּבֶךָ, *satiate us with* ***Your*** *good* — is easily understandable; since we are speaking to Hashem when we pray, we ask Him to satiate the land with His good. However, how are we to understand the other text — וְשַׂבְּעֵנוּ מִטּוּבָהּ, *satiate us with* ***its*** *good*? Which good are we speaking of?

The Vilna Gaon (*Imrei Noam, Berachos 35a*) explains that ***its*** *good* refers to the good of Eretz Yisrael. *R' Aharon Kotler* cites the Midrash (*Sifri Devarim* 11:12) that states that the success of the rest of the world depends on the prosperity of Eretz Yisrael. Hashem directly sustains Eretz Yisrael; the ancillary results of these blessings overflow to other countries, blessing them as well (the Gemara in *Taanis* 10a makes a similar observation regarding rain). Thus, when asking Hashem for prosperity, regardless of where we live, we ask Him to *satiate us with* ***its*** *good,* by blessing Eretz Yisrael, so that its blessings will spread to the entire world.

This is also the reason, explains the Vilna Gaon, why the *berachah* recited on bread is הַמּוֹצִיא לֶחֶם מִן הָאָרֶץ, *Who brings forth bread from the land,* instead of הַמּוֹצִיא לֶחֶם מִן הָאֲדָמָה, *Who brings forth bread from the earth.* He explains that we are not only tracing the bread back to the patch of earth where its wheat grew. Rather, before eating bread, which is the staple of man's existence, we are thanking Hashem for sustaining the entire world. Since the root of this sustenance is, the Vilna Gaon explains, הָאָרֶץ, *the Land* — i.e., Eretz Yisrael — we make mention of Hashem's ongoing care of Eretz Yisrael as part of our thanks to Him for bread that was grown anywhere in the world.

This dependency, concludes R' Aharon, is also the reason why Jews living around the world insert the additional prayers for rain (מַשִּׁיב הָרוּחַ וּמוֹרִיד הַגֶּשֶׁם, *He makes the wind blow and rain descend,* and וְתֵן טַל וּמָטָר לִבְרָכָה, *and grant dew and rain for blessing*) according to the seasons when Eretz Yisrael requires rain, and not based on the needs of their home countries. While it is of course true that people everywhere require prosperity, in these prayers, we ask Hashem to bestow His blessings on the source of the *berachos* that we wish to enjoy: Eretz Yisrael. Once this is fulfilled, other lands will naturally prosper as well.

A TASTE OF LOMDUS

We explained in *A Torah Thought for the Day* that the *lechem hapanim,* which miraculously remained hot and fresh after staying on the *Shulchan* for an entire week, were distributed among the Kohanim. The loaves were then eaten by the Kohanim, in fulfillment of the general mitzvah to eat *kodashim,* sanctified foods.

The Gemara (*Pesachim* 3b and *Yoma* 39a) states that there were many Kohanim who wished to partake of the *lechem hapanim,* and it often happened that each Kohen did not receive a portion bigger than the size of a bean. Even so, the miraculous qualities of the *lechem hapanim* satiated even someone who ate this minuscule amount. *Tosafos Yeshanim,* in his comments to *Yoma* 39a, raises a difficulty with the fact that the *lechem hapanim* was divided into such small pieces. He notes that in regard to other mitzvos involving eating, such as the mitzvah to eat matzah on Pesach, we find that the mitzvah is not fulfilled unless an amount equivalent to an olive's volume (*kezayis*) is eaten. This is because any commandment in the Torah *to eat* of an item is not considered fulfilled unless a *kezayis* is eaten. If this is the case, asks *Tosafos Yeshanim,* how did the Kohanim fulfill their mitzvah of eating *kodashim* by eating the *lechem hapanim,* when each Kohen was only given a bean-size piece, which is much smaller than a *kezayis*?

Beis HaLevi (1:2:7) [see also *Chasam Sofer, Orach Chaim* §49 and §140] answers *Tosafos Yeshanim's* question, explaining that there is a basic distinction between the obligation to eat *kodashim* and other eating-based obligations, such as the mitzvah to eat matzah. The directive to eat matzah on Pesach is, of course, incumbent upon every Jew. This being the case, since the Torah's command *to eat* of an item requires consumption of a *kezayis,* it is understood that a full *kezayis* of matzah must be consumed by each person. Eating *kodashim,* however, is not a mitzvah directed to a particular person. Rather, it is directed to the Kohanim as a group; the Kohanim must collectively ensure that all *korbanos* offered on the *Mizbe'ach,* and other items of *kodashim* like the *lechem hapanim,* are consumed within the proper time periods. Like all commandments involving eating, the Torah's commandment to eat *kodashim* also requires a *kezayis;* however, since this mitzvah is not directed to one individual but to the Kohanim as a whole, there is no requirement that one person must eat the entire *kezayis.* Rather, the *kezayis* amount may be divided among the many Kohanim who receive the *lechem hapanim;* the mitzvah incumbent on the group is fulfilled when a *kezayis* is eaten between them.

Beis HaLevi points out that this understanding of the mitzvah explains the Gemara's statement (in *Yoma* 39a) that the pious Kohanim (for reasons explained there) would allow their portion of the *lechem hapanim* to be taken by others. At first glance, this behavior seems puzzling; a person is not permitted to pass over the opportunity to fulfill a mitzvah. However, if we explain that the mitzvah of eating *kodashim* is not directed toward any individual, but rather to the Kohanim as a group, it is understandable why a person is permitted to allow someone else the opportunity to eat from the *lechem hapanim;* the same mitzvah of *kodashim* being eaten will be fulfilled regardless of who actually eats it.

R' Shlomo Fisher (*Beis Yishai* §23) questions *Beis HaLevi's* explanation. He argues that if the Torah does not consider consumption of less than a *kezayis* to be "eating," then it should be impossible to fulfill a communal mitzvah of eating *kodashim* by having many Kohanim eating less than a *kezayis* each. Since, in the legal sense, none of them have performed an act of "eating," how can this fulfill the mitzvah to eat *kodashim?* [In defense of *Beis HaLevi,* we may explain that in his view, a communal mitzvah does not require any single act of eating; rather, it requires that the food be *eaten.* Thus, it is not necessary for any one person to eat a *kezayis.*]

R' Fisher suggests a different approach to resolving *Tosafos Yeshanim's* question, utilizing the Talmudic principle called *achshevei,* which literally means, *he has made it significant.* This principle teaches that under certain circumstances, a person can invest an otherwise legally insignificant amount of an item with halachic significance by his actions. [An example of this principle can be found in the Mishnah in *Shabbos* 10:3 — see the *Mishnah of the Day* to Friday of *Parashas Vayeishev.*] Thus, even though eating less than a *kezayis* of *lechem hapanim* should not be considered an act of eating, the Kohen's desire that this consumption be important invests it with significance. Once the eating is halachically significant, the Kohen can fulfill the mitzvah of eating *kodashim* even through this small amount. This, however, raises a question: If less than a *kezayis* of food can be invested with halachic significance through the principle of *achshevei,* why can this not be done with respect to any mitzvah? Let a person eat a small amount of matzah with intent to fulfill the mitzvah, and *achshevei* will cause the eating to be halachically significant!

To address this question, R' Fisher also distinguishes between the

mitzvah to eat *kodashim* and other mitzvos. He explains that eating *kodashim* is considered part of the *avodah,* one of the duties that Kohanim must perform in the *Beis HaMikdash.* Thus, although the service is indeed performed by eating, the eating is not the inherent identity of the mitzvah. For this reason, it is not necessary for there to be an *actual kezayis;* even an amount that has been lent significance through the mechanism of *achshevei* is sufficient to lend this act the significance of being deemed an *avodah.* This is not so, however, with respect to a mitzvah like matzah, where the mitzvah is inherently *to eat;* therefore it is fulfilled only when an actual *kezayis* is consumed.

A TORAH THOUGHT FOR THE DAY

וְעָשִׂיתָ מְנֹרַת זָהָב טָהוֹר מִקְשָׁה תֵּיעָשֶׂה הַמְּנוֹרָה
יְרֵכָהּ וְקָנָהּ גְּבִיעֶיהָ כַּפְתֹּרֶיהָ וּפְרָחֶיהָ מִמֶּנָּה יִהְיוּ
You shall make a Menorah of pure gold,
hammered out shall the Menorah be made,
its base, its shaft, its cups, its knobs, and its blossoms,
from it they shall be made (Shemos 25:31).

Although a simple reading of the verse would seem to indicate that the *Menorah* must be fashioned of gold, the Gemara in *Menachos* (28a) concludes that it may be made of any metal. However, if it is made of gold, three conditions must be met: (1) It must have the correct type and number of ornamental goblets (22), knobs (11), and flowers (9); (2) the *Menorah* must be made from one *kikar's* weight (v. 38); and (3) the entire *Menorah* must be hammered from a single block of gold (based on *Rashi*). When the *Menorah* is made using another metal, however, these conditions are unnecessary. [*Rambam,* in fact, prohibits the modeling of the ornaments if the *Menorah* is not made of gold; see *Hil. Beis HaBechirah* 3:4.] The language of the exemption regarding מִקְשָׁה is as follows: בָּאָה זָהָב בָּאָה מִקְשָׁה אֵינָה בָּאָה זָהָב אֵינָה בָּאָה מִקְשָׁה, *If [the Menorah] is produced out of gold, then it must be produced by being hammered out; if it is not produced out of gold, then it does not have to be produced by being hammered out.* Thus, when the Gemara (ibid. 28a) states: עֲשָׂאָהּ מִן הַגְּרוּטָאוֹת פְּסוּלָה, *If [the craftsman] made it out of scraps it is invalid,* it must be referring specifically to a gold *Menorah,* and not to one made of another metal. [This is the generally accepted interpretation of the Gemara based on *Rashi.*]

Rambam (*Hil. Beis HaBechirah* 3:5), however, states that גְּרוּטָאוֹת, *scraps,* should not be used even if the *Menorah* is made of other metals, seeming to contradict the simple meaning of the Gemara. *Mishneh LaMelech* attempts to reconcile the contradiction by maintaining that *Rambam* does not mean to invalidate the *Menorah* in such a case; rather, he means to establish that the *Menorah* should not be made of scraps לְכַתְּחִלָּה, *as a first choice.* Aside from the difficulty of interpreting the *Rambam's* language in this manner, *Mishneh LaMelech* concludes that he has no source for this interpretation.

Malbim, however, suggests that *Rambam* differs with *Rashi* on the fundamental law that is derived from the word מִקְשָׁה. Rather than translating מִקְשָׁה as *hammered out,* to be teaching the halachah that the *Menorah* must be made out of one block (as *Rashi* maintains), *Rambam* holds that the main requirement of hammering is that the *Menorah* should not be hollow, i.e., it should be solid. It is for this reason, says the *Malbim,* that when discussing the exemptions for a *Menorah* made of other metals, *Rambam* says that it may be made hollow, for that is the essential point of מִקְשָׁה (which does not apply to other metals). As for the halachah that the *Menorah* must be produced from one solid block, *Rambam* derives that halachah from the end of the verse, which states: מִמֶּנָּה יִהְיוּ, *from* **it** *they shall be made,* implying that the *Menorah* must be made from one piece. And since the Gemara does not enumerate any exemptions for a non-gold *Menorah* regarding this part of the verse, the "one solid block" requirement remains a mandatory part of the *Menorah's* construction, whether it is made of gold or any other metal.

MISHNAH OF THE DAY: SHABBOS 22:4

The following Mishnah considers the cooling and heating of substances in regard to concerns other than cooking:

נוֹתְנִין תַּבְשִׁיל לְתוֹךְ הַבּוֹר בִּשְׁבִיל שֶׁיְּהֵא שָׁמוּר — ***We may place a cooked dish in a pit in order that it be preserved;***[1] וְאֶת הַמַּיִם הַיָּפִים — ***and*** a bottle of ***good*** [i.e., potable] ***water*** בְּרָעִים — ***in*** a pool of ***brackish water,*** בִּשְׁבִיל שֶׁיִּצֹּנּוּ — ***in order that it cool off;***[2] וְאֶת הַצּוֹנֵן בַּחַמָּה — ***and cold water in the sun*** בִּשְׁבִיל שֶׁיֵּחַמּוּ — ***in order that it become warm.***[3]

The Mishnah next considers a person whose clothes became wet on the Sabbath:

NOTES

1. I.e., we may place a cooked dish in a cool dry pit to prevent it from spoiling due to the heat (*Rav; Rashi; Meiri*). Our Mishnah teaches that we need not fear that a person will smooth out the depressions at the bottom of the pit in order to place the dish on level ground (*Rav; Tiferes Yisrael* from Gemara 146b; this is in contrast to the case discussed above in Mishnah 20:4, where the Rabbis did fear that this might come to happen).

2. This ruling is, in fact, obvious, since there is no reason to believe that this should be prohibited. It is stated in the Mishnah only as a prelude to the following statement, that we may place cold water in the sun in order to warm it. This statement is not obvious, as will be explained below (*Rav* from Gemara 146b).

3. The Mishnah teaches us that this is permitted because one might think that it is forbidden because it might lead to burying the container in hot ashes, which *is* prohibited on the Sabbath (*Rav* from Gemara; see above, Mishnah 3:3).

פרשת תרומה
THURSDAY
PARASHAS TERUMAH

מִי שֶׁנָּשְׁרוּ כֵלָיו בַּדֶּרֶךְ בַּמַּיִם — ***One whose*** outer ***garments fell into the water while traveling,***[4] מְהַלֵּךְ בָּהֶן — need not refrain from wearing his wet clothing. Rather, ***he may*** continue to ***walk in them,*** וְאֵינוֹ חוֹשֵׁשׁ — ***and he need not fear.***[5] הִגִּיעַ לֶחָצֵר הַחִיצוֹנָה — ***When he arrives at the outer courtyard,***[6] שׁוֹטְחָן בַּחַמָּה — ***he may spread them out in the sun*** in order to dry them, אֲבָל לֹא כְּנֶגֶד הָעָם — ***but not in front of the people.***[7]

NOTES

4. I.e., while a person was walking on the Sabbath, he dropped his cloak (or the like) into the water (*Rav; Rashi*). [An alternate reading is שֶׁנִּשְׁרוּ, *were soaked* (*Rambam Commentary*).]

5. I.e., he need not fear that people will suspect him of washing his clothes on the Sabbath (*Rav, Rashi*).

6. I.e., when he arrives at the first courtyard in which he may safely leave his garments (*Rav; Rashi*).

7. I.e., he may not spread out his clothes in a public place, lest people suspect him of having laundered them on the Sabbath. [However, this Mishnah is not the accepted halachah, as the rule is: "Anything that the Rabbis prohibited for appearance's sake (i.e., because it looks to people as if one is doing something wrong) is forbidden even in the innermost chambers." Thus, it is forbidden to spread out the clothes even in private (*Rav; Rambam, Hil. Shabbos* 22:20; *Shulchan Aruch* 301:45 from Gemara 146b).]

GEMS FROM THE GEMARA

Apropos of the Mishnah's consideration of the potential prohibition of laundering (i.e., whitening) that may be involved in the wearing of a wet garment, the Gemara (147a) considers the case of a person who shakes the dust off his cloak on the Sabbath so as to clean it. The Gemara rules that such a person is liable to a *chatas.* [*Tosafos,* disputing *Rashi,* argue that legally speaking one cannot "launder" without the use of water. They therefore assert that in our case dew had been on the person's cloak, and it was to remove these droplets that the person shook the garment. Elsewhere (141a), *Rashi* too states that water is required for the labor of laundering. He states this, however, concerning a garment that has been soiled by mud, where simply rubbing the caked mud off the garment will not remove the underlying stain. In the case of a garment that is simply dusty, though, rubbing or shaking *can* clean it effectively, and this is therefore prohibited as an act of laundering (*Beur Halachah* 302:1; see our earlier discussions of the parameters of this *melachah* in the *Halachah of the Day* section, *Parashas Shemos,* Tuesday).]

The Gemara qualifies this ruling, stating that it applies only to new garments; with regard to old ones, no transgression is involved in shaking them out. Furthermore, this ruling applies only to black garments. [Dust is clearly apparent on a black garment, and most people would not don a cloak of this color without first removing its dust (*Rashi*). The removal of this absorbed dust is an act of laundering.] But as regards white or red garments, there is no prohibition to shake them out. Moreover, this ruling applies only when the owner of the garment is particular about it, but if he generally wears these clothes even when they have not been shaken out, he does not violate the Sabbath if he shakes them. [Whereas washing a garment in water is without question a violation of laundering, the shaking of a cloak is classified as such only if the owner considers the act an important improvement to his garment. If during the week he would wear the cloak without its being shaken, then shaking it on the Sabbath (to make the garment look its finest in honor of the day) is not deemed a significant enough act to qualify as laundering (*Beis Yosef* 302:1).]

The Gemara cites an incident that confirms that when one is not particular about the dust on his garment, it is entirely permissible for him to shake the dust off on the Sabbath — i.e., there is not even a Rabbinic prohibition against doing so (*Mishnah Berurah* 302:1).

It once happened that Ulla came to the city of Pumbedisa, and he observed that the local scholars were shaking out their coats on the Sabbath. [The coats were black in color (*Rashi*), and, apparently, they were also new.] He then exclaimed, "The Rabbis are desecrating the Sabbath!" But Rav Yehudah, dean of the Pumbedisa Academy, said to the scholars: "Shake [your coats] out to his face" — i.e., pay no mind to Ulla's objections, for we are not particular about this at all. In our locale, we have no compunctions about wearing a cloak on a weekday without shaking it out, and therefore, even if we shake these garments to beautify them on the Sabbath, we commit no transgression.

QUESTION OF THE DAY:

Why did the Menorah have to be hammered from a single piece of gold?

For the answer, see page 176.

A MUSSAR THOUGHT FOR THE DAY

One of the most basic lessons regarding the importance of good deeds is found in the Mishnah in *Pirkei Avos* (4:17). It states: רַבִּי שִׁמְעוֹן אוֹמֵר: שְׁלֹשָׁה כְתָרִים הֵם: כֶּתֶר תּוֹרָה וְכֶתֶר כְּהֻנָּה וְכֶתֶר מַלְכוּת וְכֶתֶר שֵׁם טוֹב עוֹלֶה עַל גַּבֵּיהֶן, *Rabbi Shimon said: There are three crowns — the crown of Torah, the crown of priesthood, and the crown of kingship; but the crown of a good name surpasses them all.*

Rav explains that there are three types of people who hold elevated positions in Jewish life that carry certain privileges, and for whom we must have extra respect: a Torah scholar, a Kohen, and a king. In answer to the implied question, "Why is there no crown for one who is reknowned for his good deeds?," the Mishnah answers that the crown of a good name sits above each of the other crowns; meaning, it is an integral and necessary component of the three crowns. For if the scholar, Kohen, or king should behave in an unbecoming or uncouth manner, he forfeits his right to special honor.

Tiferes Yisrael adds that the symbolism of the three crowns extends to the special status of people who possess attributes similar to those of a scholar, a Kohen, or a king. Thus, the Mishnah is speaking also about a judge (scholar), one of distinguished lineage (Kohen), or a man of wealth (king). In this sense, says *Tiferes Yisrael,* the Mishnah is teaching that any such person, who is capable of using his position or special endowments for the welfare of his fellows, must do so. If he does, he is deemed to be among the crowned of Israel. If not, he is considered among the lowliest of the low, and the crown on his head is no different than the nose ring in the nose of an animal.

The Gemara in *Yoma* (72b) says that the three crowns mentioned in our Mishnah are symbolized by the three golden filigree "crowns" (each called a זֵר) that adorned three of the vessels of the Mishkan: the *Aron,* the *Shulchan,* and the Inner Altar. The crown of the Inner Altar, which represents the Kehunah, was taken by Aharon. The crown of the *Shulchan* (*Table*), which represents royalty, was taken by David. And the crown of the *Aron,* which represents Torah, is available to all, and anyone who wishes to take it may do so. Somewhat problematic, however, is that the Gemara does not mention the crown of a good name. *Maharsha* explains that this idea is conveyed in the very next passage in the Gemara, in which R' Yochanan asks why the word זֵר is read as זֵיר, *crown,* even though it is spelled without a *yud.* Seemingly, the word should be vowelized as זָר, which means *strange!* He answers that if one is deserving, his good name becomes a crown for him, but if one is not deserving, it becomes estranged from him.

Maharsha explains that the crown of a good name refers to one's fear of Heaven, which must imbue all of his behavior. Without the fear of Heaven present, the crown will depart, as one's good name will not endure.

The *Vilna Gaon,* however, in his notes to *Avos,* states cryptically that "corresponding to a good name is the *Menorah,*" without any further elucidation. The *Beurim* to the *Gra's* commentary suggests a possible explanation, based on a Midrash in *Parashas Naso* (*Bamidbar Rabbah* 14:10). The Midrash states (referring to the offerings of the *Nesiim*) that the bull, ram, and sheep that each *Nasi* brought symbolize the three crowns that Hashem gave the Jews. The Midrash then says that the goat brought by each *Nasi* as a *chatas* represents שֵׁם טוֹב, *a good name,* for the essence of a good name is good deeds, as the Mishnah (*Avos* 1:17) says: לֹא הַמִּדְרָשׁ הוּא הָעִקָּר אֶלָּא הַמַּעֲשֶׂה, *It is not the learning that is of primary importance, but the deed.* And that crown is symbolized by the *Menorah,* as it says: כִּי נֵר מִצְוָה וְתוֹרָה אוֹר, *For a commandment is a lamp, and Torah is light* (*Mishlei* 6:23). Why is the Torah called light? For it teaches one how to fulfill the will of Hashem.

Thus, the *Menorah* may be thought of as signifying the practical fulfillment of the Torah, and so it is part and parcel of the crown of Torah. This thought is further corroborated by *Haamek Davar* (*Shemos* 27:2), who says that the *Aron* symbolizes the Written Law, while the *Menorah* represents the Oral Law, upon which halachah is based and which governs all of life's activities. Accordingly, the crown of a good name can be symbolized by the *Menorah,* as the Vilna Gaon states.

HALACHAH OF THE DAY

Yesterday we discussed the conditions that have to be met in order for trapping to be prohibited by Biblical law. We stated that the animal being captured must be healthy and free, the person trapping it must intend to use the animal (e.g., its meat or hide), it must be an animal commonly trapped, and one must confine the animal into a small area for it to be considered "trapped."

As we stated yesterday, if the above criteria are not met, the trapping may still be prohibited by Rabbinic decree. The capturing of a sick or injured animal is prohibited by Rabbinic decree. The Rabbis were concerned that if the trapping of such animals would be permissible, it

might lead people to transgress the Torah law by capturing an animal that is able to flee. Similarly, one is prohibited by Rabbinic law to capture an animal for some purpose other than the use of the animal itself. It is also Rabbinically forbidden for one to trap animals even if their kind is not commonly trapped.

The fourth criterion mentioned above necessary for one to have violated the Biblical prohibition against *trapping* is confining the creature being trapped into a small area. We elaborated on this yesterday and explained that this means that one has to confine the creature into a small enough area that one may grab the animal when he wants it, without having to rest between attempts to catch the animal. In other words, the Biblical prohibition applies when one brings the animal into what we may call "close confinement." The Rabbis extended this prohibition to include confining an animal to a larger area, where one must expend more energy to actually capture it. In other words, we may say that the Sages prohibited even the bringing of an animal into "loose confinement."

Loose confinement may be defined as bringing the animal into a situation where you have limited the animal's freedom, while you still have not brought it under your control. An example of this would be one who chases a deer from the open outdoors into a spacious corral. While the animal has not been brought under his control — he cannot easily catch or restrain it — he has denied the animal a certain amount of freedom.

Since actually capturing a loosely confined animal still requires a large amount of effort, the animal is not regarded as being captured, and the Biblical prohibition against *trapping* has not been violated. Such confinement does, however, violate Rabbinic law.

A CLOSER LOOK AT THE SIDDUR

This week, we will discuss the twelfth of the Thirteen Fundamental Principles (י״ג עיקרים) enumerated by *Rambam,* which states:

אֲנִי מַאֲמִין בֶּאֱמוּנָה שְׁלֵמָה בְּבִיאַת הַמָּשִׁיחַ וְאַף עַל פִּי שֶׁיִּתְמַהְמֵהַּ עִם כָּל זֶה אֲחַכֶּה לוֹ בְּכָל יוֹם שֶׁיָּבוֹא.

I believe with complete faith in the coming of the Messiah, and even though he may delay, nevertheless, I await him every day, [for I know] that he will come.

This principle is arguably the most famous of *Rambam's* Thirteen Principles. It has stood as a banner of the Jewish belief that the day will

come when all will recognize that Hashem is the One and Only King, and the oppression of the Jewish nation will finally cease. Eternalized in song, these words were the final ones mouthed by many of our brethren as they died *al kiddush Hashem* (sanctifying the Name of God), expressing their undying belief that persecution would one day come to an end.

Rambam dwells at length on the beliefs that underlie this principle, speaking of them in two places in his *Commentary to the Mishnah* (in his Introduction to *Perek Chelek* and in the first Mishnah of that *perek*), in *Hilchos Teshuvah* and in *Hilchos Melachim.* Although a thorough discussion of these issues is beyond the scope of this work, we will attempt to touch upon the major points that *Rambam* addresses.

It is important to begin with the fact that the coming of the Messiah is alluded to (although not mentioned explicitly) in the Torah itself twice, once in the prophecy of Bilam (*Bamidbar* Ch. 24), and once in *Parashas Nitzavim* (*Devarim* Ch. 30). Thus, *Rambam* writes, one who denies that the Messiah will come is in effect denying the words of the Torah.

Moreover, the belief in the coming of the Messiah is one that must permeate our thoughts every day of our lives. When Hashem brings the Messiah at the time that He deems proper to do so, His majesty will be revealed in a way that it has not been since the early days of the Jewish nation. This revelation is one that we must hunger for. Every weekday, we pray three times in *Shemoneh Esrei:* אֶת צֶמַח דָּוִד עַבְדְּךָ מְהֵרָה תַצְמִיחַ, *May You speedily cause the offspring of David Your servant* (this refers to the Messiah, who will be a scion of the Davidic dynasty) *to flourish.* [Indeed, *Rambam* writes that part and parcel of the required belief in the coming of the Messiah is that he will be descended from Shlomo, son of David, for only such a person is fit to be the proper king over the Jews. He writes that anyone who contests the right of the Davidic line to rule is guilty of denying the words of Hashem and His prophets.]

We will continue our discussion of this principle next week.

פרשת תרומה

A TORAH THOUGHT FOR THE DAY

FRIDAY

PARASHAS TERUMAH

וְעָשִׂיתָ אֶת־הַקְּרָשִׁים לַמִּשְׁכָּן עֲצֵי שִׁטִּים עֹמְדִים

You shall make the planks of the Tabernacle of shittim wood, standing erect (*Shemos* 26:15).

An obvious difficulty with this verse, which needs clarification, is why it says הַקְּרָשִׁים, ***the*** *planks,* using the ה' הַיְדִיעָה (definite article), implying that they were well-known items.

Rashi explains, based on a Midrash, that the cedar trees used for this wood were planted by Yaakov Avinu in Egypt, expressly for the purpose of bringing them out of Egypt and using them in the construction of the Mishkan. Just prior to his death, Yaakov told his children that after leaving Egypt they would be commanded to make a Mishkan, and they were to take and use those cedars to fulfill that command. The main thrust of *Rashi's* comment is that this material was earmarked and prepared for the construction of the Mishkan.

The *Kli Yakar* notes that the *gematria,* numerical value, of הַקְּרָשִׁים לַמִּשְׁכָּן is equal to יַעֲקֹב אָבִינוּ נָטַע לָהֶם אֲרָזִים בְּמִצְרַיִם, *Yaakov Avinu planted cedars for them in Egypt,* indicating a close relationship between these two phrases. However, *Kli Yakar* maintains that Yaakov's especial interest in the preparation of the wood was due to Hashem's promise that the use of the *shittim* wood would atone for the nation's sin of the Golden Calf, and not merely to ensure that wood would be available.

Rav Yaakov Kamenetsky expands on *Rashi,* arguing that Yaakov could have instructed them to be sure and take cedar wood from Egypt when they departed during the Exodus; he did not actually have to plant the trees himself many years earlier. However, R' Yaakov explains, it was psychologically important for the cedars to be there during the exile as well. Yaakov feared that his descendants might eventually (through the pressures of bondage and the lure of assimilation) give up on their aspirations of independence, and remain in Egypt. He was afraid that the simple promise of פָּקֹד יִפְקֹד אֱלֹהִים אֶתְכֶם, *God will remember you* (*Bereishis* 50:25), would not be sufficient to inspire them. He wanted them to have a concrete, visible connection to the Redemption, to reassure them, as if to say, "We will yet be remembered, for here are the trees from which we will build the Mishkan after our redemption."

R' Yaakov elaborates further on this Midrash, pointing out that, in fact, it was Avraham Avinu who originally planted the cedars in Beer-sheva for use in the Mishkan. Yaakov went there to take them, and replanted

them in Egypt. Surely, asks R' Yaakov, all of this advance preparation was not really necessary! To answer this question, R' Yaakov cites the Gemara in *Bava Metzia* (85b) that relates that R' Chiya would sow flax, weave nets from the grown flax, trap deer with these nets, and feed their meat to orphans. Then he would prepare scrolls of parchment from the skins of these deer and write each of the *Chumashim* on one of them. Afterward, he would go to villages where there were no teachers, and teach each of five children one of the *Chumashim.* He would also teach each of six children one of the Six Orders of Mishnah. Then, each of these children would teach the others what he had learned — and, as a result, "the Torah would never be forgotten from the Jewish people." R' Yaakov says (in the name of the Vilna Gaon) that all of these tasks, from the initial sowing of the flax, were done by R' Chiya himself, to ensure that the whole process of Torah education would be performed with a pure and holy objective, untainted in any way by questionable *intent.* So too, says R' Yaakov, the structure which was to house the *Shechinah* had to be personally prepared by the *Avos,* beginning in Beer-sheva, their most holy city.

Utilizing this concept, R' Yaakov answers another question relating to our verse. What is meant by the unusual phrase, עֲצֵי שִׁטִּים עֹמְדִים, *shittim wood standing*? Now, *Rashi* interprets this to mean that the planks should be erected vertically, as opposed to horizontally. However, the Gemara in *Yoma* (72a) states that the meaning of the verse is that the beams should stand for eternity. If this is the sense of the verse, we may ask: Why does the Torah make this point in the form of a command to Moshe? Surely Moshe could do nothing to ensure that the planks would endure eternally!

According to R' Yaakov's approach, however, we can understand the nature of this command. Moshe was obligated to use *only* the wood that was prepared in purity by the *Avos,* which had the innate ability to be the foundation for the resting place of the *Shechinah* for all time.

QUESTION OF THE DAY:

Why did Hashem command that the walls of the Mishkan be made of cedar wood?

For the answer, see page 176.

MISHNAH OF THE DAY: SHABBOS 22:5

The next Mishnah considers bathing and drying on the Sabbath:

הָרוֹחֵץ בְּמֵי מְעָרָה וּבְמֵי טְבֶרְיָא — *One who bathes in the water of a cave,*[1] *or in the waters of* the *Tiberias* hot-springs,[2] וְנִסְתַּפֵּג אֲפִילוּ בְּעֶשֶׂר אֲלוּנְטִיאוֹת — *and dried himself, even with ten towels,*[3] לֹא יְבִיאֵם בְּיָדוֹ — *may not carry* the towels home *in his hand.*[4] אֲבָל עֲשָׂרָה בְּנֵי אָדָם מִסְתַּפְּגִין בַּאֲלוּנְטִית אַחַת — *However, ten people may dry themselves with one towel,* פְּנֵיהֶם יְדֵיהֶם וְרַגְלֵיהֶם — even drying *their faces, their hands, and their feet,*[5]

NOTES

1. For the purpose of bathing, water would sometimes be heated by fire and placed in an enclosed, roofed area, such as a pit inside a cave (*Rashi; Rashba;* see also *Rosh;* cf. *Rif*). [The roof of the cave would prevent the heat from dissipating.]

By phrasing the case as *one who bathes . . .* (rather than "one *may* bathe . . ."), the Mishnah indicates that the bathing itself is prohibited, and that we are dealing with the aftermath of an act that should not have taken place. This is because bathing on the Sabbath in water heated before the Sabbath is forbidden by Rabbinic decree (*Rashi*).

2. I.e., in water of the thermal springs of Tiberias. In contrast to the previous case, such bathing is permissible. It is mentioned here only to indicate that the Mishnah is discussing bathing in *hot* water, and that the cave water mentioned is, therefore, also hot water (*Tos. Yom Tov* from Gemara 40a).

The Rabbis prohibited bathing in hot water on the Sabbath even if it was heated before the Sabbath. This was prohibited because the bathhouse attendants would heat the water on the Sabbath and claim that it had been heated before the Sabbath. Subsequently, the Rabbis prohibited even entering a bathhouse in order to perspire (this was akin to entering the saunas of today), since people would enter the bathhouse to bathe under the pretext of entering merely to perspire (Gemara ibid.). Initially, even bathing in the water of thermal springs was prohibited. When the Rabbis saw that the people could not endure a total ban on hot-water bathing, they lifted the ban on bathing in thermal springs such as those of Tiberias (Gemara ibid.; see above, 3:4).

3. I.e., even though he dried himself with ten towels, thus barely wetting any of them (*Rav; Rashi*).

4. Even though the towels are barely moist, he may not carry them home with him, for fear that he will forget and wring them out on the way home, a violation of the Sabbath. [Squeezing water out of a towel, or any garment, constitutes an act of כִּבּוּס, *laundering,* a subcategory of the forbidden labor of מְלַבֵּן, *whitening.*] This prohibition applies even in cases where the carrying of the towels in and of itself is permissible — viz., in an enclosed town, where all the inhabitants are joined together in an *eruvei chatzeiros* (*Rav; Rashi*).

5. In fact, they may even dry their entire body with the same towel. The Mishnah mentions faces, hands and feet only because it is more usual for many people to use a common towel for their face, hands and feet than for their entire body (*Rav; Rashi*).

וּמְבִיאִין אוֹתָן בְּיָדָן — ***and they may carry*** the towel home ***in their hands.***[6]

NOTES

6. Although the towel is extremely wet, and one would think that we would be concerned that it would be wrung out, we are not concerned for this. Since many people are involved together, if one of them forgets that the towel may not be wrung out on the Sabbath, he will undoubtedly be reminded by the others. The ban against carrying the towel, therefore, does not apply in these circumstances (*Rav; Rashi*).

GEMS FROM THE GEMARA

Continuing our Mishnah's discussion of therapeutic baths, the Gemara (147b) discusses the therapeutic qualities of the River Diomses. The Gemara then relates an Aggadic tradition pertaining to the River Diomses: "R' Chelbo said: The wine of Prugisa and the waters of Diomses deprived Israel of the Ten Tribes." [The Ten Tribes of the Northen Kingdom of Israel were exiled to Assyria. The Gemara identifies the cause of the moral decline that precipitated their exile as excessive indulgence in material pleasures, such as the wine of Prugisa and the springs of Diomses (see *Maharal*). Becoming overly involved in these physical indulgences, they forsook the Torah and adopted dissolute lifestyles (see *Rashi*).]

The Gemara then tells of the great Tanna R' Elazar ben Arach, who was likewise enticed by the waters of Diomses. R' Elazar ben Arach once came to the region of Prugisa and Diomses and was attracted to these worldly pleasures (cf. *Koheles Rabbah* 7:7). Gradually, all his Torah knowledge faded from his mind. When he later returned from that region, and rejoined his fellow Rabbis, he rose to read from the Torah. He had intended to read the verse that begins: הַחֹדֶשׁ הַזֶּה לָכֶם, *This month shall be for you* (*Exodus* 12:2). Instead, however, he confused several letters and read it as: הֶחָרֵשׁ הָיָה לִבָּם, *Was their heart silent?* His colleagues interpreted this phrase as an oblique sign that he had forgotten much of his Torah knowledge (see *Maharal*). They beseeched Hashem to have mercy on him, and his Torah knowledge returned to him.

[The story of R' Elazar ben Arach is an object lesson for us, starkly revealing that no one is safe from the siren call of physical pleasures. R' Elazar ben Arach was the Tanna of whom it was said by Abba Shaul in the name of Rabban Yochanan ben Zakkai (*Avos* 2:12): "If all the sages of Israel, even including the great R' Eliezer ben Hyrkanos, were placed on one pan of a balance scale, and R' Elazar ben Arach were placed upon the other side, he would outweigh them all." Thus, it could be argued that he was the greatest of all the disciples of Rabban Yochanan ben Zakkai. Nevertheless, the physicality represented by the waters of Diomses affected him to such an extent that *he forgot how to read properly!* How much more must we worry that our pursuit of material things will erode our spiritual abilities.]

A MUSSAR THOUGHT FOR THE DAY

The concept that the success of an undertaking is dependent on the interest and toil that one invests in its beginning and in each subsequent step (see *A Torah Thought for the Day,* citing *Bava Metzia* 85b) is discussed by many of the masters of *mussar.*

R' Yerucham Levovitz (*Daas Torah* §210) maintains that the הַתְחָלָה, *beginning,* of any endeavor comes before any actual physical deed is performed, and indeed, even before the thought of performing that deed is formulated. The true beginning comes with the resolution to act or behave in a positive and beneficial manner, and in that decision all of the subsequent steps are contained in microcosm. This idea, says R' Yerucham, is conveyed in the prayer offered by Shlomo HaMelech after the building of the *Beis HaMikdash,* when he asks for Hashem's aid (*I Melachim* 8:58): לְהַטּוֹת לְבָבֵנוּ אֵלָיו, *to turn our hearts to Him,* that we may walk in His ways and perform the commandments. Once the heart is turned in the proper direction, says R' Yerucham, a proper beginning has been achieved.

He also cites *Avnei Eliyahu,* who says that a proper beginning represents more than half of a complete task, envelops all of its parts, and is of equal importance to the task as a whole. Thus, Moshe Rabbeinu, who was the primary agent in transmitting the Torah to the Bnei Yisrael, is considered equal to 600,000 people. Similarly, the mitzvah of *bris milah* (the first of the mitzvos dependent on the body), the mitzvah of *tzitzis* (the first Biblical mitzvah that one physically performs upon arising), and the mitzvah of Shabbos (the first prohibition to be observed after the Exodus) are all considered שְׁקוּלָה כְּנֶגֶד כָּל הַמִּצְווֹת, *of equal value to all the mitzvos.* Using this concept, he notes that the first blessing of *Shemoneh Esrei* contains eighteen praises of Hashem, and it is thus a microcosm of the whole prayer. Therefore, if one has the proper כַּוָּנָה (*kavanah*), *intent,* during the first blessing, he has fulfilled his obligation of prayer. But if he does not, then the whole prayer is invalid, even if his intent and devotion during the remainder of *Shemoneh Esrei* is perfect.

R' Aharon Kotler (*Mishnas R' Aharon* 1:179) cites a *Yalkut Shimoni* on the verse: כִּי רָאִיתִי בְּבָנָיו לִי מֶלֶךְ, *for I have seen a king for Myself among his sons* (*I Shmuel* 16:1), which refers to Hashem's command to Shmuel to anoint David to replace Shaul HaMelech as king. The *Yalkut* states that לִי, *for Myself,* means to convey that the king will perform his duties לִשְׁמִי, *for the sake of My Name.* The *Yalkut* then lists a series of entities to which the word לִי is linked, such as the Elders, Leviim, Kohanim and the Mishkan, and declares, "Each of these, delineated with the word לִי, will remain eternal."

The *Sforno* remarks that the planks of the Mishkan indeed attained eternity in a sense, for no part of the Mishkan ever fell into the hands of an enemy, whereas Shlomo's Temple was ravaged by Nevuchadnezzar. R' Aharon maintains that the glory of Hashem was more constantly observed in the Mishkan than in Shlomo's *Beis HaMikdash.* He explains that the Mishkan had greater protection because its entire construction was performed by the righteous of that generation (under the auspices of Moshe and Bezalel), while the *Beis HaMikdash* was built largely by the craftsmen and workers of Tyre. Thus, concludes R' Aharon, the *Shechinah's* residence is not dependent on the wealth or majesty of the building, but on the devotion and dedication of its builders, the layers of the foundation.

A CLOSER LOOK AT THE SIDDUR

In commenting on the phrase "*planks of cedar wood, standing erect,*" *Kli Yakar* references the verse in *Tehillim* (92:13): צַדִּיק כַּתָּמָר יִפְרָח כְּאֶרֶז בַּלְּבָנוֹן יִשְׂגֶּה, *A righteous man will flourish like a date palm, like a cedar in the Lebanon, he will grow tall.* This symbolizes that just as Hashem saw fit to rest His *Shechinah* within a wall of cedars, which is representative of the righteous, so too, he wishes to rest among the Bnei Yisrael, who are also likened to cedars.

This verse is found in the prayer מִזְמוֹר שִׁיר לְיוֹם הַשַּׁבָּת (psalm 92), and is recited immediately after לְכָה דוֹדִי on Friday night and repeated again on Shabbos morning during *Pesukei D'Zimrah.*

[Among the reasons given for reciting this psalm on Shabbos, despite the fact that there is virtually no mention of Shabbos in its text, is that of *Rashi,* who says that the psalm is speaking of the World to Come, whose essence is similar to the spirituality of Shabbos. *Malbim* maintains that the psalm is fundamentally concerned with the nature of Hashem's הַשְׁגָּחָה (*hashgachah*), *Providence,* in the world. Though the world appears to be operating solely on natural causation and laws, the intelligent eye can discern the workings of Hashem. As Shabbos represents the עֵדוּת, *testimony,* of Hashem's mastery and control of the world, it is fitting that this psalm be said on Shabbos.]

Although there are many Midrashim and Gemaras which discuss the symbolism of this verse, almost all of them relate the verse to *tzaddikim* in general, or to specific great personalities such as Aharon HaKohen or Dovid HaMelech. The Gemara in *Taanis* (25a) teaches that a characteristic of the cedar tree is that it yields no fruit, but even if cut, the stem renews itself. Conversely, a palm tree produces fruit, but once cut, its stem cannot renew itself. *Malbim* explains homiletically that the righteous person is assured of having both positive qualities: he will have children who will follow his ways, and he will have continued eternal life in the World to Come for his spiritual self. In a similar vein, *Maharsha* (*Bava Basra* 80b) states that this verse is a corroboration of the famous dictum, "The righteous will eat the fruit of their deeds in this world, while the capital will remain (unused) for the World to Come."

In keeping with this general theme of reward, many Midrashim compare these trees to the righteous, for just as their shade is distant (high up), so too is the reward for the righteous realized in the future (in the World to Come).

In addressing why the verse speaks of the cedar tree and palm, *Midrash Tanchuma* (*Bereishis, Lech Lecha* §9) says that these two types of trees can be seen from afar because of their great height, and people stand under them and cast their eyes upward at them. So too, one looks upward at the righteous, whom Hashem has elevated.

A TORAH THOUGHT FOR THE DAY

וְשַׂמְתָּ אֶת־הַשֻּׁלְחָן מִחוּץ לַפָּרֹכֶת וְאֶת־הַמְּנֹרָה נֹכַח הַשֻּׁלְחָן עַל צֶלַע הַמִּשְׁכָּן תֵּימָנָה וְהַשֻּׁלְחָן תִּתֵּן עַל־צֶלַע צָפוֹן

And you shall place the Table outside the Paroches, and the Menorah opposite the Table on the south side of the Mishkan, and the Table you shall place on the north side (*Shemos* 26:35).

R*ashi* explains that both the *Shulchan* (Table) and the *Menorah* were placed in the inner (western) half of the Mishkan, with the *Shulchan* toward the northern side of the room, two and one-half *amos* from the northern wall, and the *Menorah* opposite it, two and one-half *amos* removed from the southern wall.

Alshich notes that the wording of the verse is somewhat puzzling. First of all, he asks, why does the verse stress regarding the *Shulchan* that it was "outside the *Paroches,*" and omit this statement regarding the *Menorah*? Both of these vessels were located outside the *Paroches* (only the *Aron* was placed behind the *Paroches,* in the Holy of Holies). Furthermore, it would seem that this verse is written primarily about the placement of the *Shulchan,* as it begins and ends with a discussion of where the *Shulchan* should be placed. Yet, in the middle of the verse it interrupts with a discussion of the placement of the *Menorah*! Why does the verse not first tell us exactly where to place the *Shulchan* (in the north), and then move on to the discussion of the *Menorah*?

Alshich explains that the *Shulchan* and the *Menorah* are symbolic of wealth and wisdom, respectively. [This is alluded to in the Gemara in *Bava Basra* (25b) that tells us that although one should face toward the Holy of Holies as he prays, if he wishes to become wise, he should lean a bit toward the south (to the side where the *Menorah,* the symbol of wisdom, resides), and if he wishes to become wealthy, he should lean a bit toward the north (where the *Shulchan* resides).] Now, it is the way of human nature that one tends to offer more honor to wealth than he does to wisdom. To counter this mistaken attitude, the Torah stresses that the *Shulchan* — that is, wealth and the power that accompanies it — is "outside the *Paroches*"; that is, it is not the main purpose of life, and it should not occupy all of one's time and energy. Lest a person retort, "But the *Menorah,* too, is outside the *Paroches,*" the Torah provides us with the answer for this as well: the *Menorah* is outside the *Paroches* only because it is opposite the *Shulchan.* That is, Hashem placed the *Menorah* near the *Shulchan* to remind those who possess wealth that they are

required to support those who are able to learn, to assure that they can study Torah without lacking for their sustenance. [Indeed, this is the very reason that the wealthy are provided with their wealth.] Thus, both questions are answered. The Torah emphasizes only that the *Shulchan* is outside the *Paroches,* for the *Menorah* is there only because of the *Shulchan;* and the Torah interrupts the detailing of the placement of the *Shulchan* with the placement of the *Menorah,* because the *Menorah* is placed there specifically to be in proximity to the *Shulchan.*

For more on the relationship between the *Shulchan* and the *Menorah,* see *A Mussar Thought for the Day.*

MISHNAH OF THE DAY: SHABBOS 22:6

The next Mishnah considers various other laws relating to the care of the body on the Sabbath:

סָכִין — On the Sabbath, ***we may apply oil*** to the skin,[1] וּמְמַשְׁמְשִׁין בִּבְנֵי מֵעַיִם — ***and massage the stomach*** by hand;[2] אֲבָל לֹא מִתְעַמְּלִין — ***but we may not massage vigorously,***[3] וְלֹא מִתְגָּרְרִין — ***nor may we scrape*** the skin.[4]

אֵין יוֹרְדִין לְקוּרְדִימָא — ***We may not go down to the Kurdima*** River on the Sabbath;[5] וְאֵין עוֹשִׂין אַפִּיקְטְוִויזִין — ***and we may not take an***

NOTES

1. It was common practice to rub olive oil into the skin to keep it soft. This was often done prior to a hand massage of the body (see Gemara 147b).

2. I.e., we may massage the entire body gently for pleasure (*Rav; Rashi*). [Apparently the edition of the Mishnah used by *Rav* and *Rashi* did not contain the words בִּבְנֵי מֵעַיִם, *the stomach. Rif* and *Rosh* also did not have these words in their text of the Mishnah.]

3. This is forbidden on the Sabbath by Rabbinic decree, because it resembles an עוּבְדָא דְחוֹל, *a weekday activity* (*Tos. Yom Tov;* see *Rashi*).

4. I.e., one may not scrape the skin with a strigil, an instrument of metal, ivory or horn, that was used in those times to scrape the skin at the bath. This, too, is prohibited as a weekday-type activity (*Rav; Rashi*).

5. The banks of this river abounded with very slippery spots where one was likely to fall and soak his clothes. He would, therefore, be placing himself in a position in which he would be likely to wring out his drenched garments (*Rashi;* see *Rav;* cf. *Rambam Commentary*). [Evidently, people would avail themselves of the river or something in its vicinity for therapeutic purposes, and that is why the ban on going there on the Sabbath is included in our Mishnah.]

emetic to induce vomiting;[6] וְאֵין מְעַצְּבִין אֶת הַקָּטָן — ***and we may not straighten*** the limbs of ***an infant;***[7] וְאֵין מַחֲזִירִין אֶת הַשֶּׁבֶר — ***and we may not set a broken bone.***[8] מִי שֶׁנִּפְרְקָה יָדוֹ וְרַגְלוֹ — ***If one's hand or foot became dislocated,*** לֹא יִטְרְפֵם בְּצוֹנֵן — ***he may not vigorously rub them with cold water,***[9] אֲבָל רוֹחֵץ הוּא כְּדַרְכּוֹ — ***but he may wash*** his hands and feet with cold water ***according to his usual manner,*** וְאִם נִתְרַפֵּא נִתְרַפֵּא — ***and if he is healed*** thereby, ***he is healed.***

NOTES

6. The term אַפִּיקְטְוִיזִין is a combination of three Aramaic words: אַפִּיק — *take out;* טְוֵי — *cooked,* or *digested;* זִין — *food;* i.e., to remove the food from the stomach, where it is not being digested properly (see *Rav*). It is prohibited to induce vomiting by ingesting an emetic, since this resembles taking medicine, which is forbidden on the Sabbath (*Rashi;* see Mishnah above, 14:3).

7. I.e., if one of the vertebrae becomes dislocated, it may not be reset, since this activity is similar to the forbidden labor of building (*Rav; Tiferes Yisrael* from Gemara 147b).

8. The Gemara records an alternate reading of the Mishnah that omits the word *not* (*Rashi*). The halachah follows this reading. Accordingly, in contradistinction to the previous case that was forbidden because of its similarity to building, we may set broken bones on the Sabbath (*Rav; Tiferes Yisrael* from Gemara 148a).

9. He may not rub vigorously with cold water, since this is obviously being done for therapeutic purposes (*Rav;* see *Tur, Orach Chaim* §328).

GEMS FROM THE GEMARA

The Gemara (147b-148a) relates that R' Channa from Baghdad in the name of Shmuel ruled that a broken bone may be set on the Sabbath. [In Shmuel's version of the Mishnah, the text reads: "we *may* set a broken bone" (*Rashi*). According to this view, it is permitted to set the bone because a broken bone endangers the entire limb if it is not set immediately [and one is permitted to act to alleviate a situation where a limb is endangered] (*Ritva;* see *Mishnah Berurah* to 328:47).]

The Gemara then recounts a related episode: Rabbah bar bar Chanah, a scholar who resided in Eretz Yisrael, once came to visit Pumbedisa. While there, however, he did not go to attend the lectures given by Rav Yehudah, the head of the local academy. Rav Yehudah desired that Rabbah bar bar Chanah should come and hear the lectures. He therefore sent Adda, his attendant, to Rabbah and instructed him: "Go, confiscate Rabbah's cloak until he comes!" [Rav Yehudah strongly desired that

Rabbah bar bar Chanah attend his lectures, for since he was a prominent scholar from Eretz Yisrael, Rav Yehudah wished to hear from him what he and the scholars of Eretz Yisrael had to say about the subjects being studied at his academy (*Glosses* of *HaBoneh* to *Ein Yaakov*).] So the attendant went and confiscated Rabbah bar bar Chanah's cloak, and this had the desired effect; Rabbah bar bar Chanah then came to the lecture. When he arrived, he found Rav Yehudah expounding that it is forbidden to set a broken bone on the Sabbath. Hearing this, Rabbah bar bar Chanah said to Rav Yehudah: "So said R' Channa from Baghdad in the name of Shmuel: The law is that we may indeed set a broken bone on the Sabbath." Rav Yehudah replied to him: "Behold, Channa is ours and Shmuel is ours [i.e., Both R' Channa and Shmuel reside here in Babylonia]; and [yet, until you came and related this ruling to me,] I had not heard it! Now, was it not right that I had your garment confiscated?" [I.e., had I not employed this stratagem to impel you to attend the lecture, we would not have learned this halachah from you! (*Rashi*).]

A MUSSAR THOUGHT FOR THE DAY

In *A Torah Thought for the Day,* we discussed the placement of the *Shulchan* and the *Menorah,* and linked it to the fact that the *Shulchan* represents wealth while the *Menorah* represents wisdom. The two are placed adjacent to one another to teach that it is the task of the person who possesses wealth to ensure that the Torah scholar can continue his pursuit of wisdom without worry for his physical needs.

Imrei Yosef delves further into the relationship between the wealthy man, personified by the *Shulchan,* and the wise man, personified by the *Menorah.* He explores their intended relationship, as exemplified by the partnership between Yissachar and Zevulun, the two sons of Yaakov Avinu. Zevulun was the merchant, whose ships sailed the seas to obtain and market merchandise. And Yissachar was the man of Torah, who sat and toiled to attain wisdom. Zevulun made sure that Yissachar did not lack for bread, and for that, he was given a full share in Yissachar's Torah learning. This is alluded to in the verse (*Devarim* 33:18): שְׂמַח זְבוּלֻן בְּצֵאתֶךָ וְיִשָּׂשכָר בְּאֹהָלֶיךָ, *Rejoice, Zevulun, in your excursions and Yissachar in your tents* (see *Zohar* to *Parashas Beha'aloscha* 150:1).

Imrei Yosef states, however, that Yissachar's task in this bargain is more than simply learning and amassing wisdom. It is necessary, he explains, for Yissachar to take an active role in ensuring Zevulun's success, by praying to Hashem that Zevulun should prosper. Moreover, even praying to Hashem for Zevulun's physical success is not sufficient. It is the job of Yissachar to guarantee Zevulun's *spiritual* well-being as well, both by praying that Zevulun maintain his spiritual level, and by maintaining close ties to Zevulun and supervising him, to ensure that his way of life is proper. If both Yissachar and Zevulun do their jobs properly, both will benefit; for if Zevulun acts properly as a result of Yissachar's supervision, Hashem will allow Zevulun's business dealings to prosper, which will in turn allow him to assist Yissachar properly.

This, explains *Imrei Yosef,* is the meaning of the verse which speaks of the *Shulchan,* yet interrupts to state that the *Menorah* must be placed near the *Shulchan* (see *A Torah Thought for the Day*). It is the duty of the wise man to ensure that he remain near the wealthy man, to guide him and to pray for his welfare. He notes that this also explains why the *Shulchan* is mentioned before the *Menorah* in the verse; since the *Shulchan* represents Zevulun and the *Menorah* represents Yissachar, the verse here simply follows the pattern of the Torah in other places, for Zevulun is mentioned before Yissachar when the two are together (as in the verse in *Devarim* cited above; also, Yaakov blessed Zevulun before Yissachar, see *Bereishis* 49:13-14).

HALACHAH OF THE DAY

We will now continue our discussion of the *melachah* of *trapping,* and discuss some leniencies that pertain to this prohibition.

In some instances, it is permissible to trap an insect on Shabbos. Where there exists the possibility that an insect may inflict severe pain, such as a bee, wasp, hornet or other stinging insect, it is permissible to capture the insect. One should not, however, use a device made specifically for capturing an insect (such as a net); rather, one should capture the insect in a makeshift manner, such as by placing a cup over the insect.

With regard to insects that may bite or sting, but will not inflict significant pain or suffering, the following guidelines should be adhered to: If the insect is already on a person's body (regardless of whether or not it is biting him currently), one should try to remove it without trapping it, such as by blowing or shaking it off. If it cannot be shaken

or blown off, one may pick it off by hand (thereby capturing it) and throw it away. If the insect is not on one's body, he may drive it away (e.g., blow on it) but may not capture it.

[An animal or insect that poses a threat to human life may be killed even on Shabbos. For this reason, a person allergic to the sting of a bee or the bite of a mosquito may kill these insects on Shabbos. Furthermore, if one lives in an area where the West Nile virus is known to be carried by mosquitoes, or where Lyme disease is carried by ticks, these insects may be killed and certainly trapped on Shabbos. The details of the laws that govern the killing of animals or insects will be discussed at a later time.]

Insects that do not inflict pain, such as ants or fleas, may not be trapped on Shabbos.

One may not violate the *Biblical* prohibition of *trapping* even in order to prevent a significant monetary loss. However, there are some leniencies that come into play with regard to an act of trapping prohibited by Rabbinic law in cases where there exists risk of significant monetary loss.

One may instruct a non-Jew to perform an act forbidden by Rabbinic decree in order to prevent significant monetary loss. For this reason, one may ask a non-Jew to trap an animal where the act of *trapping* is prohibited only by Rabbinic law, and where trapping the animal will prevent one from a significant monetary loss. For example, if one has a valuable semi-domestic pet which escapes from one's house, he may instruct a non-Jew to capture it. Since the capture of a semi-domestic pet is prohibited only by Rabbinic decree, and the loss of the valuable pet constitutes a significant monetary loss, one may instruct a non-Jew to capture the pet and bring it home.

A CLOSER LOOK AT THE SIDDUR

In many shuls, there is a custom on Friday night for the *shliach tzibbur* to recite *Kiddush* after the *Shemoneh Esrei* of *Maariv.* This custom actually dates back to Talmudic times and is recorded in the Gemara (*Pesachim* 100b-101a). The Gemara cites a dispute between Amoraim as to the reason why the *Kiddush* was recited; the halachically applicable view is that of Shmuel, who maintains that the purpose of the *Kiddush* was to fulfill the *Kiddush* obligation for travelers or guests, who would typically eat their Sabbath meals and sleep in [rooms of] the shul building.

Nowadays, of course, it is rare for wayfarers to actually eat or sleep in

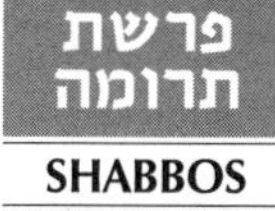

a shul building; thus, the reason for the recital of *Kiddush* in shul no longer applies. Nevertheless, *Shulchan Aruch* (*Orach Chaim* 269:1) states that there are those who still recite the *Kiddush* on Friday nights in fulfillment of the original edict (see also *Maggid Mishneh* to *Rambam, Hil. Shabbos* 29:8). He writes, however, that it is preferable not to recite the *Kiddush,* and that it is indeed the custom of those in Eretz Yisrael not to recite *Kiddush* in shul.

Nesiv Binah cites another reason for the Friday night recital of *Kiddush* in shul, from *Rav Amram Gaon.* He writes that the wine of this *Kiddush* has certain curative powers [as related in the Gemara (*Berachos* 43b), one whose eyes have been weakened by certain practices can cure this weakness by drinking the *Kiddush* wine of Friday night], and it was the custom for people to taste the wine for this reason. [It should be noted that *Rashi* to *Berachos* ibid. writes simply that this curative power resides in the wine of the Friday night *Kiddush;* seemingly, the wine from the *Kiddush* made at home should provide this benefit as well.]

Shulchan Aruch (ibid.), however, writes that those who recite *Kiddush* in shul on Friday night should give the wine to a small child to drink (if one is available), rather than drinking it themselves, since they are not eating in shul and will be making *Kiddush* again where they will eat. Interestingly, *Ohr Zarua* finds in this another reason for the Friday night recital of *Kiddush* in shul — one based on *chinuch.* He states (in the name of *Yerushalmi*) that the children are excited by the prospect of tasting the wine of the *Kiddush,* and this will engender in them a love for the mitzvah.

QUESTION OF THE DAY:

In addition to the Shulchan and the Menorah, what other vessel was located in the Heichal (Sanctuary)?

For the answer, see page 176.

ANSWERS TO QUESTIONS OF THE DAY

Sunday:

This was a sign that Hashem had forgiven them for the sin of the Golden Calf (*Rabbeinu Bachya*).

Monday:

According to *Rambam (Hil. Beis HaBechirah* 1:1), we derive from this verse a commandment to build a *Beis HaMikdash.*

Tuesday:

Chizkuni writes that it would have been too heavy to carry. [Although the *Aron* miraculously bore its own weight, it had to be constructed so that it *could* be carried.]

Wednesday:

There were two spoons of לְבֹנָה, *frankincense* (see *Vayikra* 24:7).

Thursday:

Sforno states that this teaches us the importance of אַחְדוּת, *unity* (see also *Sforno* to *Bamidbar* 8:24).

Friday:

The Midrash states that this was to teach the Jews not to use the wood of fruit-bearing trees for building houses.

Shabbos:

The Inner Altar was located between the *Shulchan* and the *Menorah,* though it was placed slightly [east], closer to the entrance of the Sanctuary.

פרשת תצוה

Parashas Tetzaveh

פרשת
תצוה

SUNDAY

PARASHAS
TETZAVEH

A TORAH THOUGHT FOR THE DAY

וְאֵלֶּה הַבְּגָדִים אֲשֶׁר יַעֲשׂוּ . . .
וְעָשׂוּ בִגְדֵי־קֹדֶשׁ לְאַהֲרֹן אָחִיךָ וּלְבָנָיו לְכַהֲנוֹ־לִי

These are the garments that they shall make . . . they shall make garments of sanctity for Aharon your brother and for his sons, to minister to Me (*Shemos* 28:4).

Special attention was given to the making of the holy garments that the Kohanim wore. Precise accuracy to every detail was the rule. Indeed, each vestment was tailored to the exact measurements of every Kohen, as the Gemara in *Zevachim* (35a) learns from the verse (*Vayikra* 6:3): מִדּוֹ בַד, *his fitted tunic.* If the clothes were even a bit too long or too short, the *avodah* that a Kohen performed while wearing them was invalid.

The *Yerushalmi* in *Shekalim* (14b) tells us that there was a certain expert by the name of Pinchas HaMalbish, who had a special touch, and could fit the clothing to each Kohen absolutely perfectly. [The Gemara there relates that a certain minister used to pay Pinchas an exorbitant price for his expertise in fitting the minister's clothing perfectly.]

We may ask: Why was such emphasis placed upon the *bigdei Kehunah*? What was the special significance of these garments that the Kohanim were required to wear during the sacrificial service? The Gemara (*Sanhedrin* 83b) even tells us that if the Kohanim were to perform the *avodah* without the *bigdei Kehunah,* it is as if they were not even Kohanim. Why do the vestments play such a vital role?

Sefer HaChinuch (Mitzvah §99) offers two reasons for the importance of these holy garments. The first is that the vestments were worn for the benefit of the Kohen himself. This is in line with the *Chinuch's* famous concept [which we discussed previously in *A Mussar Thought for the Day,* Thursday of *Parashas Bo*] that a person's inner thoughts are influenced by his outer actions. It is therefore incumbent on the messenger who is carrying out the sacred mission of providing atonement through the *avodah* to concentrate fully on the tasks he is performing. He therefore wears special clothing, so that whenever he looks at himself, he is reminded of his important mission. *Chinuch* compares this to *tefillin,* which are worn by a person to remind him of his connection to Hashem. A Kohen, although he wears *tefillin* as well, is commanded to wear special additional garments, because of the enormous responsibility placed on his shoulders. He needs a constant reminder, on every part of his body, of his vital, holy mission. *Chinuch* goes on to explain that this is also why the tunic of the Kohen was longer than the standard tunic worn by people in those times. This difference also served to remind the Kohen of his holy task.

The second reason given by the *Chinuch* for the importance of the special vestments is that they were part of the general aura of holiness that pervaded the Mishkan. This aura brought into sharp focus the sublime nature of the Mishkan, so that it would be very spiritually uplifting to those visiting or bringing a *korban.*

An additional aspect of the importance of the *bigdei Kehunah* may be learned from the words of the *Maharal.* The concept of כָּבוֹד, *honor,* explains *Maharal,* comes from the same root as כָּבֵד, which means *heavy.* To honor something is to show that it carries weight, i.e., it is an item of significance. A holy idea can be transmitted only if there is a feeling that it is one of importance and recognized substance. It is for this reason that one must honor parents and teachers of Torah; since they are the ones who will transmit the Torah to the next generation, it is necessary to invest them with significance, so that their words will be heeded.

The same is true for the Mishkan. In order for the *avodah* to have its proper impact upon us, and for the Kohen to be admired and accepted, he must wear clothing that will be לְכָבוֹד וּלְתִפְאָרֶת, *for honor and glory* (*Shemos* 28:2). In this way, a person entrusting his offering into the hands of the Kohen will have the proper regard for him, and will accept him as the agent of Hashem.

MISHNAH OF THE DAY: SHABBOS 23:1

Generally, commercial activity is forbidden on the Sabbath and on Yom Tov.[1] The following Mishnah discusses an exception to this rule:

שׁוֹאֵל אָדָם מֵחֲבֵירוֹ כַּדֵּי יַיִן וְכַדֵּי שֶׁמֶן — ***A person may borrow pitchers of wine or pitchers of oil from his friend*** on the Sabbath, **וּבִלְבַד שֶׁלֹּא יֹאמַר לוֹ הַלְוֵינִי** — ***provided that he does not say to him, "Lend*** them to

NOTES

1. There are two possible reasons for this prohibition: (1) Scripture states (*Isaiah* 58:13): מִמְּצוֹא חֶפְצְךָ וְדַבֵּר דָּבָר, [*Honor the Sabbath by refraining*] *from seeking your [personal] wants or speaking words [that are forbidden]* (see *Gemara* 150a). (2) One who engages in commerce might draw up a contract, thus performing the forbidden *melachah* of *writing* (*Rashi* to *Beitzah* 31a).

פרשת תצוה

SUNDAY

PARASHAS TETZAVEH

me."[2] וְכֵן הָאִשָּׁה מֵחֲבֵירְתָּהּ כִּכָּרוֹת — ***Similarly, a woman*** may borrow ***loaves*** of bread ***from her friend*** in the same manner.[3] וְאִם אֵינוֹ מַאֲמִינוֹ — ***And if*** the lender ***does not trust him*** to repay the wine or oil, מַנִּיחַ טַלִּיתוֹ אֶצְלוֹ — the borrower ***may leave his cloak with*** the lender,[4] וְעוֹשֶׂה עִמּוֹ חֶשְׁבּוֹן לְאַחַר שַׁבָּת — ***and make a reckoning with him after the Sabbath.***[5] וְכֵן עֶרֶב פֶּסַח בִּירוּשָׁלַיִם שֶׁחָל לִהְיוֹת בְּשַׁבָּת — ***Similarly, in Jerusalem,*** when ***the day before Pesach falls on the Sabbath,***[6] מַנִּיחַ טַלִּיתוֹ אֶצְלוֹ — the purchaser of a *pesach*-offering ***may leave his cloak with*** the seller, וְנוֹטֵל אֶת פִּסְחוֹ — ***take his pesach-offering,*** וְעוֹשֶׂה עִמּוֹ חֶשְׁבּוֹן לְאַחַר יוֹם טוֹב — ***and make a reckoning with*** the seller ***after Yom Tov.***[7]

NOTES

2. I.e., when asking for these items he may not use the term הַלְוֵנִי, *Lend to me,* because the Rabbis feared the lender might come to write up a note of this loan. [In Hebrew, there are two verbs meaning to borrow — לִשְׁאֹל and לִלְוֹת. Our Mishnah differentiates between the two. A הַלְוָאָה (*halvaah*) is for a period of thirty days, unless otherwise specified at the time of the loan. During these thirty days, the lender cannot demand repayment. A שְׁאֵלָה (*she'eilah*) may be reclaimed by the lender at any time. Since the use of the verb לִלְוֹת connotes a loan for a period of thirty days, the Rabbis were concerned that a lender, responding to a request of הַלְוֵנִי, would make a note of this loan so as not to forget about it. They therefore required that the borrower state הַשְׁאִילֵנִי, which does not imply a loan of any specific duration. Since the lender can reclaim it at any time, he will feel no necessity to make a note of it (*Rav; Rashi*).]

3. I.e., the same regulations apply to a woman who wishes to borrow loaves of bread from a friend.

4. I.e., as security for the loan. However, since the Mishnah does not state, "He may give him his cloak as security," we infer that one is not permitted to explicitly state, "Here is security." Such a statement, indicative as it is of a commercial transaction, is prohibited on the Sabbath by Rabbinic decree, because it resembles an עוּבְדָא דְחוֹל, *a weekday activity* (*Rama* 307:11, *Tiferes Yisrael*).

5. I.e., after the Sabbath they may reckon the precise amount owed (*Tiferes Yisrael*). [This may not be done on the Sabbath itself, for it falls under the prohibition of וְדַבֵּר דָּבָר, *speaking words [that are forbidden]* (*Meiri*).]

6. I.e., the first night of Pesach falls on a Saturday night. In such a case, the *pesach*-offering is brought that Sabbath afternoon. If someone forgot to acquire a lamb for his offering before the Sabbath (*Rashi*), or if he lost his animal (*Meiri*), he must buy one on the Sabbath itself.

7. Just as one may not make a reckoning on the Sabbath, he may not do so on Yom Tov. Therefore, he must wait until after the first day of Pesach (until the first day of Chol HaMoed, the Intermediate Days of the Festival) to make a reckoning for the animal.

GEMS FROM THE GEMARA

פרשת תצוה

SUNDAY

PARASHAS TETZAVEH

Our Mishnah taught that a woman may borrow loaves of bread from her friend in the same manner that a man may borrow pitchers of wine or oil — e.g., she may not say to her friend, "Lend them to me."

We may ask: Why was it necessary to teach us this law with respect to women as well as men? Surely there is no reason to assume that the laws of the Sabbath are different for women! *Shoshanim LeDavid* answers that the Mishnah adds this case to teach us that although women do not usually write down the debts owed them (and therefore there is little concern that they may come to write down the debt on the Sabbath), the Rabbis nevertheless included them in the prohibition of lending with the expression of הַלְוָאָה.

The Gemara (148b) seeks to reconcile this Mishnah with the ruling of Hillel (*Bava Metzia* 5:9) that a woman may not lend a loaf of bread to a friend unless she first establishes its monetary value. [This must be done to avoid the possibility of violating the prohibition against taking interest on a loan (רִבִּית). This can occur in cases where the price of wheat rises between the time of the loan and its repayment. By establishing the price at the time of the loan, we can ensure that the *value* of the loaf repaid will not exceed the *value* of the one borrowed; for if the value of a loaf increases, the borrower will repay a smaller loaf, equal in value to the one borrowed.] Our Mishnah, however, implies that aside from the Sabbath considerations (i.e., the possibility that someone will come to write down a debt), this type of loan is unrestricted, and one need not ascertain the value of the loaf.

The Gemara resolves this question by explaining that our Mishnah refers to a locale in which the price of a loaf of bread is constant and well-established. Thus, in the case of our Mishnah it is unnecessary to state that the value of the loaf must be determined, for everybody knows the value of the loaf. Hillel, on the other hand, refers to places where the price of a loaf tends to vary; thus, he states that to avoid the possibility of forbidden interest, the value of the loaf must be ascertained at the time of the loan.

QUESTION OF THE DAY:

***Which two of the bigdei Kehunah are omitted from the Torah's listing in the verse* (28:4)?**

For the answer, see page 236.

A MUSSAR THOUGHT FOR THE DAY

In *A Torah Thought for the Day,* we discussed the importance of the Kohanim wearing special holy garments. It is interesting to note that although it was only the Kohanim, the chosen ones from the tribe of Levi, the descendants of Aharon HaKohen, who performed the *avodah* in the Mishkan, we find that Hashem refers to all of Klal Yisrael as מַמְלֶכֶת כֹּהֲנִים וְגוֹי קָדוֹשׁ, *a kingdom of ministers and a holy nation* (*Shemos* 19:6). This was not simply a borrowed usage intended to boost Bnei Yisrael's morale; rather, it means literally that some of the qualities of the Kehunah apply to every single Jew.

This is clearly expressed in an incident related in the Gemara in *Zevachim* (19a): R' Huna bar Nassan said: I was once in the presence of the Persian king. The king, noticing that I was wearing my belt high up, close to my elbows, went ahead and lowered it, to be properly worn at my waist. He explained his actions by noting that the Torah says regarding the Jewish nation that they are *a kingdom of ministers.* Thus, said the king, you must wear the "clothing of glory," similar to the Kohanim, who are commanded to wear their belts in the proper place.

We may learn from this Gemara that it is proper for a Jew to dress in a manner that expresses honor and glory. The Gemara relates that Rav Yochanan would refer to his clothing as מְכַבְּדוֹתַי, the items that give me honor. We must understand that, as befitting our status as a kingdom of ministers, our methods of dress should always bring honor and respect to ourselves and to Hashem.

Someone who studies Torah and receives the title of *talmid chacham* reaches an even higher level. This is why the Sages tell us (see *Gittin* 62a): מַאן מַלְכֵי רַבָּנָן, *Who are true kings? The Rabbis,* who study the Torah. The Gemara in *Shabbos* (114a) says that a *talmid chacham* who wears soiled clothing deserves to be punished by death (see the Gemara there for the details of this law). A Torah scholar is supposed to wear clothing that commands respect, as this will bring honor to the Torah. A Torah scholar who is slovenly causes the opposite reaction.

Rambam in *Hilchos Dei'os* (5:1) says that a *chacham* is recognized and stands out from the rest of the nation by his speech and by his manner of dress. However, we must remember that not only the *chacham,* but every single Jew is referred to in the above-mentioned verse as part of the *mamleches Kohanim,* the kingdom of ministers. Thus, every Jew must wear clothing appropriate for this exalted status, apparel of prestige and honor.

HALACHAH OF THE DAY

Yesterday, we discussed some of the leniencies that apply with respect to the *melachah* of *trapping.* Today we will discuss an additional leniency. We will present the principle first, and then illustrate with an example.

There is a rule that in a situation where a single action contains two elements that make it exempt from a Biblical prohibition (although an action containing only one of these elements would be Rabbinically prohibited), and the action in question is necessary to avoid significant monetary loss, the Sages waive their decrees, and the action is thus permissible on Shabbos. For example: As we explained above, it is permitted under Biblical law to loosely confine an animal on Shabbos, and it is also permitted under Biblical law to trap a semi-domestic animal on Shabbos. While both of these actions are forbidden by Rabbinic decree, if a single act would combine both of these exemptions from Biblical prohibition, *and* it would prevent significant monetary loss, such an act would become permissible on Shabbos. Therefore, if one were to loosely confine a semi-domestic animal in order to avoid monetary loss, this would be permissible on Shabbos. An example of this would be chasing a dove, a semi-domestic bird, into a large room, and closing the door in order to prevent the dove from being stolen (assuming that the dove is valuable).

We will now discuss some practical applications of the *melachah* of *trapping.*

It is permissible to set any type of trap before Shabbos. On Shabbos itself, one is not allowed to set up any type of trap.

At times, one is not permitted to close the door to a room that contains an animal. While this does not apply to most domestic pets, since, as discussed earlier, most domestic pets are exempt from the *melachah* of *trapping,* a semi-domestic animal — such as a new pet that is not yet accustomed to its owner — does present halachic difficulties. If one is in a room with such an animal and desires to open the door and leave the room, to close the door behind him would be tantamount to trapping this semi-domestic animal in the room. How can one avoid this problem?

The answer is that one may open the door to the room slowly, keeping the opening blocked with his body. In this way, one never presents the animal with the possibility of escaping from the room, so that it is considered trapped the entire time. Thus, even when the door is closed again, this is not a violation of the *melachah* of *trapping.*

פרשת תצוה

SUNDAY

PARASHAS TETZAVEH

A CLOSER LOOK AT THE SIDDUR

Let us examine two of the blessings that we recite every morning as part of the *Birchas HaShachar,* the morning blessings: בָּרוּךְ אַתָּה ה׳ . . . אוֹזֵר יִשְׂרָאֵל בִּגְבוּרָה, *Blessed are You,* HASHEM *. . . Who girds Israel with strength.* בָּרוּךְ אַתָּה ה׳ . . . עוֹטֵר יִשְׂרָאֵל בְּתִפְאָרָה, *Blessed are You,* HASHEM *. . . Who crowns Israel with splendor.*

The *Shulchan Aruch* (46), in accordance with the Gemara in *Berachos* (60b), states that when one puts on his belt, which separates between his heart and the lower part of his body, he makes the blessing "Who girds Israel with strength." When he wraps his head with his head-covering [in Talmudic times, it was customary for the men to wear a type of turban], he makes the blessing "Who crowns Israel with splendor."

Bach asks: Why are these two items singled out for their own special blessings, when the person has presumably already recited the general blessing of מַלְבִּישׁ עֲרֻמִּים, *Who clothes the naked?*

Bach answers that these two items of clothing — the belt and the head-covering — are of special significance for a Jew, and that is why we mention the name "Yisrael" in these two *berachos.* While non-Jews also need clothing, and wear the same basic set of clothing that Jews do, these two items are different. The belt is symbolic of the holiness of the Jew, who must keep a line dividing his heart from the lower parts of his body, as an extra measure of modesty. A head-covering is worn to give a person a sense of *yiras Shamayim,* by reminding him constantly that there is One above him Who is watching him. [This is the reason that the head-covering we wear is called a "yarmulka"; the term is derived from the words *yarei malkah,* fear of the King (or, *yarei meiEloka,* fear of God).] Since the reasons for wearing these two items of apparel are unique to the Jews, they deserve separate blessings. [*Taz* offers the same explanation.]

The *Bnei Yisas'char* offers a unique explanation as to why special attention is given to these two items, and why we mention the name Yisrael only in these blessings.

He explains that the first *avodah* performed by the Kohen each day was the תְּרוּמַת הַדֶּשֶׁן, the removal of ashes from the Altar. Now the verse mentions only that the Kohen wore the *kesoness* (tunic) and the *michnasayim* (pants) while performing this *avodah.* Although the Gemara in *Yoma* (23b) cites the opinion of R' Yochanan that all four garments were worn for this service, only these two garments are mentioned in the verse. Why is this so?

Bnei Yisas'char answers that the Torah is hinting here at the difference between the dress of a Kohen and that of a Yisrael, in their daily *avodas Hashem.* The difference is that the Kohen must wear these two additional articles of clothing, the *kesoness* and the *michnasayim,* while the other two vestments he wears — the *avnet* (belt) and the *mitznefes* or *migbaas* (head-covering) — even a Yisrael is obligated to wear for *tefillah,* which is the *avodah* that every Jew must perform. The name "Yisrael" is used in the blessings for these two items (the belt and the head-covering) to show that these garments are worn not just by a Kohen, but by a Yisrael as well.

The *Meshech Chochmah* takes a slightly different approach. He explains according to the view that for the removal of the ashes the Kohen was indeed required to wear only two of the four *bigdei Kehunah* — the *kesoness* (tunic) and the *michnasayim* (pants). The *avnet* (belt) and the *mitznefes* (head-covering) were the two vestments that were worn for honor and splendor, while the *kesoness* and the *michnasayim* were more utilitarian garments. [He supports this from the language of the verse (*Shemos* 28:40), which (according to his understanding of the verse) mentions honor and splendor only in relation to the belt and head-covering.] For this reason, the belt and head-covering were worn only when the Kohen performed a service that was deemed more prestigious; the removal of the ashes did not require these garments.

As we explained in *A Mussar Thought for the Day,* even a Yisrael is included in the term "*mamleches Kohanim,*" and he also must wear clothing of honor. According to *Meshech Chochmah,* it is only these two garments — the belt and the head-covering — that are indicative of honor and splendor. That is why each one is accorded a special blessing, thanking Hashem for giving even a Yisrael this unique status.

A TORAH THOUGHT FOR THE DAY

וְעָשִׂיתָ חֹשֶׁן מִשְׁפָּט . . . וּמִלֵּאתָ בוֹ מִלֻּאַת אֶבֶן אַרְבָּעָה טוּרִים . . . וְנָשָׂא אַהֲרֹן אֶת־מִשְׁפַּט בְּנֵי־יִשְׂרָאֵל עַל־לִבּוֹ

You shall make the Choshen . . . and you shall fill it with stone fillings in four rows . . . And Aharon shall bear the names of the Children of Israel on his heart (*Shemos* 28:15,17,30).

The *Gra* in *Aderes Eliyahu* (to *Parashas Vezos HaBerachah*) says that Hashem gave the Bnei Yisrael two holy items: the Mishkan and the Kohanim. He states that the Mishkan derived its *kedushah* (holiness) from the sacred *Luchos* that were situated in the *Aron,* in the Holy of Holies, while the Kohanim derived their *kedushah* from the *Urim VeTumim,* the parchment inscribed with Hashem's Ineffable Name that was placed inside the *Choshen.* In a sense, then, the *Choshen* is compared to the *Aron* in the Mishkan, as it was the repository for the source of the Kohanim's *kedushah.*

Meshech Chochmah offers another insight into the significance of the *Choshen* and *Ephod.* He notes that both these items had the names of the *shevatim,* the twelve tribes of Israel, engraved upon their stones. The *Ephod* had two stones mounted on its shoulder straps (the *avnei shoham*) with six names engraved on each stone. These stones, *Meshech Chochmah* says, are compared to the head *tefillin* (as they rested on either side of the Kohen Gadol's head). The *Choshen* also had the *shevatim's* names engraved on its stones. It was worn on the Kohen Gadol's chest on top of his heart, just as the hand *tefillin* are worn near the heart. Thus, he explains, the *avnei shoham* and the *Choshen* were a sort of "*tefillin*" worn by the agent of Hashem on His behalf, to demonstrate the close connection between the Bnei Yisrael and Hashem.

If we take this analogy one step further, we can find a deeper meaning in the Kohen Gadol's wearing of the *Choshen.* We discussed in *Parashas Bo* (see *A Mussar Thought for the Day,* Shabbos) that *tefillin* are not meant merely to be *worn* on the head and on the hand opposite the heart; they are meant to remind us that Hashem is the source of all of our ideas and accomplishments. In the same way, when the Kohen Gadol wears the engraved names of the tribes of the Bnei Yisrael near his head and heart, he must feel their pain, their needs, their hopes and their aspirations. This is the real role of the Kohen Gadol.

The Gemara in *Makkos* (11a) explains why a person who killed another unwittingly and is exiled to the *arei miklat* is released upon the death of the Kohel Gadol. The Gemara explains that the Kohen Gadol bears some responsibility for the accident, because he should have prayed on behalf of his nation. A Kohen Gadol who had properly carried out his duties would not have had such a tragedy happening during his tenure, for he would have been able to protect his people with prayer.

Rashi in *Shemos* (4:14) states that Hashem told Moshe: Aharon will not resent you because you are ascending to greatness; rather, he will rejoice in his heart. Because of this, Aharon merited to wear the *Choshen,* which was placed over his heart. The connection can now be more clearly understood: A heart that is capable of feeling undiluted joy, without any trace of jealousy, for his younger brother's accomplishments, even though they eclipsed his own, is a pure heart that can feel the needs of Bnei Yisrael. This heart was fit to carry the stones of the *shevatim,* because they will be worn not only *over* that heart, but *inside* it as well.

MISHNAH OF THE DAY: SHABBOS 23:2

The following Mishnah begins with an example of a prohibition that is related to a festive meal. The Mishnah then proceeds to consider other aspects of a festive meal:

מוֹנֶה אָדָם אֶת אוֹרְחָיו — ***A person may count his guests***[1] **וְאֶת פַּרְפְּרוֹתָיו** — ***and his desserts***[2] **מִפִּיו אֲבָל לֹא מִן הַכְּתָב** — ***verbally, but not from a written note.***[3] **וּמֵפִיס עִם בָּנָיו וְעִם בְּנֵי בֵיתוֹ עַל הַשֻּׁלְחָן** — ***And***

NOTES

1. I.e., he may count the number of guests he wishes to invite for the Sabbath, in order to know how many loaves of bread [or other provisions] he will need (*Meiri*).

2. I.e., he may count the number of portions of dessert he will need to serve to his guests (*Tiferes Yisrael*).

3. I.e., from memory, but not from a guest list prepared before the Sabbath (*Rav; Rashi*). The Gemara (149a) cites two explanations for the reason for this prohibition. One is that this is a precaution against the erasure of some of the names — i.e., the possibility that upon realizing that he has inadequate food for so large a number of guests, he will decide to invite fewer people and erase the names of those to be left out (*Tos. Yom Tov* from *Rashi* 149a). The other is that this is a precaution against reading secular documents on the Sabbath. The Sages prohibited the reading of any such written notes, to insure that any reading on the Sabbath would be devoted to the reading of Torah topics — viz., the Bible, the Mishnah and Talmud, and their commentaries (*Rav, Rambam Commentary* from Gemara ibid.).

פרשת תצוה

MONDAY

PARASHAS TETZAVEH

he may cast lots with his children and the members of his household for portions ***at the table,***[4] **ובלבד שלא יתכון לעשות מנה גדולה כנגד קטנה** — ***provided that he does not intend to make*** a wager of ***a large portion against a small portion,***[5] **משום קביא** — ***because of dice.***[6] **ומטילין חלשים על הקדשים ביום טוב** — ***And*** Kohanim ***may cast lots for sacrifices on Yom Tov,***[7] **אבל לא על המנות** — ***but not for portions.***[8]

NOTES

4. This refers to children who are dependent upon their parents for food. Since one's dependents are not paying for their food, they are not overly particular about how large a portion they receive. Consequently, we need not be concerned that this will lead to measuring, weighing, or counting out exact portions on the Sabbath. With others, however, casting lots for portions is prohibited, since in their concern not to be cheated, they may come to measure, weigh, or count out exact portions, as they are normally accustomed to doing. In so doing, they would be violating the Rabbinic injunction that prohibits these activities on the Sabbath (*Tos. Yom Tov* from *Tosafos*). Furthermore, they may violate the injunction against borrowing portions using the language of a loan, which is prohibited, as we learned in the previous Mishnah (*Rav* from Gemara 149b).

5. The Gemara (ibid.) explains that there is a phrase missing from the Mishnah, and the Mishnah should be understood as follows: *And he may cast lots with his children and the members of his household* for portions *at the table, even if some portions are larger than others. With others, however, he may not cast lots even for equal portions. If he casts lots for unequal portions, this is forbidden even during the week.* The phrase in our Mishnah, "*provided that he does not intend to make* a wager of *a large portion against a small portion,*" is to be understood as referring only to those who do not belong to one's household. Its meaning is that the Sabbath prohibition against casting lots refers only to equal portions; casting lots for unequal portions is prohibited quite apart from any Sabbath considerations, since it constitutes gambling (*Rav; Rashi*).

6. I.e., because of the prohibition upon gambling. [*Dice* is a general term used by the Mishnah for all forms of gambling.] Gambling is prohibited, because the loser does not willingly part with his money. He agreed to the bet because he expected to win. Had he known that he would lose, he would not have entered into the bet. Taking his money is therefore considered by the Rabbis as akin to stealing (*Rav; Rashi*).

7. I.e., for the portions to be eaten by the Kohanim from sacrifices offered on the festival (*Rav* from Gemara ibid.). Since a Kohen fulfills a *mitzvah* when he eats those parts of the sacrifice that are designated for him, obtaining a large portion is evidence of his love and appreciation for this mitzvah (*Rambam, Hil. Yom Tov* 4:20). Therefore, eagerness on the part of Kohanim to eat from the sacrifices and to obtain a large portion is commendable. Consequently, the Rabbis permitted the casting of lots for the large portions, as an expression of that sentiment (*Rav; Rambam Commentary*).

8. I.e., not for portions of sacrifices that were offered up on the weekday preceding the festival (*Rav* from Gemara ibid. according to *Rashi*). Since it was possible to cast lots for these portions before the festival, the Rabbis did not permit doing so on the festival (*Rav; Tos. Yom Tov*).

GEMS FROM THE GEMARA

Our Mishnah taught: "[Kohanim] may cast lots for sacrifices on Yom Tov, but not for portions." The Gemara (149b) asks: What is the meaning of the words "but not for portions"? R' Yaakov the son of Yaakov's daughter responds that it means that Kohanim may not cast lots on Yom Tov for portions of sacrifices that were offered on the preceding weekday. [R' Yaakov's father is not named here; instead, R' Yaakov is identified as the son of his *mother,* who is also not named, but merely called "Yaakov's daughter" (R' Yaakov's maternal grandfather was also named Yaakov). *Rashi* (to *Eruvin* 80a) states that R' Yaakov's father was not identified by name because he was unworthy.]

Having cited one teaching of R' Yaakov the son of Yaakov's daughter, the Gemara presents another statement in his name: "Anyone whose friend was punished on his account, is not admitted into the enclosure of the Holy One, Blessed is He." [I.e., one who causes punishment to befall his fellow is excluded from a certain degree of closeness to the Divine Presence in the World to Come.]

The Gemara then asks: From where do we know this? The Gemara cites several possibilities, only to reject them. Eventually, the Gemara concludes that proof can be adduced for the teaching of R' Yaakov the son of Yaakov's daughter from the following verse (*Proverbs* 17:26): גַּם עֲנוֹשׁ לַצַּדִּיק לֹא־טוֹב, *Also to punish is not good for a righteous man.* Posits the Gemara: the term *not good* means nothing other than evil, and it is written about evil (*Psalms* 5:5): כִּי לֹא אֵל־חָפֵץ רֶשַׁע אָתָּה לֹא יְגֻרְךָ רָע, *For You are not a God Who desires wickedness; evil does not abide with You,* which means: You, Hashem, are righteous (see *Jeremiah* 12:1), therefore, an evil one shall not be allowed in Your abode. Since one who causes the punishment of another is defined as "evil," it follows that such a person is not allowed into God's abode. This confirms the statement of R' Yaakov.

[R' Yaakov's statement applies even in the case of a victim whose oppressor was punished by God for oppressing him. Since the victim was the cause of another's suffering (albeit justifiably), he too must suffer (see *Bava Basra* 22a). However, this applies only where the victim actually did something to bring about the other's punishment — viz., he prayed that God would punish his oppressor (see *Iyun Yaakov* and *Sfas Emes* ibid.). By doing this the victim has acted incorrectly — for one should pray only that his suffering cease, and not that his oppressor be punished.]

פרשת תצוה

MONDAY

PARASHAS TETZAVEH

A MUSSAR THOUGHT FOR THE DAY

Rabbeinu Bachya gives a lengthy description of all the stones that were on the *Choshen,* and connects each of their colors and attributes to the appropriate tribe. Let us examine the stone that represented the tribe of Yissachar, and the lesson that it carried.

The Torah tells us that Yissachar's stone was the sapphire, which is the bluish color of *techeiles.* This stone was selected to represent this particular tribe because the men of Yissachar were great Torah scholars. *Rabbeinu Bachya* notes that the *Luchos* (Tablets of the Law) were also made from sapphire. He notes as well that when the Torah describes the vision of Hashem that appeared to Moshe, Aharon and the elders of Bnei Yisrael when the Torah was given at Har Sinai, the verse states (*Shemos* 24:10): וְתַחַת רַגְלָיו כְּמַעֲשֵׂה לִבְנַת הַסַּפִּיר, *and under His feet was that which had the form of a sapphire brick.* The souls of those who delve deeply into Torah, adds *Rabbeinu Bachya,* are directly linked to the Holy Throne of Hashem's Glory that also has the appearance of the sapphire stone, as is stated in *Yechezkel* (Ch. 1).

He goes on to explain that the color blue indicates humility and is appropriate for both young and old (unlike the colors red and green that he characterizes as more haughty colors).

Rabbeinu Bachya states that the sapphire stone carries within it a *segulah* for good eyesight. In this, the sapphire is also comparable to Torah, of which the verse states (*Tehillim* 19:9): מִצְוַת ה׳ בָּרָה מְאִירַת עֵינָיִם, *the command of* H*ASHEM* *is clear, enlightening the eyes.* He notes further that this stone can be used to cure any pain or swelling in the body. The Torah has this ability as well, as the Gemara states (*Eruvin* 54a): If someone has a pain in his head, he should learn Torah. Because of the many similarities between the sapphire stone and Torah, it was selected as Yissachar's stone.

A lesson that may be learned from this *Rabbeinu Bachya* is the importance of humility in a Torah scholar. The only attribute of Moshe Rabbeinu that the Torah explicitly acknowledges is his *middah* of עֲנָוָה, *humility.* As the Torah testifies in *Parashas Beha'aloscha* (*Bamidbar* 12:3): וְהָאִישׁ מֹשֶׁה עָנָו מְאֹד מִכֹּל הָאָדָם אֲשֶׁר עַל־פְּנֵי הָאֲדָמָה, *Moshe was exceedingly humble, more than any person on the face of the earth.* The Gemara in *Shabbos* (89a) tells us that because of this *middah,* he merited that the Torah is identified with his name, as "Toras Moshe." This fits well with the idea that humility is a prerequisite for becoming a true Torah scholar.

Although we may not perceive the quality of humility that is present in the color of sapphire or *techeiles,* nevertheless, the lesson of humility is one that we can absorb. As we say in the prayer of *Elokai Netzor* at the end of *Shemoneh Esrei*: נַפְשִׁי כֶּעָפָר לַכֹּל תִּהְיֶה פְּתַח לִבִּי בְּתוֹרָתֶךָ, *let my soul be like dust to everyone, open my heart to Your Torah.* These two prayers are connected, for humility — epitomized by the dust, which is the most humble of creations — is the gateway through which one must enter to succeed in his Torah study.

HALACHAH OF THE DAY

Yesterday, we discussed the potential problem with closing a door to a room that contains a non-domestic (or semi-domestic) animal, and how this may be done without transgressing the *melachah* of *trapping.*

A similar situation arises when closing the door of an occupied birdcage on Shabbos. Closing the cage door is considered trapping the bird which is inside it. If one must open the door to the cage on Shabbos, he can avoid transgressing the *melachah* of *trapping* by opening the door while blocking the opening with his hand, so that the bird is regarded as trapped the entire time. In this way, there is no violation of Shabbos when reclosing the door.

In contrast to these above-mentioned cases where there is an issue of *trapping,* one is permitted to close the door of a large room on Shabbos if an insect is flying about inside the room. An insect free to fly around a large room is considered to be completely free. Closing the door is therefore permitted under both Biblical and Rabbinic law.

A common scenario where questions of trapping arise is that of trapping an insect between a window and a screen. If one's window is open and there is a fly on the screen, one may not close the window, since he will thereby be trapping the fly between the window and the screen. If the screen has large holes in it, or if there are other significant gaps that will allow the insect to easily find its way outside, one may close the window, since then the insect is not considered trapped at all. Additionally, if one's intention in closing the window is not to trap the fly, but rather to keep out the cold or the noise from the outside, he may close the window even though the insect will perforce be trapped.

[Although the above would seem to be a case of פְּסִיק רֵישֵׁיהּ (*p'sik reishei*), *the inevitable consequence,* which is forbidden on Shabbos even when there is no intent to accomplish the forbidden activity, closing the

window to keep out the cold is still permissible. The reason for this is as follows: We explained above that in order for *trapping* to be forbidden on a Biblical level, one of the criteria is that the trapped animal must be one that is commonly trapped. Another criteria is that the animal must be confined in such a way that it can be easily taken hold of. Neither of these criteria are met in the case of a fly trapped between a window and a screen. Since there are two reasons to exempt this act from the Biblical prohibition of trapping, it is permissible despite the fact that it is a *p'sik reishei.*]

It is permissible to free an animal from a trap on Shabbos.

This concludes our discussion of the *melachah* of *trapping.*

A CLOSER LOOK AT THE SIDDUR

In the third chapter of *Krias Shema,* we recite the verse: וְנָתְנוּ עַל־צִיצִת הַכָּנָף פְּתִיל תְּכֵלֶת... וּרְאִיתֶם אֹתוֹ וּזְכַרְתֶּם אֶת־כָּל־מִצְוֹת ה׳, *They are to place upon the tzitzis of each corner a thread of techeiles [sky-blue wool] . . . and you will see it and remember all the commandments of HASHEM.*

In *A Mussar Thought for the Day,* we discussed the connection between the color of *techeiles* and the *shevet* of Yissachar. We will now examine the reason we are commanded to place a *techeiles* thread on our *tzitzis* garment, and its meaningful lesson.

The Gemara in *Menachos* (43b) asks: Why is *techeiles* different than any other color [i.e., why was it the only color chosen to be included (along with the white strings) in the mitzvah of *tzitzis*]? Because *techeiles* is similar to the color of the ocean, which reflects the color of the sky, which is similar to the Holy Throne of Hashem's Glory [which, as we learned above, was made of sapphire stone, which has a bluish color].

The color association related by the Gemara (*techeiles* to ocean to sky to Hashem's Throne of Glory) will obviously occur only to one who actually thinks about the *techeiles* when he looks at it. This is indeed alluded to in the verse in the *parashah* of *tzitzis* (the third paragraph of *Krias Shema,* which states [*Bamidbar* 15:39]: וּרְאִיתֶם אֹתוֹ וּזְכַרְתֶּם אֶת־כָּל־מִצְוֹת ה׳ וַעֲשִׂיתֶם אֹתָם וְלֹא תָתוּרוּ אַחֲרֵי לְבַבְכֶם וְאַחֲרֵי עֵינֵיכֶם, *And you will see it* [see *Ramban* ibid., who understands the verse to be referring to the *techeiles;* cf., however, *Rashi* ibid.], *and remember all the commandments of HASHEM and perform them; and you will not explore after your heart and after your eyes*). If a person looks at and studies the *techeiles* when he says the *Shema,* this will serve as a reminder for him throughout the day.

If he has any temptation to sin, the *techeiles* will remind him that Hashem, sitting on His Holy Throne that is the same shade as the *techeiles,* is watching him, and this thought will prevent him from sinning. [As we learned earlier (see *A Mussar Thought for the Day*), *Rabbeinu Bachya* explains that the color of *techeiles* signifies humility. This can also be understood in light of the fact that the *techeiles* reminds one of Hashem sitting on His Throne of Glory. For when a person who is contemplating sin thinks about the greatness of Hashem, he will be overcome by fear and embarrassment at his own inadequacy, and this can bring him to humility.]

The Gemara relates an incident where the mitzvah of *techeiles* did actually prevent a person from doing a sin. In *Menachos* (44a), the Gemara tells of a man who was very careful in the mitzvah of *tzitzis,* but was tempted to commit the terrible sin of adultery. The Gemara relates that before the man was able to commit the sin, his *tzitzis* hit him on his face. He took that as a message from Hashem, saying: אֲנִי ה׳, *I am HASHEM* Who will punish sinners, and *I am HASHEM* Who will reward those who do not sin, but perform My mitzvos.

We see from this Gemara that someone who takes the mitzvah of *tzitzis* seriously possesses a constant reminder that Hashem is watching his every action, and that he will be punished for every sin and rewarded for every mitzvah. This reminder will help to keep a person on the right track in his service of Hashem.

QUESTION OF THE DAY:

In addition to the names of the shevatim, what else was engraved upon the stones of the Choshen?

For the answer, see page 236.

A TORAH THOUGHT FOR THE DAY

וְעָשִׂיתָ אֶת־מְעִיל הָאֵפוֹד . . . פַּעֲמֹן זָהָב וְרִמּוֹן . . .
עַל־שׁוּלֵי הַמְּעִיל סָבִיב. וְהָיָה עַל־אַהֲרֹן לְשָׁרֵת
וְנִשְׁמַע קוֹלוֹ בְּבֹאוֹ אֶל־הַקֹּדֶשׁ לִפְנֵי ה׳ וּבְצֵאתוֹ וְלֹא יָמוּת

You shall make the Robe of the Ephod . . . a golden bell and a pomegranate . . . on the hem of the robe all around. It shall be upon Aharon in order to serve, and its sound shall be heard when he enters the Holy before HASHEM *and when he leaves, so that he not die* (*Shemos* 28:31, 34-35).

R*ashi* teaches us that this verse (v. 35) is the source for the law that a Kohen — even a Kohen *hedyot* (ordinary Kohen) — who performs the *avodah* without wearing the proper vestments is liable to death at the hands of Heaven. As the Gemara (*Zevachim* 17b, *Sanhedrin* 83b) states: When their holy vestments are upon them, they have their Kehunah upon them, but if they are not wearing those vestments, they are considered as non-Kohanim and are not fit to serve.

Ramban questions this explanation. He asks: Why did the Torah interrupt the listing of all the *bigdei Kehunah* to teach us this law? Furthermore, why does the Torah teach us this law in the passage that speaks of the *Me'il* (robe), and not after listing all the garments? This is especially difficult, given that the *Me'il* is not even one of the four garments worn by a Kohen *hedyot*!

Ramban therefore interprets the phrase וְלֹא יָמוּת, *and he shall not die,* that appears in v. 35, as referring to something that pertains only to the *Me'il.* He explains that the verse is not coming to subject the Kohen to the punishment of Divinely imposed death if he does not wear the vestments. Rather, it is guaranteeing the Kohen that he will not die if he does as the Torah commands. *Ramban* notes that bells really have no place on the clothing of noble people; yet, the Torah commanded the Kohen to wear bells upon the hem of the *Me'il,* to announce his arrival in the holy areas. We know from reading *Megillas Esther* that someone who enters the king's chambers suddenly, without first being summoned, deserves to be killed. Here, too, when the Kohen enters the Holy of Holies, he is coming to Hashem's private chamber. Even the angels do not enter there unannounced, and the Kohen would be in terrible danger if he were to do so. Therefore, the Torah commanded him to put bells on the *Me'il* to signal his arrival, that he is coming to do Hashem's *avodah.* This will protect him from any harm. [Although, as the *Ramban* points out, the Kohen Gadol did not wear the *Me'il* when he entered the Holy of Holies (for the inner service on Yom Kippur, the Kohen Gadol wore a special set of white garments, not the eight golden garments that were his customary vestments), he still needed the bells to announce his arrival into the *Ohel Mo'ed,* for which service the golden garments were indeed worn.]

Ohr HaChaim also takes issue with *Rashi*'s contention that this verse is the source for the law that a Kohen is punishable by death for performing the *avodah* without the *bigdei Kehunah.* He understands, as does the *Ramban,* that the subject of the verse is only the *Me'il,* but his approach is slightly different. In his view, the verse is emphasizing that every detail of the making of the *Me'il* is critical, and the design must be executed exactly as described by the Torah. If even seemingly small details, such as the bells on the hem, are lacking, the Kohen Gadol will be liable to death for performing the *avodah* while so attired. Even though he is wearing all the proper garments, including the *Me'il,* since he is lacking the bells, he is subject to death. *Gur Aryeh* adds: Do not think that the bells are only for beauty and are not an essential part of the *Me'il;* rather, if they are not present, it is as if he is not wearing the *Me'il* at all, and he is subject to death.

MISHNAH OF THE DAY: SHABBOS 23:3

This Mishnah considers laws that emerge from the verse (*Isaiah* 58:13): מִמְּצוֹא חֶפְצְךָ וְדַבֵּר דָּבָר, *[Honor the Sabbath by refraining] from seeking your [personal] wants, or speaking words [that are forbidden]* (*Rav; Rashi*):

לֹא יִשְׂכּוֹר אָדָם פּוֹעֲלִים בְּשַׁבָּת — *A person may not hire workers on the Sabbath,*[1] וְלֹא יֹאמַר אָדָם לַחֲבֵירוֹ לִשְׂכּוֹר לוֹ פּוֹעֲלִים — *and a person may not tell his friend to hire workers for him.*[2] אֵין מַחְשִׁיכִין עַל הַתְּחוּם לִשְׂכּוֹר פּוֹעֲלִים וּלְהָבִיא פֵּירוֹת — *We may not go to await nightfall*

NOTES

1. It is forbidden to hire workers on the Sabbath, even for work that is to be done after the Sabbath (*Shulchan Aruch, Orach Chaim* 307:2), and even if one does not mention the fee (*Beur Halachah* ibid.).

2. This ruling is obvious. Since his friend is himself a Jew, and is also forbidden to hire workers on the Sabbath, one may not cause him to commit a sin by telling him to do so. Rather, the lesson of this Mishnah is in its inference, that the prohibition is only to explicitly *tell* another to hire workers. He may, however, say to his friend, "Let us see whether you will join me in the evening" — even though it is thereby understood that he wishes to hire him as a worker. This is permissible, since Scripture prohibits only speech, not thought. Since he merely intimates that he wishes to hire him, this is regarded, with respect to this halachah, as thought and not speech (*Rav* from Gemara 150a).

at the Sabbath boundary for the purpose of ***hiring workers or bringing produce*** after the Sabbath,[3] אֲבָל מַחְשִׁיךְ הוּא לִשְׁמוֹר — ***but one may go to await nightfall*** at the Sabbath boundary ***for*** the purpose of ***guarding*** his property after the Sabbath,[4] וּמֵבִיא פֵּירוֹת בְּיָדוֹ — ***and he may bring back produce in his hand.***[5] כְּלָל אָמַר אַבָּא שָׁאוּל כֹּל שֶׁאֲנִי זַכַּאי בַּאֲמִירָתוֹ רַשַּׁאי אֲנִי לְהַחְשִׁיךְ עָלָיו — ***Abba Shaul stated a general rule: Whatever I am permitted to discuss,***[6] ***I am permitted to await nightfall for it*** as well.[7]

NOTES

3. As we have learned (above, Mishnah 2:7), the Rabbis limited the distance one may travel on the Sabbath, forbidding a person from going farther than 2,000 *amos* [cubits] from the place he camps or from the edge of the city in which he resides on the Sabbath. This limit is known as תְּחוּם שַׁבָּת, *the Sabbath boundary.* Thus, our Mishnah is teaching that a person may not go on the Sabbath to the end of his Sabbath boundary — i.e., to just within the limit of 2,000 *amos* — to await nightfall in order to reach the people he wishes to hire as soon after the Sabbath as possible, or to reach the field or orchard from which he wishes to take produce as soon after the Sabbath as possible. Since hiring workers and gathering produce are prohibited on the Sabbath, they fall into the category of the *wants* which one is prohibited from seeking on the Sabbath. Attending to the preliminaries necessary for the accomplishment of these objectives — e.g., by traveling toward their place on the Sabbath — constitutes *seeking your personal wants* (*Tos. Yom Tov* from *Rambam, Hil. Shabbos* 24:2).

4. I.e., he may await nightfall at the boundary in order to reach his field soon after the Sabbath to guard its produce. Since the act of guarding produce is permitted even on the Sabbath itself (if it is within the boundary), one may await nightfall at the boundary for that purpose (*Rashi*).

5. One who waited at the Sabbath boundary to be able to guard his produce after nightfall may, upon returning home, bring some produce with him. This is permitted because his intent was primarily to guard his produce, not to bring it (*Rav; Rashi*).

6. I.e., whatever I may instruct someone on the Sabbath to do either after the Sabbath — such as to bring a coffin and shrouds for the dead (see following Mishnah) — or on the Sabbath itself — such as to watch produce within his boundary (*Rav; Rashi; Tosafos* to 151a).

7. The Tanna Kamma permits awaiting nightfall at the Sabbath boundary only for acts permissible on the Sabbath, whether those acts are optional or mitzvah-related. Abba Shaul's rule, however, permits awaiting nightfall for matters of mitzvah (viz., attending to the needs of the deceased, etc., as explained in the next Mishnah), under all circumstances — i.e., even though they may not actually be attended to on the Sabbath. Abba Shaul's reasoning is that since Scripture prohibits only *seeking your personal wants,* the implication is that the wants of Heaven — i.e., mitzvah matters — may be pursued on the Sabbath. We may therefore await nightfall at the boundary for such purposes (*Tos. Yom Tov* from Gemara 150a). The Tanna Kamma, however, restricts awaiting nightfall even for purposes of a mitzvah. Accordingly, the next Mishnah, that permits awaiting nightfall at the boundary to attend to the affairs of a bride or the affairs of a deceased, accords with Abba Shaul, not the Tanna Kamma (*Rav; Rashi; Tosafos* to 151a; cf. *Meiri*).

GEMS FROM THE GEMARA

Our Mishnah deals only with produce that is still attached to the ground, or with detached produce that is for some reason *muktzeh.* Since one is forbidden to pick the produce or to move it on the Sabbath, his awaiting nightfall for that purpose is also prohibited.

If the produce is within the Sabbath boundary, one may go to it on the Sabbath in order to pick it after nightfall. Since he does not go to the limits of the Sabbath boundary, it is not apparent that his traveling is for picking produce. Such travel was therefore not banned (*Tiferes Yisrael* from *Shulchan Aruch* 307:9).

The Gemara (150b), elaborating on our Mishnah, states that if the produce he wishes to bring in from the field is detached and not *muktzeh,* but it is beyond the Sabbath boundary, one is permitted to await nightfall at the boundary to take it immediately after the Sabbath. This is because the hauling of such produce is only *circumstantially,* not *intrinsically,* prohibited — i.e., the act of transporting detached non-*muktzeh* produce is permissible under certain circumstances. An example is when there is a wall or an *eruv* enclosing the entire area between the field and the place to which one wishes to bring the produce. This would remove both the problem of carrying through a public domain or *karmelis* and the problem of traveling outside the *techum.* Therefore, even when the area is unenclosed, and one is consequently prohibited from transporting the produce, that prohibition is not *intrinsic* to the act of hauling, but is rather a product of circumstances, namely, the lack of an enclosure. Since the activity is not intrinsically prohibited, it cannot be defined as *seeking your wants,* which refers only to wants which are in themselves incompatible with Sabbath behavior. One is, however, prohibited from awaiting nightfall to take produce that is still growing or *muktzeh,* because no conceivable circumstances can be imagined that would enable one to engage in that activity on the Sabbath.

This rule applies as well to any other activity for which conceivable circumstances exist which would permit one to pick or transport that produce on the Sabbath. While circumstances may prohibit one from actually engaging in that activity, one is permitted to travel to the boundary to await nightfall in order to engage in it. Similarly, one is permitted to discuss performing such an act, as long as one does not say that he intends to do so in a prohibited manner. For example, one may say that he intends to bring his produce in from the field after the Sabbath, as long as he does not specify that he will carry it through a public domain.

פרשת תצוה

TUESDAY

PARASHAS TETZAVEH

A MUSSAR THOUGHT FOR THE DAY

The Gemara (*Arachin* 16a) says that the *Me'il* is worn to bring atonement for the sin of *lashon hara* (harmful speech). In the words of the Gemara: Let an item like a bell, that gives off sound, come and atone for a sin done with sound.

It seems interesting that to atone for a sin done with sound, the Torah commands the Kohen Gadol to wear something that produces sound. Seemingly, the atonement should come from something that does not make any sound, to teach a person not to make those improper sounds!

The *Chofetz Chaim* would often say that the Torah does not want a person to act like a mute and refrain from speech altogether. On the contrary, the Torah gave us the gift of speech as the power which elevates us over the animals. When the verse states in *Bereishis* (2:7): וַיְהִי הָאָדָם לְנֶפֶשׁ חַיָּה, *and man became a living soul, Targum Onkelos* translates the phrase *a living soul* as: רוּחַ מְמַלְּלָא, *a creature able to speak.* The Torah does not want us to neglect or ignore this ability. Instead, we must safeguard it and be sure to use it only for holy things such as Torah, prayer, and helping others.

The Chofetz Chaim says, though, that we must learn a lesson not only from the bells of the *Me'il,* but also from the woolen pomegranates that hung from its hem along with the bells. The *Me'il* was adorned with both of these items to teach us a double lesson. The bells give off sound and make noise, to allude that the Torah wants us to use our power of speech for Torah and prayer. However, when we are not learning or praying, we must take on the attribute of the silent pomegranates, and cherish silence. As R' Shimon says in *Avos* (1:17): כָּל יָמַי גָּדַלְתִּי בֵּין הַחֲכָמִים וְלֹא מָצָאתִי לְגוּף טוֹב אֶלָּא שְׁתִיקָה, *I was brought up my entire life in the company of the Sages, and I found no better trait than* שְׁתִיקָה, *silence.* Thus, both lessons are available to us, to be learned from the hem of the *Me'il.*

It is well-known that the Chofetz Chaim would constantly speak to people, both individuals and groups, about the importance of *shemiras halashon,* guarding one's speech. Although he dedicated his life to spreading awareness of the evils of *lashon hara* and to halting the spread of evil gossip, he himself did not spend his days in solitude, without speaking to people. He taught that a person must take control of his speech and know when to be a פַּעֲמוֹן (*bell*), to give off the sound of Torah, and when to be a רִמּוֹן (*pomegranate*) and adopt the trait of שְׁתִיקָה. He lived as he preached, and was either speaking words of Torah to strengthen his fellow Jews, or engaged in prayer.

The stone that represented Binyamin on the *Choshen* was called יָשְׁפֵה, *yoshfei.* The commentators explain that the name of this stone is expounded and read as two words: יֵשׁ פֶּה *(yeish peh), there is a mouth.* This is a reference to the fact that Binyamin did not reveal to Yaakov that Yosef was still alive, although he possessed this information and was never forbidden to reveal it. He knew, however, that if Hashem did not reveal it to Yaakov, it was not his place to do so either. As a reward, Binyamin merited the stone of *yoshfei.* Now, one might ask: for not using his mouth, why would Binyamin be rewarded with a stone whose name means *there is a mouth*? The commentators answer, as we have explained, that one can be considered a true owner of his mouth when he demonstrates that he understands when to use it and when to remain silent. Such a person truly has the gift of speech. Someone who has no guidelines, and speaks whenever he decides to do so, is abusing the power of speech. He does not truly possess the gift of speech, because he does not control it.

Kli Yakar notes that the *Me'il* teaches another lesson regarding proper speech. As the Gemara (*Arachin* 15b) states: Hashem gave our mouth two gates — the lips and the teeth — to remind us to think twice before we speak. The opening at the neck of the *Me'il* also had such a "gate," for the Torah tells us that the neckline of the *Me'il* was woven in double thickness so there would be a border around the opening. The Torah describes this border as שָׂפָה יִהְיֶה לְפִיו, which literally means, *a lip to its mouth.* And the Torah issues a prohibition regarding it — לֹא יִקָּרֵעַ, *it shall not be torn*! This lesson must be taken to heart with regard to our speech as well. We must always be vigilant, and not allow ourselves to lose control and commit sins through speech.

HALACHAH OF THE DAY

The next of the thirty-nine *avos melachos* is the *melachah* of שׁוֹחֵט, *slaughtering.* As is the case with all of the thirty-nine forbidden labors, *slaughtering* was an activity performed during construction of the Mishkan. Prior to constructing the Mishkan, rams and other animals were slaughtered in order to provide the skins that were used to make the roof-coverings of the Mishkan.

The *melachah* of *slaughtering,* in respect to the laws of Shabbos, is defined as the taking of any life, whether animal or bird, fish or reptile, wild or domestic. One who kills even the smallest insect may be in violation of the *melachah* of *slaughtering.*

Under Torah law, the prohibition of *slaughtering* applies only when one kills a creature in order to derive benefit from it; for example, in order to consume it or to use its hide. The Sages, however, extended the prohibition to include even slaughtering any creature for no beneficial purpose at all. For this reason, one may not kill a living creature on Shabbos even if it is a purposeless act.

While the Hebrew word for slaughtering, שְׁחִיטָה, is generally associated with killing through the use of a blade, the prohibited *melachah* includes any form of killing at all.

Removing a fish from water is a violation of the *melachah* of *slaughtering,* because this will cause the fish to suffocate and expire. If one removes the fish from water long enough for the liquid between its fins to begin to dry out (it has reached this state if the liquid between the fins begins to adhere to one's finger, and is drawn after the finger in a sticky thread), he violates the *melachah* of *slaughtering* even if he replaces the fish in water before it dies. Since a fish that has been out of water for this length of time will certainly die, taking it out of water for this length of time is akin to killing it.

While until now we have defined the *melachah* of *slaughtering* as the taking of a life, the Sages derive from the verse that the drawing of blood from any living being is also prohibited under the *melachah* of *slaughtering.* The verse states (*Vayikra* 17:11): כִּי־נֶפֶשׁ הַבָּשָׂר בַּדָּם הִוא, *For the soul of the flesh is in the blood.* This verse teaches that the life-force of a living creature is contained in its blood. It therefore follows that causing blood to flow from a living creature is akin to removing some of its life — a violation of the *melachah* of *slaughtering.*

The Biblical prohibition against the drawing of blood applies only if the blood is drawn for some beneficial purpose (such as blood drawn for testing purposes). The Sages, however, forbade the drawing of blood even for non-beneficial purposes.

QUESTION OF THE DAY:

What was unique about the material of the Me'il?

For the answer, see page 236.

A CLOSER LOOK AT THE SIDDUR

Immediately before the opening blessing of *Shemoneh Esrei* we recite the following prayer: ה׳ שְׂפָתַי תִּפְתָּח וּפִי יַגִּיד תְּהִלָּתֶךָ, *My Lord, open my lips, that my mouth may declare Your praise.* It is a request (from the verse in *Tehillim* 51:17) to Hashem that He grant us the ability to pray properly.

The Gemara in *Berachos* (4b) raises a halachic issue with this practice. We know that one is forbidden to interrupt his prayer between the blessing of גָּאַל יִשְׂרָאֵל and the beginning of *Shemoneh Esrei.* Why is it permitted, then, to recite this verse from *Tehillim*? The Gemara answers that we consider this recital, along with *Shemoneh Esrei,* to be a תְּפִלָּה אֲרִיכְתָּא, *one long prayer.* Essentially, then, the Gemara is answering that reciting this verse is critical to our prayer and is therefore not considered an interruption.

We may ask: What is the meaning behind this verse, and why is it so important that it be recited before every *Shemoneh Esrei*?

The *Yaaros Devash* explains that when one recites this verse, he should have in mind that Hashem created his lips as guardians for his mouth, to protect him from speaking improperly, just as everyone has a lock on his door to protect himself from danger. Life and death can depend on what comes out of a person's mouth. The lips are like שְׁעָרִים, *gates;* the only way the שַׁעֲרֵי צֶדֶק, *righteous gates,* will open up for a person in prayer is if he safeguards the gates of his mouth and does not allow it to be easily opened to speak *lashon hara,* gossip, improper talk, mockery, lies etc., but reserves it for Torah, prayer, and words of kindness. He notes the hypocrisy of someone asking Hashem to open his lips in prayer, while during the rest of the day the floodgates of his lips are open wide, and he says whatever his heart desires, including sinful speech! The angels in heaven laugh at such a request.

This, too, is a powerful reminder of the need to safeguard our speech. Only if we are vigilant in how we speak are we entitled to ask Hashem to help us praise Him properly in prayer, and to help us ask Him in the correct manner for all of our personal needs.

In *A Mussar Thought for the Day,* we discussed how the *Me'il* teaches us the correct manner of speech. The *Chofetz Chaim* cites a beautiful homiletic interpretation of the verse containing this very idea. The verse states concerning the *Me'il* (*Shemos* 28:35): וְהָיָה עַל־אַהֲרֹן לְשָׁרֵת וְנִשְׁמַע קוֹלוֹ בְּבֹאוֹ אֶל־הַקֹּדֶשׁ לִפְנֵי ה׳ וּבְצֵאתוֹ וְלֹא יָמוּת, *It shall be upon Aharon in order to serve, and its sound shall be heard when he enters the Holy before HASHEM and when he leaves, so that he not die.* The Chofetz Chaim

explains as follows: If a person will wear the lessons of the *Me'il* — that is, if he uses his power of speech properly and speaks when he should and keeps silent when he should — then "his voice will be heard when he comes to the Holy," i.e., his prayers will be hearkened to. And when such a person leaves this world, this will not be a real death for him; the Torah study and prayer that he performed with his pure mouth will help him to merit eternal life, because every word of Torah and prayer that was uttered by a person endures forever. His words, spoken with *kedushah,* will help to elevate him to the place of his eternal reward.

[It is worthwhile to note that proper guarding of one's speech is not only a prerequisite for acceptance of one's prayers. Torah study that is performed with a mouth soiled by speech-related sins is also adversely affected. The Chofetz Chaim mentions in several places that keeping one's mouth pure raises his Torah study to a much higher level.]

A TORAH THOUGHT FOR THE DAY

וּבִגְדֵי הַקֹּדֶשׁ אֲשֶׁר לְאַהֲרֹן יִהְיוּ לְבָנָיו אַחֲרָיו לְמָשְׁחָה בָהֶם וּלְמַלֵּא־בָם אֶת־יָדָם. שִׁבְעַת יָמִים יִלְבָּשָׁם הַכֹּהֵן תַּחְתָּיו מִבָּנָיו אֲשֶׁר יָבֹא אֶל־אֹהֶל מוֹעֵד לְשָׁרֵת בַּקֹּדֶשׁ

The holy vestments of Aharon shall belong to his sons after him, to become elevated through them, to become inaugurated through them. For a seven-day period, the Kohen who succeeds him from his sons, who shall enter the Tent of Meeting to serve in the Holy, shall don them (*Shemos* 29:29-30).

The Torah tells us that Aharon, to be inaugurated as Kohen Gadol, was to wear the *bigdei Kehunah Gedolah* — the Kohen Gadol's vestments — and be anointed with שֶׁמֶן הַמִּשְׁחָה (*shemen hamishchah*), *the anointing oil,* for seven days. With respect to the instruction to wear these vestments for seven days, *Rashi* comments that these days must be consecutive.

The commentaries address the question: From where did *Rashi* know this to be so? Perhaps the Torah is just stating that the wearing of the vestments and being anointed must be done for a total of seven days. Where is it made clear that the days must be consecutive?

R' Eliyahu Mizrachi suggests that *Rashi* derives the need for consecutive days from a different commandment — Moshe's instructions to Aharon during the period of the Mishkan's inauguration. The verse relates that Moshe told Aharon (*Vayikra* 8:35): וּפֶתַח אֹהֶל מוֹעֵד תֵּשְׁבוּ יוֹמָם וָלַיְלָה שִׁבְעַת יָמִים, *At the entrance of the Tent of Meeting you shall dwell day and night, for a seven-day period.* Since the verse states that Aharon was to dwell there day and night, this clearly implies a continuous period of time. And just as the Mishkan's inauguration was performed during a set, consecutive period of time, it can be deduced that Aharon's personal inauguration for service in the Mishkan was no different.

Maharal and *HaKesav VeHaKabbalah* take a different approach. They explain that *Rashi's* source for the need for the seven days to be consecutive is from the Torah's wording in our verse. Instead of commanding Aharon to wear the vestments for שִׁבְעָה יָמִים, *seven days,* the Torah employs a different expression – שִׁבְעַת יָמִים, *a seven-day period.* These commentaries explain that whenever the Torah uses this syntax [for example שִׁבְעַת יָמִים מַצּוֹת תֹּאכֵלוּ, *For a seven-day period you shall eat matzos* (*Shemos* 12:15)], it is not instructing simply that something must be done for a number of days. Rather, by adding the letter ת to the end of a number —

making שִׁבְעָה into שִׁבְעַת — the Torah changes the meaning of the phrase, giving it an entirely new implication. Instead of the number simply being used to express a quantity of units (in this case, days), thus commanding Aharon to wear the *bigdei Kehunah* for *seven days*, the added ת transforms the phrase into a noun describing a unit that is larger than the combined sum of its parts. Thus, שִׁבְעַת יָמִים does not mean *seven days*, but *a seven-day period;* Aharon was commanded to wear these vestments for this unit of time.

This definition of שִׁבְעַת יָמִים, commanding Aharon to wear these vestments for a single seven-day unit of time, conclude *Maharal* and *HaKesav VeHaKabbalah*, is the source for *Rashi's* explanation that the days on which Aharon was commanded to wear the *bigdei Kehunah* had to be consecutive.

Tzror HaMor provides an insight into *why* Aharon was in fact commanded to wear the *bigdei Kehunah* for seven consecutive days. He notes that the verse states (*Shemos* 29:35): וְעָשִׂיתָ לְאַהֲרֹן וּלְבָנָיו כָּכָה כְּכֹל אֲשֶׁר־צִוִּיתִי אֹתָכָה שִׁבְעַת יָמִים תְּמַלֵּא יָדָם, *You shall do thus for Aharon and his sons, like everything that I have commanded you; for a seven-day period you shall inaugurate them. Tzror HaMor* (see also *Rabbeinu Bachya* to *Shemos* 38:21) explains that the purpose of the Mishkan was to bring humanity closer to the lofty relationship that we enjoyed with Hashem prior to Adam's sin. Thus, every facet of the Mishkan — and ultimately, the sacrificial service as well — was designed to rebuild the spiritual aspects of the world that Hashem created, and that Adam, through his sin, damaged. Accordingly, the world that was created in seven days required a seven-day inauguration period for these foundations to be recreated, in order to achieve a renewed spiritual relationship with Hashem. The Mishkan, which would fulfill this purpose, therefore needed seven days of inauguration. It is perhaps for this reason that the Torah specifically commanded that the days when Aharon donned the *bigdei Kehunah* to become inaugurated as Kohen Gadol be a consecutive *seven-day period* as well. Since seven days was the time period used to create the world, it was also the unit needed for Aharon to become inaugurated for the job that would help rebuild the spiritual world anew.

QUESTION OF THE DAY:

Which Torah prohibition was overridden when the bigdei Kehunah were worn?

For the answer, see page 236.

MISHNAH OF THE DAY: SHABBOS 23:4

As we learned at the end of the previous Mishnah, one is permitted to await nightfall at the boundary of his Sabbath residence for the purpose of the affairs of Heaven even when he is forbidden to do so for his own purposes. The coming Mishnah illustrates that ruling:

מַחְשִׁיכִין עַל הַתְּחוּם לְפַקֵּחַ עַל עִסְקֵי כַלָּה — ***We may await nightfall at the*** Sabbath ***boundary to oversee the affairs of a bride,***[1] **וְעַל עִסְקֵי הַמֵּת לְהָבִיא לוֹ אָרוֹן וְתַכְרִיכִים** — ***or for the affairs of a deceased person,*** such as ***to bring a coffin and shrouds for him.***[2]

The Mishnah considers other laws that concern preparations for a funeral on the Sabbath:

נָכְרִי שֶׁהֵבִיא חֲלִילִין בְּשַׁבָּת — If ***a non-Jew brought flutes on the Sabbath,***[3] **לֹא יִסְפּוֹד בָּהֶן יִשְׂרָאֵל** — ***a Jew may not bewail with them*** after the Sabbath,[4] **אֶלָּא אִם כֵּן בָּאוּ מִמָּקוֹם קָרוֹב** — ***unless they came from a nearby place.***[5] **עָשׂוּ לוֹ אָרוֹן וְחָפְרוּ לוֹ קֶבֶר** — If ***[non-Jews] made a coffin for him, or dug a grave for him*** on the Sabbath,[6] **יִקָּבֵר בּוֹ יִשְׂרָאֵל** —

NOTES

1. I.e., to ascertain what is necessary for her forthcoming nuptials (*Rav*).

2. Even if the coffin and shrouds are not yet made, so that there is forbidden labor involved in their preparation, one may nevertheless await nightfall at the boundary to arrange for it, since it is a mitzvah matter.

This is in accordance with the view of Abba Shaul (see the previous Mishnah). According to the Tanna Kamma of the previous Mishnah, one may not await nightfall at the boundary for an act forbidden on the Sabbath, even if one is doing so for a mitzvah.

3. He brought the flutes for a Jew to use at a funeral (*Rashi*). The sound of these flutes aroused wailing and mourning (*Rambam Commentary*), and it was customary to play them at funeral processions (*Rav; Tiferes Yisrael*).

4. They may not be used even after the Sabbath, because it is possible that the flutes were brought from beyond the Sabbath boundary (*Tiferes Yisrael*). *Rashi* states that since it is obvious that the flutes were expressly brought for the funeral (as these instruments were not used for other purposes), the Rabbis penalized those involved by forever banning their use for *any* Jewish funeral. However, according to most authorities, the ban lasts only as long as would be required to obtain new ones after the Sabbath. After that time, one no longer benefits from the desecration of the Sabbath, since he could, in any case, have obtained new ones. There is, therefore, no reason to prohibit the use of those brought on the Sabbath (*Tosafos; Rambam, Hil. Shabbos* 6:6; *Ran*).

5. I.e., unless we are certain that they came from a place within the Sabbath boundary (*Rav*).

6. I.e., if non-Jews constructed coffins or dug graves on the Sabbath for their own purposes, either to bury another non-Jew or to sell (*Rav; Rashi*).

a Jew may be interred in it.[7] וְאִם בִּשְׁבִיל יִשְׂרָאֵל — ***But if*** they did it ***for a Jew,***[8] לֹא יִקָּבֵר בּוֹ עוֹלָמִית — ***he may never be interred in it.***[9]

NOTES

7. I.e., immediately after the Sabbath (*Ran*).

8. I.e., if the non-Jews constructed the coffin or dug the grave on the Sabbath expressly for a Jew.

9. I.e., the Jew for whom the coffin was made, or for whom the grave was dug, may never be buried in it. [Other Jews may be buried in it after enough time has elapsed to have dug the grave or built the coffin after the Sabbath (*Rashba; Meiri; Shulchan Aruch, Orach Chaim* 325:14).]

GEMS FROM THE GEMARA

Our Mishnah taught that if a non-Jew brought flutes on the Sabbath for use at a Jewish funeral, a Jew may not bewail with them, unless we are certain that they came from a place within the Sabbath boundary (see *Rav*). This follows the explanation of the Mishnah offered by the Amora Rav in the Gemara (151a), who understands the Mishnah to be permitting only flutes that we know were in the non-Jew's house, within the city. Shmuel, however, differs with Rav, and explains the Mishnah as permitting even the use of flutes that were brought from outside the city, since they *may* have been brought from within the Sabbath boundary. According to Shmuel, the only flutes that may not be used are those that are *known* to have been brought from outside the boundary (*Rashi*).

Other *Rishonim* explain the dispute of Rav and Shmuel differently. In their view, Rav's opinion is the more lenient one, as he rules that as long as we see that the non-Jew brought the flutes from his house on the Sabbath day, we may assume that they were there from before the Sabbath, and they may therefore be used after the Sabbath. Shmuel, however, disagrees, and maintains that the fact that the non-Jew brought them from his house on the Sabbath day does not prove that they were there from the onset of the Sabbath, for it is possible that they were brought from outside the Sabbath boundary on Friday night. According to this interpretation, Shmuel's view is the more stringent of the two (*Rif* as explained by *Ran; Rambam, Hil. Shabbos* 6:6 as explained by *Maggid Mishneh*).

It should be noted that if the flutes were definitely brought from within the Sabbath boundary, they may be used immediately after the Sabbath, even though they were carried through a public domain. *Tosafos* account for this leniency by stating that since they were brought from nearby, one saves very little time, and therefore derives little benefit, from their having been brought on the Sabbath. The Rabbis therefore did not require a person to wait that small amount of time before using them after the Sabbath. Other authorities, however, rule that if they were carried through a public domain, they may indeed not be used until the time when they could have been brought from that place after nightfall (*Tos. Yom Tov* from *Ran, Rambam* and *Tur* §325).

A MUSSAR THOUGHT FOR THE DAY

We explained in *A Torah Thought for the Day* that an inherent difference exists between the phrase שִׁבְעָה יָמִים, *seven days,* and the similar phrase שִׁבְעַת יָמִים, which means *a seven-day period;* while the former is a tally of individual units of days, the latter is a new unit that is greater than the sum of its individual parts. The *Telzer Rav* and *R' Chaim Shmulevitz* explain that the difference between individual units and a greater, uninterrupted whole is best illustrated by an episode that the Gemara (*Kesubos* 62b) relates about the Tanna R' Akiva.

R' Akiva was an unlearned forty-year-old shepherd when he married his wife Rachel, and, at her urging, he traveled to learn Torah and spent many years away from home. After twelve years of continuous Torah study, R' Akiva, already a great Torah scholar, decided to return home. As he approached the entrance to his house, he overheard a neighbor telling his wife, "Until when will you continue to live as a widow? It has already been twelve years that you have not seen your husband!" As R' Akiva stood there listening, he heard his wife respond, "If it were up to me, he would spend another twelve years fully immersed in Torah study!" At once, R' Akiva turned around and returned to yeshivah, and did not come home for another twelve years, thus spending a total of twenty-four years immersed in uninterrupted Torah study.

It is understandable, comment the *Telzer Rav* and *R' Chaim Shmulevitz,* why, after hearing his wife's encouraging words, R' Akiva chose to return to the yeshivah; his great desire to study Torah, coupled with his wife's unswerving self-sacrifice and encouragement, allowed him to devote many years of his life to uninterrupted Torah study. However, if he was already standing on his doorstep, why did he have to turn around and go back immediately? Could he not spare the few moments it would have taken him to enter his house and greet his wife, who had done so much for him, and whom he had not seen in so many years? He could have returned to the yeshivah after a brief reunion. Why did he choose not to even enter the house?

The answer to this question, explain the Telzer Rav and R' Chaim Shmulevitz, is that twelve years of Torah study plus another twelve years of Torah study is not the same as an uninterrupted twenty-four years of Torah study. There is no question that, after spending a few moments at home, R' Akiva would once again have traveled to his yeshivah to spend a second twelve years studying Torah. However, doing so would have started a new era, for the enthusiasm and momentum of the first, twelve-year period of study would have concluded when he entered his house. Upon his return to yeshivah, the development of the attachment to Torah that can be acquired only through twelve years of uninterrupted study would have had to be started anew. The second twelve years would not have been a continuation of the first. Even though the minutes of time spent in study of two twelve-year periods of Torah study are perhaps identical to the minutes spent in a twenty-four-year period of study, Torah that is learned when having to begin once again cannot be compared to Torah that is learned while one is immersed in a framework of continuous Torah study. [R' Chaim Shmulevitz comments that it is clear that R' Akiva understood that his wife would have agreed with this assessment, for, had he felt that she might not, it is inconceivable that R' Akiva, who later told his wife, "All the Torah that I and my students have studied is because of you," in total gratitude, would not have entered the house and asked her permission. Rather, he understood that her devotion to his total continued immersion in Torah overcame her desire to see her husband even after their long separation.]

R' Chaim Shmulevitz provides a practical example of the difference between two groups of twelve and one uninterrupted unit of twenty-four — boiling a kettle of water. A person who puts a kettle on the fire for five-minute periods, only to remove it and once again place it onto the fire after several more minutes, will never obtain any boiling water, even if the flame is intense. It is only when the pot is left on the flame for an extended period of time that the water will become boiled. The same is true with Torah study. Although we are of course unable to devote twenty-four uninterrupted years to toil in Torah, as did R' Akiva, it is axiomatic that uninterrupted periods of learning are much more valuable than fragmented ones, even if the amounts of time spent are identical.

HALACHAH OF THE DAY

As we discussed yesterday, the drawing of blood from a living creature is forbidden as part of the *melachah* of *slaughtering.*

Inflicting a bruise upon a human being, or any other living creature that possesses a thick skin or hide, is a violation of the prohibition against the drawing of blood even if there is no apparent loss of blood resulting from the bruise. This is because the characteristic discoloration of a bruise is the result of blood seeping from blood vessels that have ruptured beneath the surface of the skin. While this blood does not drain outside the body, neither is it reabsorbed into the bloodstream; the body eliminates it through natural processes. Thus, we can see that bruising involves the removal of some blood from the body. It is therefore forbidden as part of the *melachah* of *slaughtering.*

There are instances where killing is permissible on Shabbos. One may kill any animal or insect that poses a danger to human life, even if the creature is not presently pursuing anyone, and even if the creature is trying to run away. Some examples of animals that may be killed are: a mad dog, a snake that may be venomous, a scorpion, a bee in the presence of someone who is allergic to its sting, and insects that may be carrying dangerous diseases (e.g., mosquitoes in certain areas, or certain types of ticks).

Animals and insects that do not pose a danger to life, but whose bites can cause severe injury, may be killed on Shabbos only if they are pursuing someone. If they are not presently pursuing anyone, they may not be killed.

While the killing of any animal or insect is generally forbidden on Shabbos, there are *poskim* who maintain that lice are an exception to this rule, and they may be killed on Shabbos. Therefore, if lice are causing a person pain on Shabbos, the lice may be killed in accordance with the opinion of these *poskim,* in order to alleviate the pain.

Now that we have discussed the principles that govern this *melachah,* we will begin to analyze some practical applications of these prohibitions.

If one is confronted by a swarm of insects that are not dangerous, such as a swarm of common ants, he may not kill them. However, if he is disgusted by them and is worried that they may spread, he may place or spray poison *around* the area in which the insects are found, to prevent them from spreading further. If at all possible, the poison should be placed by a non-Jew.

A CLOSER LOOK AT THE SIDDUR

The Gemara (*Yoma* 5a) understands the Torah's commandment: לְמָשְׁחָה בָהֶם, literally, *to be anointed in them,* to be teaching that Aharon and all future Kohanim Gedolim were anointed for seven days as part of their inauguration ceremony (see *A Taste of Lomdus*). Nevertheless, *Rashi* explains the words לְמָשְׁחָה בָהֶם to be connected to the verse's earlier mention of the vestments of Aharon, and he translates the verse as saying that the garments are to be worn by the Kohen Gadol ***to become elevated through them.***

This usage of the word לְמָשְׁחָה (and its cognate forms), explains *Rashi,* is also found in a verse that we recite in the *tefillah* of *Hodu,* during *Pesukei D'Zimrah*: אַל־תִּגְּעוּ בִּמְשִׁיחָי וּבִנְבִיאַי אַל־תָּרֵעוּ, *Dare not touch My esteemed ones, and to My prophets do no harm* (*I Divrei HaYamim* 16:22). This verse speaks of Hashem's warnings to Pharaoh and Avimelech not to harm Sarah and to return her to Avraham (as is described in *Bereishis* 12:15-17 and 20:2-3). [This is evident from the verses that precede it in *Divrei HaYamim* (vs. 19-21): בִּהְיוֹתְכֶם מְתֵי מִסְפָּר כִּמְעַט וְגָרִים בָּהּ. וַיִּתְהַלְּכוּ מִגּוֹי אֶל־גּוֹי וּמִמַּמְלָכָה אֶל־עַם אַחֵר. לֹא־הִנִּיחַ לְאִישׁ לְעָשְׁקָם וַיּוֹכַח עֲלֵיהֶם מְלָכִים, *When you were few in number, hardly dwelling there, and they wandered from nation to nation, and from one kingdom to another people; He allowed no man to rob them, and He rebuked kings for their sake.*] Since Avraham was of course never anointed, מְשִׁיחָי cannot be understood to mean *My anointed ones.* Rather, maintains *Rashi,* the proper translation is *My esteemed ones.*

Ramban argues with *Rashi,* explaining that while it is unquestionably true that since holders of important Jewish positions — such as the king and the Kohen Gadol — are anointed with *shemen hamishchah,* anointing oil, the term can be used in a borrowed sense to refer to any position of power, even those that do not involve actual anointment. Thus, he argues that the literal translation of לְמָשְׁחָה is not, as *Rashi* explains, *to become elevated;* rather, it indeed means *to be anointed.* This, stresses *Ramban* (as explained by *Shaarei Aharon*), is especially true in our verse, which refers to the Kohen Gadol; for the Gemara in fact states that the Kohen Gadol was anointed as part of his inauguration ceremony. *Ramban* therefore understands the words לְמָשְׁחָה בָהֶם in our verse to mean *to be anointed in them;* and aside from teaching us the law that a Kohen Gadol is anointed during his inauguration, the Torah is also teaching us that this anointing must be performed while he is wearing the *bigdei Kehunah Gedolah.*

Ramban concludes by offering an explanation of why Hashem's warning to Pharaoh and Avimelech was couched in terms of אַל־תִּגְּעוּ בִמְשִׁיחָי, *Dare not touch my anointed ones.* Although it is true that Avraham was never anointed, the warning not to harm Sarah was not given only to protect Avraham from harm. Rather, since Sarah was the matriarch of the entire Jewish nation, Hashem was warning Pharaoh and Avimelech that although they would of course be held culpable for *any* attack on a married woman, the gravity of attacking Sarah was far greater. For any abuse that Sarah would suffer at their hands would have corrupted the purity of the entire Bnei Yisrael, including *the anointed ones,* i.e., the kings that Sarah — through her lofty descendants — would ultimately bear.

A TASTE OF LOMDUS

The Gemara in *Yoma* (5a) states that the verses in Chapter 29 of *Shemos* that describe the order of Aharon's inauguration as Kohen Gadol teach the laws of inaugurating future Kohanim Gedolim as well. Just as Aharon, in order to be inaugurated as Kohen Gadol, required seven consecutive days of wearing the *bigdei Kehunah Gedolah* (the Kohen Gadol's vestments), and seven consecutive days of anointment with *shemen hamishchah* (the anointing oil), the Torah is teaching that these criteria also apply to Aharon's descendants who will fill his role as Kohen Gadol in future generations. They too are enjoined to wear the vestments and be anointed with the oil for seven days. The Gemara continues, stating that although ideally a newly appointed Kohen Gadol is commanded to wear the *bigdei Kehunah Gedolah* and be anointed for seven days, in a case where the new Kohen Gadol wore the *bigdei Kehunah Gedolah* for seven days but was anointed with the *shemen hamishchah* for only one day, or was anointed for the full period but only wore the *bigdei Kehunah Gedolah* on the day that he served as Kohen Gadol, his service is acceptable nonetheless. (The Gemara derives this from a verse in *Parashas Acharei Mos;* see there for the exact Scriptural exegesis.)

Rambam and *Raavad* (*Hilchos Klei HaMikdash* 4:13) differ as to when the guidelines described in this Gemara apply. *Rambam* maintains that these laws are absolute; a Kohen Gadol who did not perform at least one of the inauguration elements — seven days of anointing or seven days of wearing the *bigdei Kehunah Gedolah* — is prohibited from serving as

Kohen Gadol. It is only when he fulfills at least one of these conditions that his service is acceptable after the fact. *Raavad* argues, maintaining that this Gemara understands the Torah's instructions to be specifically speaking about the Kohen Gadol's service on Yom Kippur. Thus, it is only for these duties to be acceptable that the Kohen Gadol must have completed at least one of the inauguration elements of seven days (either wearing *bigdei Kehunah Gedolah* or anointment). The rest of the year, however, a new Kohen Gadol is permitted to perform the service in the *Beis HaMikdash* in the full *bigdei Kehunah Gedolah* starting from the first day of his inauguration process, and he need not wait seven days.

The commentaries struggle to explain *Raavad's* distinction between Yom Kippur and the rest of the year. If the Gemara stated that the new Kohen Gadol must wait seven days to complete at least one element of inauguration before beginning to officiate as Kohen Gadol, why should this law apply only to Yom Kippur?

R' Chaim Soloveitchik explains *Raavad's* opinion as follows: Since the only time that the Torah is particular that the service be performed specifically by the Kohen Gadol is on Yom Kippur (many aspects of the Yom Kippur service are valid only when performed by the Kohen Gadol), during other times, a Kohen Gadol, strictly speaking, is not needed. While it is true that during the rest of the year the Kohen Gadol is given priority in performing any service in the *Beis HaMikdash* that he desires, Temple service is not exclusive to a Kohen Gadol and can be performed just as well by a regular Kohen. This being the case, there is no reason why the soon-to-be Kohen Gadol should not serve in the *Beis HaMikdash* during his inauguration period, for during the week that he begins wearing *bigdei Kehunah Gedolah* and is anointed each day, he remains an ordinary Kohen who is permitted to perform the *Beis HaMikdash* service. Accordingly, understands *Raavad,* the Gemara stating that the Temple service is valid only after a week of at least one of the inauguration elements (wearing *bigdei Kehunah Gedolah* or anointment with the *shemen hamishchah*) can be speaking only about a time when a Kohen Gadol is needed — namely, for the Yom Kippur service.

After explaining the opinion of *Raavad,* R' Chaim Soloveitchik notes an apparent difficulty with his explanation. The Gemara states that it was forbidden for a Kohen to perform the service in the *Beis HaMikdash* while wearing extra *bigdei Kehunah,* and any service performed while dressed in extra clothing was invalid. [Likewise, serving while dressed in too few *bigdei Kehunah* is also forbidden.] Although this law applies to an ordinary Kohen and a Kohen Gadol alike, the appropriate *bigdei*

Kehunah that must be worn varied according to the Kohen's station; a Kohen Gadol is liable only if he wears more than his eight specified garments, while an ordinary Kohen transgresses this prohibition if he performs the service in anything more than four garments. If this is the case, asks R' Chaim, how was the soon-to-be Kohen Gadol, who, as we explained, was still an ordinary Kohen for the week of his inauguration, allowed to serve in the full eight garments of the *bigdei Kehunah Gedolah*?

R' Chaim Soloveitchik explains that *Raavad* evidently understands the prohibition of serving in too many priestly garments differently. In his view, the prohibition to wear an inappropriate amount of vestments when serving in the *Beis HaMikdash* is not dependent on what kind of a Kohen this person is, for the prohibition is not defined as wearing *too many* vestments, but as wearing ***unnecessary*** vestments. Now, since the vestments that the soon-to-be Kohen Gadol wore were not *unnecessary* — for he was actually commanded to wear them for the week of his inauguration — performing the service in them would in no way violate the prohibition of serving in extra vestments.

פרשת תצוה

THURSDAY

PARASHAS TETZAVEH

A TORAH THOUGHT FOR THE DAY

וְהָיָה הַמִּזְבֵּחַ קֹדֶשׁ קָדָשִׁים כָּל־הַנֹּגֵעַ בַּמִּזְבֵּחַ יִקְדָּשׁ

The Altar shall be holy of holies; whatever touches the Altar shall become consecrated (*Shemos* 29:37).

R*ashi* explains that the two statements in the verse are connected. The Torah tells us that the Altar is holy. And in what way is this holiness manifest? In the fact that *whatever touches the Altar shall become consecrated.* This refers to the law that even a disqualified offering (for example, an offering that became *tamei*) that is mistakenly placed upon the Altar is thereby rendered fit to be burned upon the Altar, and is not removed.

R' Moshe Feinstein (in *Darash Moshe*) notes that in this verse, as well as in *Parashas Pekudei* (*Shemos* 40:10), the Altar is referred to as being "holy of holies." He asks: These verses refer to the *Outer* Altar, which was situated in the Courtyard of the Mishkan, outside the Sanctuary. Yet, the verse refers to that Altar as "holy of holies." The Inner Altar, by way of contrast, stood *inside* the Sanctuary, and yet the Torah (ibid. v. 9) refers to that Altar simply as being "holy"! What lesson can we derive from this?

R' Moshe offers two lessons that may be learned from the Torah's characterization of only the Outer Altar as "holy of holies." The first is that it is most important for one to ensure that his actions are above reproach when he is "outside the Sanctuary"; that is, when he is in the company of people who are not on his spiritual level. Thus, while one must always act properly, if his actions while he is in a Torah setting are "holy," when he is *not* in a Torah setting, they must be "holy of holies." For in such a setting he is likely to meet up with people whose standards are not as high as his, and he may be influenced by their ways.

How does one accomplish this? R' Moshe explains that when one does find himself in a true Torah setting, he must expend the effort to make Torah ideals and values truly a part of himself, so that he will not be subject to adverse influences even when he is away from spiritually superior circumstances. He must strive to emulate the example of the Altar, which had the power to consecrate whatever came into contact with it. A person whose Torah values have become part of his very fiber can do the same — he has the ability to inspire those who interact with him to repent of their sins and reach for higher levels in their service of Hashem.

The second lesson, says R' Moshe, is that one must always be cognizant of how others regard him. Every Torah student must realize that even if he is not viewed as the greatest Torah scholar in the circles of a yeshivah, the outside world will still view him as a representative of the Torah, and will judge the Torah by the way he acts. Thus, even one who is merely "holy" when he is inside the world of Torah must act outside those circles as if he is "holy of holies," so that he will increase the honor of Hashem and the Torah with his actions. This is a lesson that every Torah scholar should always bear in mind, for neglecting it can bring disgrace to the Name of Hashem.

For another lesson that can be learned from the Altar's ability to consecrate, see *A Mussar Thought for the Day.*

MISHNAH OF THE DAY: SHABBOS 23:5

This coming Mishnah considers how to deal with the body of a deceased person on the Sabbath:

עוֹשִׂין כָּל צָרְכֵי הַמֵּת — ***We may attend to all the needs of the deceased*** on the Sabbath:[1] סָכִין — ***We may anoint*** him with oil,[2] וּמְדִיחִין אוֹתוֹ — ***and rinse him*** with water, וּבִלְבַד שֶׁלֹּא יָזִיז בּוֹ אֵבֶר — ***provided we do not move any of his limbs.***[3] שׁוֹמְטִין אֶת הַכַּר מִתַּחְתָּיו — ***We may pull the pillow from under him*** וּמַטִּילִין אוֹתוֹ עַל הַחוֹל — ***and we may lay him on the sand,***[4] בִּשְׁבִיל שֶׁיַּמְתִּין — ***in order that*** his body ***remain moist.***[5] קוֹשְׁרִין אֶת הַלֶּחִי — ***We may bind up the***

NOTES

1. I.e., all that is necessary to retard the body's decomposition before the funeral, or to prevent its lying in an undignified state.

2. The body was anointed with balsam oil to mask the odor of decomposition (*Tiferes Yisrael*).

3. I.e., one may not lift a hand, a foot, or even an eyelid of the body (*Rashi*), because a corpse is *muktzeh.* [From here we learn that the prohibition against moving a *muktzeh* object applies to moving even a part of the object (see *Ramban, Ritva, Ran*). However, a corpse, as well as any other *muktzeh* object, may be *touched* on the Sabbath, as long as it is not moved (*Rav*).]

4. I.e., the pillow or mattress upon which the deceased is lying may be pulled out from under him, so the body will thereby be lying on the cool sand or dirt near his bed. However, since the Mishnah states above that not even one limb of the deceased may be moved, he may not be picked up to be placed on the sand (*Rav; Rambam Commentary*).

5. A body kept in a warm place decomposes more rapidly than one in a cool place. Since the pillows and the mattress keep the body relatively warm, the body is moved to the cooler dirt floor to retard the rate of decomposition (*Rav; Rashi; Aruch* cited by *Tos. Yom Tov; Tiferes Yisrael*).

פרשת תצוה

THURSDAY

PARASHAS TETZAVEH

jaw,[6] לֹא שֶׁיַּעֲלֶה — *not that it should rise,*[7] אֶלָּא שֶׁלֹּא יוֹסִיף — *but that it should not continue* to drop.[8]

The Mishnah considers a similar law:

וְכֵן קוֹרָה שֶׁנִּשְׁבְּרָה — ***And so too*** is the law in the case of ***a beam that broke:*** סוֹמְכִין אוֹתָהּ בְּסַפְסָל אוֹ בַאֲרוּכוֹת הַמִּטָּה — ***We may support it with a bench or with the side-pieces of a bed,***[9] לֹא שֶׁתַּעֲלֶה — ***not that it should rise,*** אֶלָּא שֶׁלֹּא תוֹסִיף — ***but that it should not continue*** to drop.[10]

The Mishnah returns to discussing how to deal with the body of a deceased person on the Sabbath:

אֵין מְעַמְּצִין אֶת הַמֵּת בְּשַׁבָּת — ***We may not close the eyes of the deceased on the Sabbath,***[11] וְלֹא בְחוֹל עִם יְצִיאַת נֶפֶשׁ — ***nor*** may we do so even ***on a weekday at the moment of death.***[12] וְהַמְעַמֵּץ עִם יְצִיאַת הַנֶּפֶשׁ — ***And whoever closes*** the eyes of a dying person ***with the departure of the soul,***[13] הֲרֵי זֶה שׁוֹפֵךְ דָּמִים — ***this*** person ***is a murderer.***[14]

NOTES

6. I.e., if the mouth had begun to sag open as a result of the relaxing of the muscles, the jaw may be bound up (*Rav; Rashi*).

7. I.e., not to close the part that has already opened, since, as stated above, no limb of a corpse may be moved on the Sabbath (*Rav; Tiferes Yisrael*).

8. I.e., one may tie a strip of cloth around the head and jaw tightly enough to prevent any further sagging of the jaw, but not so tightly as to force it closed.

9. One may move only a non-*muktzeh* item to support the broken beam. Therefore, a bench may be used, since it is a utensil and therefore not *muktzeh* (*Rav; Rashi*). The same is true of the side-pieces of a bed (*Tiferes Yisrael*).

10. I.e., the support may be inserted only to the level where it prevents the beam from sagging any lower. We may not wedge the bench in such a manner as to raise it toward its original position, since that is akin to building (*Rav; Rashi*).

11. One normally closes the eyes of a corpse before burial (*Yoreh Deah* 352:4). However, this is not done on the Sabbath, because moving an eyelid is the equivalent of moving a limb of the corpse — and, as we learned above, this is prohibited, because the corpse is *muktzeh* (*Rashi*).

12. This is prohibited because we fear that he may not be quite dead yet, but in a deep coma. In such a state, even the slightest movement can hasten his death (*Rav; Rashi*). One is obligated, therefore, to wait a while after the presumed moment of death before moving the body (*Tiferes Yisrael; Shulchan Aruch, Yoreh Deah* 339:1). [Not only may we not close the eyes, but we may not move any part of the body. The Mishnah mentions closing the eyes because it is customary to do so for the dead (*Tiferes Yisrael*).]

13. I.e., at the moment of death.

14. In such a state, even the slightest movement can hasten his death (*Rashi*). One must therefore wait an appropriate length of time before closing the eyes, since the "dead" person may in fact not yet be dead but merely unconscious (*Rambam, Hil. Aveilus* 4:5). If one does not wait, he is considered a murderer, because causing someone to die even a moment earlier than necessary is considered murder (*Rav; Rashi*).

GEMS FROM THE GEMARA

The Gemara (151b) challenges the Mishnah's ruling that allows the anointing or rinsing of a corpse on the Sabbath. The Gemara cites Rav Yehudah's statement in the name of Shmuel: There was an incident involving a student of R' Meir [*Yerushalmi* identifies the student as R' Shimon ben Elazar], who followed R' Meir into a bathhouse on the Sabbath. The student wanted to wash the floor of the bathhouse for R' Meir. R' Meir admonished him, "One may not wash!" The student then wanted to spread fragrant oil on the stones of the floor of the bathhouse, whereupon R' Meir said to him, "One may not spread!"

The Gemara initially assumes that the reason R' Meir forbade the student to spread oil on the floor was because the stones on the floor were *muktzeh,* and the student would be handling the stones while spreading oil on them. Why, then, does our Mishnah permit one to spread oil on a corpse, which is also *muktzeh*?

The Gemara answers that in fact it is permitted to spread oil on a *muktzeh* object as long as one does not move it, and for this reason one may spread oil on a corpse, as long as one takes care not to move it while doing so. The reason for R' Meir's instruction to the student not to spread oil on the stones of the floor was a different one. R' Meir held that if we were to permit the spreading of oil on a stone floor, a person might come to spread oil on a dirt floor, which *is* forbidden; we are concerned that a person will come to level out uneven spots in the floor — which is prohibited as a derivative of the *melachah* of *building.* [Although the only type of floor that a person would level out is a dirt floor, the Rabbis nevertheless banned washing or spreading oil on any type of floor, because people do not differentiate between one type of floor and another *(Rashi)*.] A corpse, however, is not associated with a floor. Even if one is allowed to spread oil on a corpse, he will not come to do so to a floor; therefore, the Sages did not forbid anointing a corpse with oil (as long as the corpse is not moved thereby).

QUESTION OF THE DAY:

How tall was the Outer Altar?

For the answer, see page 236.

A MUSSAR THOUGHT FOR THE DAY

In *A Torah Thought for the Day,* we mentioned the law that the Altar can consecrate even a disqualified offering, and render it fit to be burned before Hashem. *Rashi,* citing the Gemara in *Zevachim* (83a-84a), notes that this does not apply to all invalid sacrifices. While the Altar can render fit those offerings that became disqualified after they had already been consecrated (such as an offering that became *tamei,* or the sacrificial parts of an offering that were disqualified because they became left-over [*nossar*]), it cannot render fit those offerings whose disqualifications did not occur after a consecration (for example, an animal that was worshiped as a deity, or an animal that was blemished before it was consecrated).

We may ask: If the Altar is given the ability to render fit even those offerings that are unfit with severe invalidations such as *nossar* (an invalidation that carries a penalty of *kares,* Divinely imposed premature death, for one who eats of it), why can it not render fit animals that have disqualifications that are seemingly less severe, such as an animal that was blemished before it was consecrated?

R' Moshe Feinstein explains that an offering that once had valid consecration, even if it is now suffering from a severe flaw, is still inherently more fit for offering than an animal that could never be consecrated properly. For that reason, the Altar's touch can "cure" the once-consecrated offering, while it can do nothing for that which was never worthy.

R' Moshe draws a parallel to those wishing to repent. Although all repentance is accepted and cherished by Hashem, it is easier for one who once studied Torah to repent, even if his sins are great, for the holiness of the Torah that is within him will provide him with the impetus to do so. One who has never learned Torah, on the other hand, is less likely to repent, even if he has committed relatively minor transgressions.

R' Moshe cautions, therefore, that one should never make the mistake of thinking that it is not important to teach his children Torah because he reasons that they will not become Torah scholars in any event. The value of the holiness of Torah goes beyond the purpose of becoming a scholar, as its holiness helps to ensure that one will always be able to find the proper path in life, even if he strays along the way.

HALACHAH OF THE DAY

As we mentioned above, any form of killing is forbidden under the prohibition against *slaughtering.* It is, therefore, forbidden to throw an insect into water on Shabbos, because doing so will cause the insect to drown. For this reason, if an insect is found on a utensil on Shabbos, one may not place the utensil into a washbasin full of water in order to wash it. Likewise, one may not wash a vegetable that has an insect on it, because the washing will kill the insect. If one desires to remove the insect from the vegetable on Shabbos, he must cut off a piece of the vegetable upon which the insect is found and remove it along with the insect, in order to avoid transgressing the *melachah* of *borer,* selecting.

If an insect is located in a toilet, the toilet may be flushed in order to flush away the waste matter, even though the insect will be killed as a result of the flush. However, this is permitted only in cases where this is necessary in order to maintain human dignity.

One may spray insecticide in the room of a sick person or baby in order to drive insects away from the occupant. One should exercise care not to spray the insecticide directly on the insects, so as not to kill them through a direct act. Additionally, one must leave a door or window open, in order to allow them a possible way to escape the deadly fumes.

We will now turn our attention to some practical applications of the prohibition against drawing blood on Shabbos.

It is forbidden to remove a scab from a wound on Shabbos if this will cause the wound to bleed. If removal of the scab will not cause the wound to bleed, the scab may be removed.

Extracting teeth typically causes bleeding. It is therefore forbidden to pull teeth on Shabbos.

One may not use a toothpick on Shabbos if he knows that use of the pick will cause his gums to bleed. If one is unsure whether or not the toothpick will cause bleeding, he may use it on Shabbos.

A Jewish doctor may not draw blood on Shabbos from a patient who is not seriously ill, even if this entails no more than a simple finger prick. However, one may draw blood for medical purposes from a patient who is, or who may be, seriously ill. This is permitted even if the results of the blood work will not be known for several days. [Where blood must be drawn on Shabbos, it is preferable (when medically acceptable) to draw all the required blood at one time, as each puncture to draw blood is another violation of the *melachah.*]

One may not suck blood from a wound on Shabbos.

פרשת תצוה

THURSDAY

PARASHAS TETZAVEH

A CLOSER LOOK AT THE SIDDUR

This week, we will continue our discussion of the twelfth of the Thirteen Fundamental Principles (י"ג עיקרים) enumerated by *Rambam,* which states:

אֲנִי מַאֲמִין בֶּאֱמוּנָה שְׁלֵמָה בְּבִיאַת הַמָּשִׁיחַ וְאַף עַל פִּי שֶׁיִּתְמַהְמֵהַּ עִם כָּל זֶה אֲחַכֶּה לוֹ בְּכָל יוֹם שֶׁיָּבוֹא.

I believe with complete faith in the coming of the Messiah, and even though he may delay, nevertheless, I await him every day, [for I know] that he will come.

There is extensive discussion in the *Rishonim* regarding the exact nature of the future era. Many Gemaras speak of יְמוֹת הַמָּשִׁיחַ (*the Messianic Era*), לֶעָתִיד לָבֹא (*the Future to Come*), עוֹלָם הַבָּא (*the World to Come*), and גַּן עֵדֶן, (*the Garden of Eden*). There are many different views as to the exact nature of each of these periods: whether they each refer to a different time or are different names for one (or two) epochs, and the sequence in which they will occur if they are different periods. For the purpose of the explanation of the Fundamental Principle under discussion, we will provide a definition of the Messianic era as it was apparently understood by *Rambam.*

In his *Commentary to the Mishnah* (*Sanhedrin* 10:1), *Rambam* writes that the main change that the advent of the Messianic era will bring about is that the Jews will regain their independence and will no longer be subjugated by other nations. It will be a time when sustenance will be easy to obtain and the Jews will be able to keep the Torah with ease, as the nations will no longer oppress them. Wars will be a thing of the past, and people will live in peace, using their leisure to increase their wisdom.

In *Hilchos Melachim* (Chapter 11), *Rambam* adds that the Messiah will be a scion of the house of David, who will restore the monarchy of the Davidic dynasty to its former glory. He will gather the Jewish exiles from the scattered lands in which they are found and return them to Eretz Yisrael, where he will rebuild the *Beis HaMikdash* and rule over them as their king.

Rambam (ibid.) makes a point in emphasizing that the coming of the Messiah will not change the Torah at all. All the mitzvos of the Torah will remain the same, and nothing will be added to it or removed from it. Moreover, man will still possess the same material desires and free will that he does now. However, the understanding of Hashem that will fill the world will be so total that evil will cease to be, and the peoples of the world, who will coexist in peace and harmony, will work in unison to perfect themselves and become as close as possible to Hashem (see *R' Moshe Chaim Luzzato* in *Ma'amar HaIkkarim* §8; see also *Sanhedrin* 91b).

We will continue our discussion of this principle next week.

A TORAH THOUGHT FOR THE DAY

וְזֶה אֲשֶׁר תַּעֲשֶׂה עַל־הַמִּזְבֵּחַ כְּבָשִׂים בְּנֵי־שָׁנָה
שְׁנַיִם לַיּוֹם תָּמִיד. אֶת־הַכֶּבֶשׂ הָאֶחָד תַּעֲשֶׂה
בַבֹּקֶר וְאֵת הַכֶּבֶשׂ הַשֵּׁנִי תַּעֲשֶׂה בֵּין הָעַרְבָּיִם

*This is what you shall offer upon the Altar:
two sheep within their first year every day, continually.
You shall offer the one sheep in the morning, and the second
sheep you shall offer in the afternoon* (*Shemos* 29:38-39).

Although this commandment to bring a daily *olas tamid,* continual offering, is repeated in *Parashas Pinchas,* it is stated here for the purpose of teaching that the *tamid* was brought daily, even in the *Midbar* (Wilderness). The *Netziv* explains that the *tamid* was brought in the *Midbar* for the purpose of bringing down the *Shechinah.* That is why the Gemara (see *Taanis* 30b) says that after the sin of the *meraglim,* when Bnei Yisrael were in a state of excommunication, they stopped bringing the *tamid.*

In *Parashas Pinchas,* on the other hand, the Torah teaches the mitzvah of bringing the *tamid* in Eretz Yisrael. The offering of the *tamid* there was to bring down the flow of פַּרְנָסָה, *sustenance,* from Heaven. Indeed, the Mishnah says that in the merit of the daily *tamid* offering on the Altar, the Bnei Yisrael will have sufficient food on their tables.

Basing himself on this thought, the *Netziv* explains some of the discrepancies between the two *parshiyos.* For example, the words לַחְמִי לְאִשַּׁי, *My bread for My offering,* is omitted in our *parashah,* because only when the *tamid* was offered in Eretz Yisrael did it have the purpose of ensuring the food supply of the Jews.

The *tamid* had another purpose as well. The verse states in *Yeshayah* (1:21): אֵיכָה הָיְתָה לְזוֹנָה קִרְיָה נֶאֱמָנָה מְלֵאֲתִי מִשְׁפָּט צֶדֶק יָלִין בָּהּ, *How the faithful city has become a harlot! She had been full of justice, righteousness lodged in her. Rashi* explains the words *righteousness lodged in her* as follows: The *tamid* offered in the morning would atone for sins committed throughout the night, while the *tamid* offered in the evening would atone for sins carried out by day. Thus, the citizens of the city were always righteous. [Of course, a *korban* does not atone without repentance. Still, the inhabitants of Jerusalem were fortunate in that they had two daily *korbanos* that would bring them atonement for any sins as soon as they repented. This allowed them to always have a clean slate, without an accumulation of sins.]

Although in our times we unfortunately do not have the *Beis HaMikdash* and the *tamid* cannot be offered, this concept of seeking forgiveness for our sins every day is a worthy one. We can and should think of *teshuvah* before retiring every night, so that we do not "lodge with sin." We can also receive the merits of the *tamid* through prayer, which today is our substitute for the *avodah* of the *korbanos.* See further in *A Closer Look at the Siddur.*

MISHNAH OF THE DAY: SHABBOS 24:1

The coming Mishnah teaches that although a Jew is forbidden to carry four *amos* in a public domain on the Sabbath, nevertheless, if he finds himself on the road at the onset of the Sabbath, he need not abandon his purse there:

מִי שֶׁהֶחְשִׁיךְ בַּדֶּרֶךְ — ***One who was on the road as dusk approached*** on Friday, נוֹתֵן כִּיסוֹ לְנָכְרִי — ***should give his purse to a non-Jew*** to carry.[1] וְאִם אֵין עִמּוֹ נָכְרִי — ***And if there is no*** non-Jew ***with him,*** מַנִּיחוֹ עַל הַחֲמוֹר — ***he should place*** the purse ***on*** his ***donkey.***[2]

NOTES

1. I.e., he may give his purse to a non-Jew before nightfall to carry for him (*Rav; Rashi*). Even though money is *muktzeh* (see preface to Ch. 21), the Rabbis permitted handling it in order to avoid incurring a loss (*Tos. Yom Tov*). An element of leniency is involved in this ruling, since he is making the non-Jew his agent to carry his purse on the Sabbath, an act ordinarily prohibited (as we learned above, 16:6). Under these circumstances, however, the Rabbis permitted it, because they realized that most people do not willingly part with their money, and that some people, unable to abandon their purses, would end up carrying them through a public domain on the Sabbath, where carrying a distance of four *amos* [cubits] is a capital transgression. To forestall this possibility, the Rabbis permitted a person to save his money in such a situation by resorting to activities that are normally Rabbinically prohibited (*Rav* from Gemara 153a).

2. Where he has the option of giving it to a non-Jew, however, he may not place the purse on the donkey, but must give it to the non-Jew. This is because a person has a Biblical obligation to allow his animals to rest on the Sabbath (*Shemos* 20:10,23; 23:12), while he has no such obligation toward a non-Jew. [The prohibition to tell a non-Jew to perform a forbidden labor on the Sabbath is entirely of Rabbinic origin.]

Moreover, since there is a Biblical prohibition involved in causing an animal to work on the Sabbath, it follows that even when one is permitted to place his purse on the animal, he must do so in such a way as to avoid any Biblical violation. [It is not within the power of the Rabbis to permit something Biblically prohibited.] However, the Biblical prohibition against causing an animal to perform forbidden labor applies only to those acts which a person himself is Biblically prohibited to perform. The forbidden labor of transferring from one domain to another consists of three parts: (1) an *akirah* — picking up an article in one domain; (2) the actual transfer;

The next part of the Mishnah deals with a person who was traveling on Friday with a donkey laden with packages, and was then overtaken by darkness and the onset of the Sabbath (*Rav; Rambam Commentary*):
הִגִּיעַ לֶחָצֵר הַחִיצוֹנָה — ***When he reaches the outermost courtyard,***[3] **נוֹטֵל אֶת הַכֵּלִים הַנִּיטָּלִין בְּשַׁבָּת** — ***he may take*** off ***any utensils that may*** normally ***be moved on the Sabbath.***[4] **וְשֶׁאֵינָן נִיטָּלִין בְּשַׁבָּת** — ***However, those*** utensils ***that may not be moved on the Sabbath*** because they are *muktzeh,* he may not take himself; **מַתִּיר הַחֲבָלִים וְהַשַּׂקִּין נוֹפְלִין מֵאֵילֵיהֶם** — instead, ***he undoes the ropes*** that hold them fastened to the saddle, ***and the sacks fall*** down ***on their own.***[5]

NOTES

and (3) a *hanachah* — placing the article down in the second domain (see Mishnah 1:1). In the case of transferring four *amos* in a public domain (a derivative of transferring from one domain to another) it consists of *akirah* (picking up the object, or beginning to move), moving the article four *amos,* and *hanachah* (setting the object down). Hence, to avoid a Biblical prohibition, one should place the purse on the donkey *after* it has commenced walking — so that there is no real *akirah* — and remove it *before* it stops — so that there is no real *hanachah* (*Rav; Rambam Commentary; Tos. Yom Tov* from Gemara 153b).

3. I.e., when he reaches the first courtyard at the outskirts of the city in which it is safe to unload his bags (*Rav; Rashi*).

4. I.e., those articles that are not *muktzeh* may be removed by hand from the donkey's back (*Rav*).

5. Once he has reached a secure area, he can no longer make use of the above dispensation, and cannot allow the donkey to carry his valuables any further through the streets of the town.

GEMS FROM THE GEMARA

The Gemara (153b) states that a traveler who finds himself on the road as the Sabbath is about to begin actually has at his disposal several means of transporting his purse on the Sabbath. These are, in order of preference: giving it to a non-Jew to carry for him; placing it on his donkey; giving it to a deranged person to carry; giving it to a deaf-mute or a minor to carry.

The Gemara then inquires: If there is neither a non-Jew, nor a donkey, nor a deaf-mute, nor a deranged person there with him, what should he do with the purse?

The Gemara answers that R' Yitzchak said that there was yet another method by which the person would be allowed to save the purse in this case, but the Sages did not wish to reveal it.

The Gemara explains: To what does "there was yet another method" refer? To the fact that, if he has no other choice, he may carry it himself, in increments of less than four *amos.* [From a Biblical standpoint, one is permitted to carry an object even several miles in a public domain, as long as he does so in increments of less than four *amos* — i.e., as long as he stops every step or two, so that he never traverses four *amos* in a single act of carrying. Although it is Rabbinically forbidden to carry in the public domain even in this manner, the Rabbis were lenient, and allowed a traveler to use this method to transport his purse if he finds himself in a situation where none of the other methods outlined earlier are available.]

The Gemara asks: Why did the Sages not want to reveal [this method]? The Gemara replies: They applied to this matter the following verse (*Proverbs* 25:2): כְּבֹד אֱלֹהִים הַסְתֵּר דָּבָר וּכְבֹד מְלָכִים חֲקֹר דָּבָר, *[Regarding] the honor of God, you should conceal a matter, but [regarding] the honor of kings, you should investigate a matter.* Because publicizing this method would compromise the honor of God, the Sages did not want to reveal it.

The Gemara then asks: What threat to the honor of God is there in publicizing this method? The Gemara answers: Because one who uses this method might come to carry the purse a full four *amos* in the public domain without pause, and thereby desecrate the Sabbath and slight the honor of God, they decided that it would be better not to reveal it. [However, it is permitted in exceptional circumstances, as explained above.]

A MUSSAR THOUGHT FOR THE DAY

In *A Torah Thought for the Day,* we discussed some of the lessons of the *korban tamid.* However, another important lesson of the *tamid* is implicit in its very name. *Tamid* means continuous, without pause, every single day. Unlike other *korbanos* that are either brought on specific days or for unusual occurrences, the *tamid* was brought every day of the year. In fact, this phenomenon is so significant that one of the reasons we fast on *Shivah Asar B'Tammuz* is because on this day, the unbroken string of many consecutive days that the *tamid* had been offered came to an end. Now, if we look at some of the other reasons for this fast day, such a misfortune seems to pale in comparison. For example, *Shivah*

Asar B'Tammuz was the date on which the *Luchos* were broken after the sin of the Golden Calf, and the date on which a structure of *avodah zarah* was placed in the *Heichal.* These were significant spiritual tragedies that caused the Sages to implement a day of *teshuvah* and fasting. Why was the cessation of the continuous offering of the *tamid* considered so significant that it took its place alongside these major misfortunes?

The answer lies in the understanding that for something to be considered *tamid,* it must be done *every single day.* Even if only one day out of the year is missing, the whole chain of *tamid* is broken; none of the days are considered *tamid.* A thing is *tamid* if it exists without interruption from the time of its implementation. Thus, when the continuous line of the *korban tamid* came to a halt on that bitter day, it did not only mean that Bnei Yisrael would no longer have a *korban tamid;* it put in jeopardy all previous *tamids* that were brought. And when that link was broken, the Jews lost something very precious — their constant bond and connection to *avodas Hashem,* which existed as long as the *tamid* was being offered.

The Bach in *Hilchos Chanukah* teaches us that whenever an *avodah* is done constantly, there are advantages and disadvantages. The fact that an *avodah* is always there means that a person is always connected to *avodas Hashem.* However, there is always the danger that an *avodah* performed constantly will become routine, and that one will fulfill it as one acting out of habit, without feeling and devotion. It is very difficult to perform the same *avodah* every day with freshness. Indeed, we find that Aharon HaKohen was praised: שֶׁלֹּא שִׁנָּה, *for he did not change.* This refers to the fact that he lit the *Menorah* daily with the same enthusiasm as he did the very first time. If a person strives to always find a new approach to his daily *avodah,* he will have both advantages.

Rav Chaim Volozhin writes very penetrating words in his *sefer Ruach Chaim* on *Avos* (2:1): If a person wants to improve his performance in *avodas Hashem,* he should see to it that all his acts are performed according to a set schedule. His time for learning should be established and constant. In fact, it is brought down in *Shulchan Aruch* (*Orach Chaim* 155:1) that a person should set aside a fixed time daily for learning Torah, and it should not be canceled even for a great business opportunity. R' Chaim states that even if a person feels that keeping to this set schedule does not allow him to always learn with his full concentration, it is better to continue without breaking the schedule than to stop completely in an attempt to gain greater returns. A person, he explains, will naturally have ups and downs. It is human nature that when a person is feeling low he feels that everything he is doing in Torah or *avodah* is counterproductive. Thus, it is natural for him to think, "Let me rest and relax until I get back my enthusiasm." However, this is the advice of the *yetzer hara.* As soon as a person pauses in his *avodah,* the *yetzer hara* has him in its clutches; and, unless it is repelled, it will increase its grasp upon the person until it totally extinguishes the fire of Torah study in him.

HALACHAH OF THE DAY

We now continue discussing the practical applications of the *melachah* of *slaughtering.*

If a person is in pain due to a collection of pus in an abscess, he may puncture the abscess in order to extract the pus, even if this will cause some blood to drain from the abscess along with the pus. This is permitted because the prohibition against drawing blood on Shabbos applies only to blood that is part of the circulating bloodstream. Blood that has collected in an abscess has already left the bloodstream, and is now only being extracted from the abscess. Once the abscess has been drained, one should take care not to continue to squeeze it, since this may cause fresh blood to be extracted from the blood vessels of the adjoining tissue, which would be a violation of the *melachah* of *slaughtering.*

Inserting an intravenous line into a patient's vein on Shabbos may involve several halachic questions. First, the mere insertion of the needle into the vein usually results in the release of a small amount of blood. Second, after inserting the needle, one generally draws some blood into the syringe in order to ascertain that the needle is properly placed. In cases where it may be necessary to start an intravenous line, a competent halachic authority should be consulted. The same advice applies to administering injections on Shabbos.

The brushing of teeth on Shabbos presents us with two different halachic difficulties. If the brush is moistened prior to its use, there is a question as to whether using the brush involves a violation of the *melachah* of סְחִיטָה (*sechitah*), *squeezing. HaRav Moshe Feinstein* writes that it is best not to use a moistened toothbrush on Shabbos. While other *poskim* disagree, it is best to abide by the more stringent view. If the toothbrush is dry, its use may cause the gums to bleed, which would involve a violation of the prohibition against drawing blood on Shabbos.

Therefore, one should not use even a dry toothbrush on Shabbos if it will cause his gums to bleed.

It is permissible to remove a splinter on Shabbos even if the removal may cause some bleeding. However, one should make every effort to avoid causing bleeding on Shabbos. If removing the splinter will definitely cause bleeding, the splinter may be removed only if it is causing pain. In the absence of pain, the splinter should be left in place and removed only after Shabbos.

This concludes our discussion of the *melachah* of *slaughtering.*

A CLOSER LOOK AT THE SIDDUR

The *Tur* (§48) states: The Sages instituted that one should read the Torah passage describing the offering of the *tamid* during the daily prayers, as it says in the Midrash (*Taanis* 27b): Avraham Avinu was concerned, and asked Hashem, "What will happen if my children will sin as did the Generation of the Flood?" Hashem replied, "They will bring *korbanos,* which will atone for their sins." Avraham questioned further, "And what will be when they will not have a *Beis HaMikdash* in which to bring *korbanos*?" Hashem answered, "I have established *Seder HaKorbanos.* Whenever they will read the verses of the *korbanos,* I will consider it as if they brought those sacrifices, and I will forgive them."

This great promise was made to Avraham Avinu before he even had a child. Hashem promised him that even in *galus* we will still possess the power to harness the atonement of *korbanos* by reading the relevant passages.

The *Tur* writes that we should say a short prayer after reciting the *parashah* of the *tamid;* it reads as follows: "Master of the Worlds! You commanded us to bring the *tamid* offering at its set time, and that the Kohanim be at their assigned service . . . But now through our sins our Holy Temple is destroyed and the continual offering is discontinued . . . But You said, *'Let our lips compensate for the bulls';* therefore, may it be Your Will . . . that the prayer of our lips be worthy, acceptable, and favorable before You as if we had brought the continual offerings."

[*Rav Chaim Kanievski* notes that the language of the *Shulchan Aruch* seems to indicate that the recital of the passage of the *tamid* is not merely a good practice (as he says regarding the passage of the *Akeidah*), but an essential part of prayer.]

The *Shulchan Aruch* says that after reciting the passage of the *tamid,*

one should recite the verse (*Vayikra* 1:11): וְשָׁחַט אֹתוֹ עַל יֶרֶךְ הַמִּזְבֵּחַ צָפֹנָה לִפְנֵי ה׳, *He shall slaughter it at the side of the Altar, on the north, before* HASHEM. Most *siddurim* print this verse together with the *parashah* of the *tamid.* However, there is a difficulty. What is the purpose of reciting this verse, which is speaking about all *korbenos olah,* and not specifically the *tamid* offering?

The *Gra* in *Shulchan Aruch* cites a Midrash that notes that the command to slaughter an *olah* in the north is written in the Torah with respect to an *olah* that is an אַיִל, *a ram;* this, explains the Midrash, is an allusion to *Akeidas Yitzchak.* When Avraham bound Yitzchak on the altar, Hashem set in place the two *tamid* offerings, and promised that whenever the Jews would bring the *tamid* and recite the words צָפֹנָה לִפְנֵי ה׳, Hashem would remember the merit of the *Akeidah.* The Midrash continues, stating that Hashem made the heavens and earth witnesses that no matter which Jew — be it man, woman, or slave — would recite this verse, He would remember this merit.

This, explains *Gra,* is why we recite this verse with the *parashas hatamid* — to get the full benefit of the *parashah* itself, which stands in place of the actual *korban,* and to maximize the power of our prayer, by combining it with the merit of the *Akeidah.*

QUESTION OF THE DAY:

Who offered the first korban tamid?

For the answer, see page 236.

A TORAH THOUGHT FOR THE DAY

וְעָשִׂיתָ מִזְבֵּחַ מִקְטַר קְטֹרֶת עֲצֵי שִׁטִּים תַּעֲשֶׂה אֹתוֹ
You shall make an Altar on which to bring incense up in smoke, of shittim wood shall you make it (*Shemos* 30:1).

The commentators grapple with an obvious question here. Why does the Torah not discuss the construction of this Altar (the Inner Altar, also known as the *Mizbach HaKetores* or the Incense Altar) in *Parashas Terumah*, which deals with all the other vessels of the Mishkan? The *Shulchan* and *Menorah,* which share the same room of the Sanctuary (*Heichal*) with the Inner Altar, are all discussed there. Why does the Torah wait until the end of *Parashas Tetzaveh* — after listing all the clothing of the Kohanim and relating which sacrifices are to be brought during the opening ceremonies of the Mishkan — to command the Jews to make the *Mizbach HaKetores*? It is clear that this separation indicates that the function of this *Mizbe'ach* is fundamentally different from that of the other vessels of the Mishkan. But what is the nature of this difference?

Daas Zekeinim in *Parashas Terumah* raises another question. Why, he asks, is *ketores* mentioned in the list of materials that were needed for building the Mishkan? The *ketores* was not necessary for the construction of the Mishkan — it was required *after* the Mishkan was completed, just as animals were required for use as sacrifices. Seemingly, then, it does not belong in the list of items enumerated as necessary building materials!

Daas Zekeinim explains that the *ketores* was indeed viewed as a construction necessity, because incense is used as soon as the construction is completed, as a means of announcing that the king will now be arriving. Just as it was the custom to burn incense in a palace prior to the arrival of the king, it is appropriate to prepare *ketores* in anticipation of the arrival of the *Shechinah.* Further, it is for this reason that *ketores* is brought into the Holy of Holies on Yom Kippur. Since the Kohen Gadol enters into the abode of the *Shechinah,* it is proper that he offer incense to welcome Its Presence. This is also the reason that the Altar upon which the incense is offered is not mentioned until after the discussion of the opening ceremonies of the Mishkan — the point at which the *Shechinah* would descend to remain in the Mishkan. This was the proper place and time to mention the function of this Altar.

Sforno takes a different approach. He states that while all the other vessels were part of the blueprint of the Mishkan and were necessary in order to bring about the reposing of the *Shechinah* in the Mishkan, the service upon this Altar had a different purpose: it was simply to honor Hashem. After completing the service of the *korbanos* every morning and night, the incense was offered as an additional tribute to Hashem's honor. It was therefore discussed only after mention of all the vessels and all the details pertaining to the regular sacrificial service had been completed.

Meshech Chochmah notes the following simple difference between this Altar and the other Mishkan vessels. All the other vessels were needed so that their related service could be performed, or for a specific function to be fulfilled. For instance, the *Aron* was constructed to house the *Luchos;* without the *Aron,* the *Luchos* would have no resting place. Without the *Shulchan,* there would be no repository for the *lechem hapanim.* The same is true of the vestments of the Kohanim — without them, a Kohen is unfit to do *avodah.* But the Altar of the *ketores* was not critical to the offering of the *ketores* — for the law is that even if the Altar is unavailable for some reason, the *ketores* is brought upon its place (*Zevachim* 59b). For this reason, it is mentioned after the other vessels — for their absence renders their related functions impossible, while the *Mizbach HaKetores* is needed only *lechatchilah,* as the best option.

MISHNAH OF THE DAY: SHABBOS 24:2

The coming Mishnah considers the preparation of animal feed on the Sabbath:

מַתִּירִין פְּקִיעֵי עָמִיר לִפְנֵי בְהֵמָה — ***We may untie bundles of straw before an animal,***[1] **וּמְפַסְפְּסִין אֶת הַכִּיפִּין** — ***and we may scatter tender cedar boughs*** for it,[2] **אֲבָל לֹא אֶת הַזִּירִין** — ***but not triply bound bundles of***

NOTES

1. As long as the bundles are tied, the straw is not fit for the animal's consumption. Untying them, therefore, makes it edible. As long as no forbidden labor is performed, it is permissible to make food edible for livestock on the Sabbath (*Rav; Rashi*).

2. Normally, when one gives such bundles to an animal, one scatters them first in order to render them more appetizing; if they are packed together, they become warm and fail to release much of a scent. As a result, the animal finds them unpalatable (*Rav; Rashi*).

straw.[3] אֵין מְרַסְּקִין — *We may not shred*[4] לֹא אֶת הַשַּׁחַת — *neither fodder*[5] וְלֹא אֶת הֶחָרוּבִין — *nor carobs*[6] לִפְנֵי בְהֵמָה — *before an animal,*[7] בֵּין דַּקָּה וּבֵין גַּסָּה — *whether* it is *small or large.*[8] רַבִּי יְהוּדָה מַתִּיר בֶּחָרוּבִין לְדַקָּה — *R' Yehudah permits* shredding *carobs for a lightweight* animal.[9]

NOTES

3. These are the same as the *bundles of straw* mentioned in the beginning of the Mishnah, except that whereas those are tied only at both ends, these are tied in the middle as well (*Rav*). The Mishnah states that although these bundles may be untied, they may not be scattered. Since, due to their being packed tightly by being triply bound, these bundles become excessively warm and are not especially appetizing to the animals, on weekdays it was generally the custom to scatter these bundles. However, since after untying them they are already edible, on the Sabbath they may not be scattered to make them more palatable to the livestock. This is regarded as an unnecessary effort on behalf of the animal and is prohibited for a food that is already edible (*Rav,* in accordance with the opinion of Rav Yehudah in the Gemara, 155a).

4. I.e., cut into small pieces (*Rav*).

5. This refers to straw from immature grain that is soft enough for an animal to eat as is, without further preparation.

6. The Mishnah refers to tender carob-pods that are edible in their natural state and need not be cut up (*Tos. Yom Tov* from Gemara).

7. Although the shredding makes the fodder and carobs easier to eat, nevertheless, it is prohibited as excessive exertion (*Rav; Rashi* in accordance with Rav Yehudah, ibid.). [Since the fodder and carobs are already edible in their present state, any effort expended on their improvement is unnecessary, and therefore proscribed on the Sabbath.]

8. Literally, *thin or fat.* These are idiomatic terms used throughout Mishnah to describe the two categories of kosher animals generally raised for meat. "Small" animals are sheep and goats; "large" animals are cattle.

9. The teeth of sheep and goats are small, and it would be difficult for such an animal to chew through tough carobs unless these are first shredded (*Rav; Rashi*).

GEMS FROM THE GEMARA

The interpretation of our Mishnah is subject to a dispute in the Gemara (155a). We have explained the Mishnah according to Rav Yehudah the Amora [not to be confused with R' Yehudah the Tanna, who is mentioned in the Mishnah], who permits making a substance into food for livestock as long as it was not edible before. If a food is edible as is, however, he prohibits excessive toil for the purpose of making the already edible food more attractive or palatable. Rav Huna, however, holds the opposite. In his view, it is prohibited to do anything to make a substance that is now inedible into a food, since that involves creating something new. On the other hand, if the substance is already fit to eat, he permits taking the extra effort to make it more attractive for the animal. According to Rav Huna, the explanation of the Mishnah is as follows:

We may untie bundles of sheaves before an animal, and we may scatter them as well. Since they are normally intended for food, performing these tasks is not regarded as creating new foodstuffs. Likewise, triply bound bundles of straw may be untied and scattered. Cedar boughs, however, may *not* be untied or scattered on the Sabbath. Since these are generally intended for kindling, untying or scattering them converts them into food and is prohibited. [Rav Huna reverses the meanings of כִּיפִּין and זִירְין from the definitions given above. According to his interpretation, כִּיפִּין are *triply bound bundles of straw,* while זִירְין are *cedar boughs.*]

The Mishnah continues: We may not shred neither fodder nor carobs for animals. According to Rav Huna, the Mishnah refers to hard carobs and hard fodder, which are not edible in their natural state until they are cut into small pieces. Therefore, they may not be shredded, since this makes them edible.

The Gemara concedes, however, that the end of the Mishnah presents a difficulty for Rav Huna. The Tanna R' Yehudah evidently permits shredding hard carobs for small animals who are unable to eat them otherwise. This would seem to present a difficulty according to Rav Huna, who does not allow the performance of acts that make something edible. Nor can Rav Huna explain that R' Yehudah is referring here to carobs that are already fit for eating, for then it would certainly be permitted to cut up the carobs for a large animal, and R' Yehudah permits it only for a small animal.

A MUSSAR THOUGHT FOR THE DAY

The *Kli Yakar* makes the following observation. All the vessels in the Mishkan existed without duplicates except for the Altars, of which there were two — the Outer Altar in the Courtyard of the Mishkan upon which the sacrifices were offered, and the Inner Altar upon which the *ketores* (incense) was offered. He explains that although the two Altars had different functions, they both shared a common goal — to help bring atonement to a person who had sinned.

Kli Yakar explains: Whenever a person sins, the sin is a joint act of the body and soul. Both body and soul suffer from the sin, and both require atonement. The function of the Outer Altar is to afford atonement to the body. Thus, its height (according to one view) was three *amos,* which is the height of an average person. We offer animals as sacrifices on this Altar, to remind a person that what is happening to that animal should really be happening to him, as a result of his sin (see *Ramban* to the beginning of *Parashas Vayikra*). Thus, the Outer Altar provides atonement for the outer portion of a person — his physical body.

However, the soul is also adversely affected by sins, and it needs atonement as well. The sacrifice of the tangible, physical body of the animal has no relation to the soul. But the smoke of the *ketores,* which corresponds to the *ruach* of a person, can bring atonement to the soul — and this is the function of the Inner Altar. It provides atonement to the inner essence of the person.

The Inner Altar was one *amah* wide and one *amah* long — this parallels the oneness of the soul. Also, the *ketores* was offered at the same time that the *Menorah* was prepared and lit, for a candle is used as the symbol for a person's soul.

Kli Yakar explains further that the *ketores* was offered half in the morning and half in the evening. This is done to remind each person that he received his soul fresh and pure as the morning and that he must see to it that "in the evening," when a person enters the final stages of his life, his soul should be as close as possible to the pristine state in which it was received.

HALACHAH OF THE DAY

S*kinning* is the next of the thirty-nine *avos melachos* that are prohibited on Shabbos. After the rams and the *techashim* prepared for use in the Mishkan were slaughtered, they were skinned, so that their hides could be used for the coverings of the Mishkan.

In order to process an animal's hide into leather, parchment, or fur, the hide must first be removed. The definition of the *melachah* of *skinning* is the removal of the hide or skin of any animal, fish or bird, be it kosher or nonkosher.

According to Biblical law, the prohibition of *skinning* applies only if one intends to use the skin or hide after it is removed. If the skins will be discarded, the skinning is prohibited only by Rabbinic decree.

The prohibition of skinning does not apply to cooked food. When cooked, the skin is considered to be a part of the food. Thus, for instance, if chicken or fish are cooked together with their skins, it is not a violation of the *melachah* of *skinning* to remove these skins. One must be careful when doing so, however, not to violate the *melachah* of *borer*, selecting. (For details on how to remove skin while avoiding issues of *borer*, see our earlier discussions of that *melachah*.)

Following *slaughtering* and *skinning* in the list of the thirty-nine forbidden labors of Shabbos is the *melachah* of מְעַבֵּד, *tanning.* During the time of the Mishkan, the hides of the rams and *techashim* were tanned after they were skinned, as part of the process to prepare them as coverings for the Mishkan.

Tanning is the method through which hides are converted into leather. The *melachah* of *tanning* includes all actions necessary to convert an animal hide into leather.

We will now discuss the process of converting hides into leather, and the activities it includes.

Animal hides intended for use as leather must be preserved so that they do not rot or decompose. In order to accomplish this the hides are first soaked in various liquids, such as water, brine (saltwater) and tannic solutions. Alternately, the hides are covered in salt. Both these methods are used to preserve the hide from decaying. One is forbidden to place hides into any of these liquids, or into salt, on Shabbos.

Another part of the tanning process is to trample the hides. This hardens and strengthens the leather. Nowadays, this process is accomplished by the use of rolling machines. One may not trample hides on Shabbos, whether by manual process or by machine.

A CLOSER LOOK AT THE SIDDUR

After the conclusion of the Friday night *Maariv* service, there is a widespread custom for parents to bless their children. This custom has many forms. Some bless their children immediately after the prayers conclude, while others do so upon arriving home, before making *Kiddush.* Some bless only small children, while others bless even their married children. In some places, only the father blesses the children, while in others both parents do so. Some place both hands upon the child's head during the blessing, while others use only one hand, and still others distinguish between married and unmarried children in this regard. All of these customs have their roots, and while a thorough discussion is beyond the scope of our work, we will explore the framework and source for the basic custom.

This blessing is given at the onset of the Sabbath because it is a time of special Divine blessing, when Hashem allows His beneficence to flow freely upon His nation. We therefore try to take advantage of this auspicious time of Divine favor by blessing our offspring.

Most parents bless their sons with the phrase: יְשִׂמְךָ אֱלֹהִים כְּאֶפְרַיִם וְכִמְנַשֶּׁה, *May God make you like Ephraim and Menasheh.* This was the blessing that Yaakov gave to the sons of Yosef before his death. Yaakov prefaced his blessing to the children with the words: בְּךָ יְבָרֵךְ יִשְׂרָאֵל, *By you shall Israel bless* (*Bereishis* 48:20). *Rashi* there explains this to mean that Yaakov indicated that one who wishes to bless his sons would use this formula to do so.

Many interpretations have been advanced as to the significance of wishing that our children should be as Ephraim and Menasheh. Perhaps the simplest one is that these two young men, despite having been raised in the midst of the corrupt miasma of Egyptian society, not only became *tzaddkim,* but ascended to a level where they merited treatment equal to their great uncles, receiving portions in Eretz Yisrael alongside the *shevatim.* Thus, we wish that our offspring enjoy the same success and accomplishment.

It is customary, when blessing one's daughters, to use the form: יְשִׂמֵךְ אֱלֹהִים כְּשָׂרָה רִבְקָה רָחֵל וְלֵאָה, *May God make you as Sarah, Rivkah, Rachel, and Leah.* Although no Scriptural source exists for this formula, it is logical to wish that our daughters should grow up in the mold of the Matriarchs, who were the maternal foundation of our nation. [The omission of Bilhah and Zilpah is apparently based upon the Gemara in *Berachos* (16b) that states that only the four mentioned above are to be accorded the title of *Imahos* (Matriarchs).]

After these verses, many conclude the blessing by reciting the verses of the *Birchas Kohanim,* the Priestly Blessings (*Bamidbar* 6:24-26). These verses are identified as those through which the Kohanim channel Divine blessing upon the Jews; it is appropriate, therefore, that parents recite them to channel the Divine blessing that is present on the Sabbath upon their children.

QUESTION OF THE DAY:

Why was the top of the Inner Altar made of gold plated wood, while the top of the Outer Altar was earth?

For the answer, see page 236.

ANSWERS TO QUESTIONS OF THE DAY

Sunday:

The *tzitz* (the golden headplate worn by the Kohen Gadol) and the *michnasayim* (short pants) are omitted.[See *Ohr HaChaim* and *Rashbam* for reasons why they are not mentioned here.]

Monday:

The names of the *Avos* (Avraham, Yitzchak and Yaakov), and the words שִׁבְטֵי יְשׁוּרוּן (*Yoma* 73b) were engraved on the stones of the *Choshen.*

Tuesday:

It was the only one of the *bigdei Kehunah* that was made completely of *techeiles*.

Wednesday:

The prohibition (*Devarim* 22:11) against wearing *shaatnez* (a mixture of wool and linen) was overridden.

Thursday:

The Gemara (*Zevachim* 59b) records a dispute: R' Yehudah held it was five *amos* high, while R' Yose maintained that it was ten *amos* high.

Friday:

During the week of the inauguration of the Mishkan, the *tamid* was brought by Moshe himself (see *Ibn Ezra*).

Shabbos:

The large fires of the Outer Altar would have destroyed a surface of gold-plated wood. The fire needed to burn the incense, however, was minimal (*Sforno*).